Lecture Notes in Computer Science 10356

Commenced Publication in 1973
Founding and Former Series Editors:
Gerhard Goos, Juris Hartmanis, and Jan van Leeuwen

Daphne Tuncer · Robert Koch
Rémi Badonnel · Burkhard Stiller (Eds.)

Security of Networks and Services in an All-Connected World

11th IFIP WG 6.6 International Conference
on Autonomous Infrastructure, Management, and Security, AIMS 2017
Zurich, Switzerland, July 10–13, 2017
Proceedings

Springer Open

Editors
Daphne Tuncer
University College London
London
UK

Robert Koch
Universität der Bundeswehr München
Neubiberg
Germany

Rémi Badonnel
LORIA - Inria
Villers-lès-Nancy
France

Burkhard Stiller
University of Zurich
Zurich
Switzerland

ISSN 0302-9743   ISSN 1611-3349 (electronic)
Lecture Notes in Computer Science
ISBN 978-3-319-60773-3   ISBN 978-3-319-60774-0 (eBook)
DOI 10.1007/978-3-319-60774-0

Library of Congress Control Number: 2017943842

LNCS Sublibrary: SL5 – Computer Communication Networks and Telecommunications

Printed on acid-free paper

This Springer imprint is published by Springer Nature
The registered company is Springer International Publishing AG
The registered company address is: Gewerbestrasse 11, 6330 Cham, Switzerland

Preface

The International Conference on Autonomous Infrastructure, Management, and Security (AIMS 2017) is a single-track event targeted at junior researchers and PhD students in network and service management and security. It features a range of sessions including conference paper presentations, hands-on lab courses, and educational keynotes. One of the key goals of AIMS is to offer junior researchers and PhD students a dedicated place where they can discuss their research work and experience, receive constructive feedback from senior scientists, and benefit from practical hands-on sessions on emerging technologies. By putting the focus on junior researchers and PhD students, AIMS acts as a complementary piece in the set of international conferences in the network and service management community, providing an optimal environment for in-depth discussions and networking.

AIMS 2017 — which took place during July 10-13, 2017, in Zürich, Switzerland, and was hosted by the University of Zürich — was the 11th edition of a conference series on management and security aspects of distributed and autonomous systems. It followed the already established tradition of an unusually vivid and interactive conference series, after successful events in Munich, Germany, in 2016, Ghent, Belgium, in 2015, Brno, Czech Republic, in 2014, Barcelona, Spain, in 2013, Luxembourg, Luxembourg, in 2012, Nancy, France, in 2011, Zürich, Switzerland, in 2010, Enschede, The Netherlands, in 2009, Bremen, Germany, in 2008, and Oslo, Norway, in 2007.

AIMS 2017 focused on security of networks and services in an all-connected world. To address these challenges, solutions for the design, monitoring, configuration, and protection of the next generation of networked systems in an efficient, secure, and smart manner are investigated. The theme is reflected in the technical program with papers presenting novel approaches and evaluation studies for the security management of rich network services and environments. AIMS 2017 was organized as a 4-day program to encourage the active participation of and interaction with the audience. The program consisted of technical sessions for the main track and PhD sessions, interleaved with three lab sessions and two keynotes.

The lab sessions offered hands-on experience in the topics of security and advanced network management techniques, and were organized in on-site labs preceded by short tutorial-style teaching sessions. The first lab session was run by Martin Drašar (Masaryk University, Czech Republic) and focused on an introduction to security games. The second lab session was supervised by Thomas Bocek and Moritz Schneider (University of Zürich, Switzerland) and presented how to program smart contracts. Finally, the last session was held by Salvatore Signorello (University of Luxembourg, Luxembourg) and Jérôme François (Inria, France) and explored P4, the emerging high-level data plane programing language and its applicability to packet processors.

The keynotes were presented by two experts in their domain: Marcel Waldvogel (University of Konstanz, Germany), who discussed "Getting Rid of IoT Insecurity," and Matthias Bossardt (KPMG, Switzerland), who shared his view with the audience on "Cyber Security Challenges – A Business Perspective."

The technical program consisted of six sessions, divided into three full-paper sessions and three short-paper sessions. The three full-paper sessions covered technical presentations on the themes of: (1) Security Management, (2) Management of Cloud Environments and Services, and (3) Evaluation and Experimental Study of Rich Network Services. They included a total of eight full papers, which were selected after a thorough reviewing process out of 24 submissions. Each paper received at least three independent reviews. The three short-paper sessions included 11 short papers. These covered PhD research papers on the themes of "Methods for the Protection of Infrastructure and Services," and "Autonomic and Self-Management Solutions" as well as six short presentations on the topic of "Security, Intrusion Detection, and Configuration."

During all the PhD research presentations, doctoral students had the opportunity to present and discuss their research ideas, and more importantly to obtain valuable feedback from the AIMS audience about their PhD research work. All PhD research proposals included in this volume describe the current state of these investigations, including well-defined research problem statements, proposed approaches, and an outline of emerging and promising results achieved to date.

The present volume of the *Lecture Notes in Computer Science* series includes all papers presented at AIMS 2017 as defined within the overall final program. It demonstrates again the European scope of this conference series, since most of the accepted papers originate from European research groups. In addition, by hosting two tracks specifically dedicated to research proposals, AIMS 2017 stayed true to its defined DNA of a conference with a strong educational goal, focusing especially on issues and challenges associated with the security of networks and services.

The editors would like to thank the many people who helped to make AIMS 2017 such a high-quality and successful event. Firstly, many thanks are extended to all authors who submitted their contributions to AIMS 2017, and to the lab session speakers as well as the keynote speakers. The great review work performed by the members of the AIMS Technical Program Committee as well as additional reviewers is greatly acknowledged. Thanks also to Thomas Bocek and Martin Drašar for organizing the lab sessions. Additionally, many thanks are extended to the local organizers for handling logistics and hosting the AIMS 2017 event.

Finally, the editors would like to express their thanks to Springer, especially Anna Kramer, for the smooth cooperation in finalizing these proceedings. Additionally, special thanks go to the AIMS 2017 supporters, University of Zürich UZH, Communication Systems Group CSG, Research Institute for Cyber Defense and Smart Data CODE, München, Germany, and the European FP7 NoE FLAMINGO under Grant No. 318488.

May 2017

Daphne Tuncer
Robert Koch
Rémi Badonnel
Burkhard Stiller

Organization

General Chair AIMS 2017

Burkhard Stiller   University of Zürich, Switzerland

Technical Program Committee Co-chairs

Daphne Tuncer   University College London, UK
Robert Koch   Universität der Bundeswehr München, Germany

Labs Co-chairs

Martin Drašar   Masaryk University, Czech Republic
Thomas Bocek   University of Zürich, Switzerland

Publications Co-chairs

Rémi Badonnel   LORIA, Inria, France
Burkhard Stiller   University of Zürich, Switzerland

Local Chair

Barbara Jost   University of Zürich, Switzerland

Publicity Chair and Web Master

Corinna Schmitt   University of Zürich, Switzerland

AIMS Steering Committee

Anna Sperotto   University of Twente, The Netherlands
Pavel Čeleda   Masaryk University, Czech Republic
Filip De Turck   Ghent University - iMinds, Belgium
Rémi Badonnel   LORIA, Inria, France
Aiko Pras   University of Twente, The Netherlands
Burkhard Stiller   University of Zürich, Switzerland
Robert Koch   Universität der Bundeswehr München, Germany

Technical Program Committee

Alexander Clemm   Huawai, USA
Alexander Keller   IBM Global Technology Services, USA

Alva L. Couch	Tufts University, USA
Anandha Gopalan	Imperial College London, UK
Anna Sperotto	University of Twente, The Netherlands
Bertrand Mathieu	Orange Labs, France
Bruno Quoitin	Université de Mons, Belgium
Burkhard Stiller	University of Zürich, Switzerland
Daniele Sgandurra	Imperial College London, UK
David Hausheer	Otto-von-Guericke Universität Magdeburg, Germany
Filip De Turck	Ghent University - iMinds, Belgium
Gabi Dreo Rodosek	Universität der Bundeswehr München, Germany
Guillaume Doyen	Troyes University of Technology, France
Isabelle Chrisment	TELECOM Nancy, Université de Lorraine, France
Jan Kořenek	Brno University of Technology, Czech Republic
Jérôme François	Inria Nancy Grand Est, France
Joan Serrat	Universitat Politècnica de Catalunya, Spain
Jürgen Schönwälder	Jacobs University Bremen, Germany
Kurt Tutschku	Blekinge Institute of Technology, Sweden
Lisandro Zambenedetti Granville	UFRGS, Brazil
Mario Golling	Universität der Bundeswehr München, Germany
Martin Barrère	Imperial College London, UK
Mauro Tortonesi	University of Ferrara, Italy
Michelle Sibilla	Paul Sabatier University, France
Olivier Festor	INRIA Nancy Grand Est, France
Pavel Čeleda	Masaryk University, Czech Republic
Philippe Owezarski	LAAS-CNRS, France
Rashid Mijumbi	Waterford Institute of Technology, Ireland
Rémi Badonnel	Telecom Nancy, Université de Lorraine, France
Ricardo Schmidt	University of Twente, The Netherlands
Roberto Riggio	CREATE-NET, Italy
Steven Latré	University of Antwerp, iMinds, Belgium
Thomas Bocek	University of Zürich, Switzerland

Additional Reviewers

Detailed reviews for papers submitted to AIMS 2017 were undertaken by the Technical Program Committee as listed above and additionally by the following reviewers:

Messaoud Aouadj, Jeremias Blendin, Remi Cogranne, Ariel Dalla-Costa, Muriel Franco, Borislava Gajic, Christian Jacquenet, Christian Koch, Radek Krejci, Genaro Longoria, Christian Mannweiler, Hassnaa Moustafa, Tan Nguyen, Leonhard Nobach, Vinícius Schaurich, and Eder John Scheid.

Keynotes

Getting Rid of IoT Insecurity

Marcel Waldvogel

University of Konstanz, Distributed Systems Group, Universitätsstr. 10/229,
78457 Konstanz, Germany
Marcel.Waldvogel@uni-konstanz.de

Abstract. The Internet-of-Things (IoT) is already everywhere, but even then, there is still much more to come. Right now, IoT security is a mess, chaotic, unsustainable, and unmanageable. To prevent this is going to remain like this, and that these devices will continue to risk or endanger increasing amounts of our and everybody's lives, we need coordinated actions by manufacturers, vendors, integrators, ISPs, and customers.

But it is the researchers, you, who need to make a long-term difference: how to create blueprints, on which new products may be based, which may include design for privacy, security, manageability, while not overwhelming the users is probably the biggest challenge of them all.

This talk will present three examples, which clearly outlines the challenges, describes open problems, and proposes a coherent framework, into which your next solutions hopefully will fit.

Cyber Security Challenges –
A Business Perspective

Matthias Bossardt

Lead Partner for Cyber Security, KPMG Switzerland, Zürich, Switzerland
mbossardt@kpmg.com

Abstract. This keynote will shed light on real world challenges that companies face when dealing with cyber threats on a global scale. In global organizations and where cyber security has to scale to hundred thousands of employees, contractors, suppliers, and clients as well as thousands of business processes and applications, understanding the organization's risk exposure and implementing effective protection measures is very complex.

And the plethora of challenges related to the (Industrial) Internet-of-Things and managing cyber security becomes a daunting task. To secure an organization, understanding human behavior and mastering organizational change is as important as implementing security technology. This talk will discuss those security capabilities needed in an organization and it will highlight those topics that can benefit greatly from additional research.

Lab Sessions

Hacking your Way to Safety – A Beginner's Guide to Security Games

Martin Drašar

CSIRT-MU, Masaryk University, Brno, Czech Republic
drasar@ics.muni.cz

Abstract. Maintaining infrastructure security or hardening a system is never a simple task. Nor it is a one-click operation. Often it requires the adoption of attacker's mindset to identify correctly weak spots or to even understand that a threat is imminent. This, however, is not possible without acquiring a large body of knowledge, which is usually dispersed around the Internet or available only as dry technical reports. While the process of assembling these bits of information may appeal to somebody, a majority will prefer something more entertaining. Security games are one such approach.

This lab is aimed at beginners and will serve as a brief introduction to hacking as a way to better understand computer security. It will discuss available learning resources and focus mostly on security games: why, which, where, and how to play them for maximum benefit? It will also give participants an opportunity to try out some of these games in a guided manner. These games will be executed both locally as virtual machines on attendees' laptops and remotely in a virtual sandbox environment [1]. Attendees will also be asked to participate in a survey regarding skill self-assessment and effectiveness of knowledge transfer, which fosters further research as presented in [2].

References

1. Kourill, D., Rebok, T., Jirsik, T., Čegan, J., Drasar, M., Vizvary, M., Vykopal, J.: Cloud-based Testbed for Simulation of Cyber Attacks. In: IFIP/IEEE Network Operations and Management Symposium. NOMS 2014, Krakow, Poland, May 2016
2. Ykopal, J., Bartak, M.: On the Design of Security Games: From Frustrating to Engaging Learning, In: USENIX Workshop on Advances in Security Education. ASE 2016, Austin, Texas, USA, August 2016

Programming Smart Contracts

Thomas Bocek and Moritz Schneider

University of Zürich UZH, Department of Informatics IfI, Communication Systems Group CSG, Binzmühlestrasse 14, 8050 Zürich, Switzerland
bocek@ifi.uzh.ch, moritz.schneider3@uzh.ch

Abstract. Blockchains and smart contracts have gained a lot of attention. Public blockchains are considered secure and exist without centralized control. As one of the most prominent blockchain examples, Bitcoin has the potential to disrupt financial services. However, the blockchain technology is applicable to a wider range of application domains, such as smart contracts, public registries, registry of deeds, or virtual organizations.

Another prominent blockchain example, Ethereum, which is considered a general approach for smart contracts, is the second biggest public blockchain with respect to market capitalization. A smart contract in Ethereum [1] is written in the language Solidity [2]. These contracts allow not only sending and receiving funds, but since Solidity its a Turing-complete language, it allows for the definition of any kind of rules.

The introduction of this lab session will address the history and an overview of blockchains as well as their categorization. Blockchain basics are explained in terms of basic building blocks and how they work, including the essential consensus mechanisms. Thus, the Solidity language is introduced in terms of syntax and main constructs, combined with simple code snippets and examples [3]. The audience will compile and deploy a simple smart contract with the goal to familiarize itself with the language and the development environment. Furthermore, the lab shows on the basis of Ethereum smart contracts how to create your own tokens or cryptocurrency [4]. The tokens or cryptocurrency initiator can create initial tokens that can be transferred to any address.

References

1. Homestead Release: ethereum. https://www.ethereum.org/. Accessed May 1, 2017
2. Solidity. http://solidity.readthedocs.io. Accessed May 1, 2017
3. Contract examples for Ethereum. https://github.com/fivedogit/solidity-baby-steps. Accessed May 1, 2017
4. Create your own crypto-currency with Ethereum. https://www.ethereum.org/token. Accessed May 1, 2017

Programming Data Planes in P4 – A High-level Language for Packet Processors

Salvatore Signorello[1] and Jérôme François[2]

[1] SnT, University of Luxembourg, Luxembourg, and LORIA,
University of Nancy, Nancy, France
[2] MADYNES Team at INRIA, Nancy Grand-Est, France
salvatore.signorello@uni.lu, jerome.francois@inria.fr

Abstract. This lab will introduce the audience to the P4 language [1], providing them with the knowledge necessary to develop and prototype their own research ideas in P4. The lab starts by providing an overview of the research that led to the emergence of the language and by illustrating the P4 language consortium objectives and related ongoing activities. Additionally, the lab explains the P4 language programming model and introduces an open source development environment [2], which can be used to write and test P4 programs on a single machine. The presented software toolset includes a P4 front-end compiler, a P4 software target, and the Command Line Interface (CLI) used to program this target at run-time. Finally, the lab interactively presents the language's syntax and main constructs.

Throughout the entire lab, simple P4 code snippets and examples are written, compiled, and executed by the participants. Furthermore, full assignments of increasing complexity are proposed to strengthen the understanding of the programming model and of the main language constructs. More in detail, simple tasks, like the definition of a custom encapsulation protocol and the implementation of an access control list, help the audience to familiarize itself with the definition and the parsing of new protocols and with the definition of the control flow of a P4 program. While more complex assignments, like the implementation of a port-knock firewall, are meant to explore advanced language constructs, which can be used to implement stateful network functions.

References

1. Bosshart, P., Daly, D., Gibb, G., Izzard, M., McKeown, N., Rexford, J., Schlesinger, C., Talayco, D., Vahdat, A., Varghese, G., Walker, D.: P4: Programming Protocol-independent Packet Processors. Comput. Commun. Rev. **44**(3), 87–95
2. P4. http://p4.org/join-us

Contents

Security Management

Making Flow-Based Security Detection Parallel 3
  Marek Švepeš and Tomáš Čejka

A Blockchain-Based Architecture for Collaborative DDoS Mitigation
with Smart Contracts 16
  Bruno Rodrigues, Thomas Bocek, Andri Lareida, David Hausheer,
  Sina Rafati, and Burkhard Stiller

Achieving Reproducible Network Environments with INSALATA 30
  Nadine Herold, Matthias Wachs, Marko Dorfhuber, Christoph Rudolf,
  Stefan Liebald, and Georg Carle

Management of Cloud Environments and Services

Towards a Software-Defined Security Framework for Supporting
Distributed Cloud 47
  Maxime Compastié, Rémi Badonnel, Olivier Festor, Ruan He,
  and Mohamed Kassi-Lahlou

Optimal Service Function Chain Composition in Network
Functions Virtualization 62
  Andrés F. Ocampo, Juliver Gil-Herrera, Pedro H. Isolani,
  Miguel C. Neves, Juan F. Botero, Steven Latré, Lisandro Zambenedetti,
  Marinho P. Barcellos, and Luciano P. Gaspary

Evaluation and Experimental Study of Rich Network Services

An Optimized Resilient Advance Bandwidth Scheduling for Media
Delivery Services 79
  Maryam Barshan, Hendrik Moens, Bruno Volckaert, and Filip De Turck

The Evaluation of the V2VUNet Concept to Improve
Inter-vehicle Communications 94
  Lisa Kristiana, Corinna Schmitt, and Burkhard Stiller

Towards Internet Scale Quality-of-Experience Measurement with Twitter . . . 108
  Dennis Kergl, Robert Roedler, and Gabi Dreo Rodosek

Short Papers: Security, Intrusion Detection, and Configuration

Hunting SIP Authentication Attacks Efficiently.   125
    Tomáš Jansky, Tomáš Čejka, and Václav Bartoš

MoDeNA: Enhancing User Security for Devices in Wireless Personal
and Local Area Networks.   131
    Robert Müller, Marcel Waldvogel, and Corinna Schmitt

Flow-Based Detection of IPv6-specific Network Layer Attacks.   137
    Luuk Hendriks, Petr Velan, Ricardo de O. Schmidt,
    Pieter-Tjerk de Boer, and Aiko Pras

Towards a Hybrid Cloud Platform Using Apache Mesos   143
    Noha Xue, Hårek Haugerud, and Anis Yazidi

Visual Analytics for Network Security and Critical Infrastructures.   149
    Karolína Burská and Radek Ošlejšek

Preserving Relations in Parallel Flow Data Processing.   153
    Tomáš Čejka and Martin Žádník

Ph.D. Track: Autonomic and Self-Management Solutions

SmartDEMAP: A Smart Contract Deployment and Management Platform . . .   159
    Markus Knecht and Burkhard Stiller

Optimizing the Integration of Agent-Based Cloud Orchestrators
and Higher-Level Workloads   165
    Merlijn Sebrechts, Gregory Van Seghbroeck, and Filip De Turck

Ph.D. Track: Methods for the Protection of Infrastructure and Services

Situational Awareness: Detecting Critical Dependencies and Devices
in a Network   173
    Martin Laštovička and Pavel Čeleda

A Framework for SFC Integrity in NFV Environments   179
    Lucas Bondan, Tim Wauters, Bruno Volckaert, Filip De Turck,
    and Lisandro Zambenedetti Granville

Multi-domain DDoS Mitigation Based on Blockchains   185
    Bruno Rodrigues, Thomas Bocek, and Burkhard Stiller

Author Index   191

Security Management

Making Flow-Based Security Detection Parallel

Marek Švepeš[1] and Tomáš Čejka[2(✉)]

[1] FIT, CTU in Prague, Thakurova 9, 160 00 Prague 6, Czech Republic
svepemar@fit.cvut.cz
[2] CESNET, a.l.e., Zikova 4, 160 00 Prague 6, Czech Republic
cejkat@cesnet.cz

Abstract. Flow based monitoring is currently a standard approach suitable for large networks of ISP size. The main advantage of flow processing is a smaller amount of data due to aggregation. There are many reasons (such as huge volume of transferred data, attacks represented by many flow records) to develop scalable systems that can process flow data in parallel. This paper deals with splitting a stream of flow data in order to perform parallel anomaly detection on distributed computational nodes. Flow data distribution is focused not only on uniformity but mainly on successful detection. The results of an experimental analysis show that the proposed approach does not break important semantic relations between individual flow records and therefore it preserves detection results. All experiments were performed using real data traces from Czech National Education and Research Network.

1 Introduction

Flow-based monitoring plays a key role in network management. Not only it provides an overview of the traffic mix, it greatly helps with network security issues such as malicious traffic detection.

There are many types of malicious traffic that should be detected in real networks. As the speed and size of computer networks grow, it is necessary for network operators to process more and more data to be informed about the status of their network. However, with the increasing traffic volume, it is difficult to run lots of detection algorithms at once using just a single machine. The more data, the more computing resources are needed and the longer time the processing takes.

In order to overcome resource limits of a single machine, parallelism plays an important role. Various types of scalable architecture have been invented to process data in parallel. Generally, to be able to process more data, analyzer has to either run parts of its algorithms in parallel or split data for separate processing units.

Since the parallelization of individual detection algorithms is very dependent on the nature of the algorithm and, additionally, according to Amdahl's law,

© The Author(s) 2017
D. Tuncer et al. (Eds.): AIMS 2017, LNCS 10356, pp. 3–15, 2017.
DOI: 10.1007/978-3-319-60774-0_1

there are parts of algorithms that can't be run in parallel, we have decided to focus on data distribution for independent processing units. Our aim is to split a continuous stream of network data (more specifically flow records, i.e. aggregated packet headers) into much smaller subsets that are being processed separately in parallel. We also focus on evaluation of the impact of data splitting on the security analysis results.

The contribution of this paper is to present our experiments with processing data traces from the real backbone network. The aim is to use existing algorithms from a single machine processing and deploy them in a distributed environment. This paper shows, that data splitting for such purpose is complicated due to semantic relations in data which should be preserved. Breaking the relations can cause that the obtained detection results are significantly worse than using a single processing machine. The paper also shows a feasible way how to split flow data with respect to semantic relations. Proposed approach preserves detection results and allows a scalable deployment.

This paper is organized as follows. Sect. 2 describes existing related work, i.e. systems for anomaly detection, traffic sampling and network traffic processing in parallel. Sect. 3 describes scattering methods that can be used to split flow records into a separate groups for parallel processing by independent computational nodes. Sect. 4 describes our testing environment that was created for our experiments. The section also presents results of measurement of described scattering methods. Sect. 5 concludes the paper.

2   Related Work

This section describes related approaches of parallel network traffic analysis and anomaly detection usually done using Network Intrusion Detection System (NIDS) or Network Intrusion Prevention System (NIPS).

There are many existing systems for network traffic analysis and anomaly detection that are modular by design. For instance, TOPAS [1] and NEMEA [2] are flow-based systems that consists of modules that process data. When there is a big volume of flow data, running the systems on a single machine may reach resource limits of the machine. The systems do not support data distribution natively as it is available for various big data frameworks. However, NEMEA modules can be easily run and connected in a distributed environment.

Xinidis et al. in [3] presented an architecture with Active Splitter for distributed NIDS aiming for performance optimization of the detection sensors running Snort [4] (packet-based system performing deep packet inspection). The splitter uses hash functions for packet distribution and three techniques to optimize the performance of the sensors. Cumulative Acknowledgements reduce redundant sending of packets between splitter and sensors, Early Filtering in splitter applies Snort rule subset on packet headers (no payload inspection) and finally Locality Buffering reorders packets in a way that improves the locality of sensors memory accesses.

Sallay et al. in [5] made the network traffic analysis distributed using switch/router. The architecture contains dedicated sensors for individual services (e.g. FTP) and the incoming traffic is forwarded to them according to switching table of the switch/router. Sensors are running Snort but only with needed rule subset for their service. Since the volume of traffic of individual services can differ significantly, the load of computational nodes wouldn't be uniform. Therefore, this approach is not suitable for us.

Kim et al. in [6] compare static and dynamic hash-based load balancing schemes and propose dynamic (i.e. adaptive) load-balancing scheme for NIDS. It uses a lookup table which is periodically reorganized according to historical packet distribution and current load of individual nodes. If needed, flows with the smallest volume are reorganized. Proposed method distributes packets in a way that does not break the flow stream, however, they don't take into account relations between individual flow records and the impact of splitting on detection results is not evaluated.

Valentin et al. in [7] presented a NIDS cluster for scalable intrusion detection. It consists of frontend nodes that distribute packets between backend nodes running Bro [8] for intrusion detection. Moreover, there are proxy nodes propagating state information of backend nodes and also one central manager node for collecting and aggregating results. Each frontend node distributes data from one monitored line and uses a hashing distribution scheme with a single hash function. The architecture requires backend nodes and proxy nodes to exchange data with detection subresults. In our approach, we are dealing with splitting a stream of flow records instead of packets. Our hashing distribution scheme is adjusted to provide all needed data to the detection methods for correct intrusion detection. Therefore, our computational nodes running intrusion detection are independent and don't communicate with each other. Finally, our proposed hashing distribution scheme represents a general way, how to split flow data with respect to detection results.

Big data frameworks such as Hadoop [9] or Spark [10] are distributed by nature. They are based on storage of data onto some distributed file system. A special designed parallel algorithm can be used to run on many distributed nodes and process all data. A universal and the most popular approach of distributed processing is MapReduce. However, the overall result of this kind of computation usually depends on the Reduce phase that merges local results from all nodes. Therefore, only low attention is paid to any relations or semantics during the data distribution and storage. An improved data distribution in Hadoop was presented as Hashdoop in [11]. Contrary, our approach is more general and it is applicable even on stream-wise processing with multiple different algorithms. Even though the main focus of ours is to make non-distributed system working in parallel, the principle described in our paper can be used for improvement of data distribution in big data frameworks as well.

Sampling has a common goal with parallel processing – capability to handle more data at the same time. Mai in [12] shows impact of the packet sampling on detection of portscanning and Bartos in [13] deals with flow sampling techniques for anomaly detection. However none of these approaches can be applied on data splitting.

3   Flow Distribution Scheme

When designing a distribution scheme, several aspects have to be taken into account: (i) the data should be distributed uniformly between all computational nodes, (ii) the distribution algorithm should be as fast as possible in order to process as much data as possible, (iii) the impact of splitting the data on detection results should be minimized.

In general, there are two ways how to distribute the data, statically or dynamically (also called static and dynamic load-balancing) and both have some pros and cons when applied in parallel NIDS. Static distribution has immutable rules for splitting the data e.g. a packet with source IP address 1.2.3.4 goes to node 1 and a packet with source IP address 5.6.7.8 goes to node 2. This preserves the data stream with possible security incident. However, it cannot affect the load of individual computational nodes when the distribution is not uniform. On the other hand dynamic distribution can perform some actions in order to make the load uniform (e.g. redirect some packets to less loaded computational nodes). Unfortunately, this behaviour can make the security incident invisible. Therefore, we have decided to use static distribution and focus on uniformity.

Figure 1 shows high level view of the infrastructure of scalable and distributed network flows analysis using NIDS. The following subsections describe several splitting mechanisms used in the flow scatter.

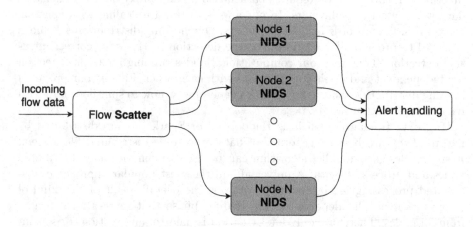

Fig. 1. A high level view of the infrastructure of scalable and distributed network flows analysis using NIDS.

3.1   Random Scattering

Lets assume the detection results are not dependent on any semantic relations between flow data, i.e. scattering mechanism can distribute the data regardless of the information from flow records. In that case, the flow scatter can distribute the flow records between nodes using statistical uniform distribution, which is optimal for load-balancing. Received records by flow scatter are forwarded to computational nodes according to random number generator. It is clear that every random distribution splits the flow records into different subsets. However, as we discuss in Evaluation (Sect. 4), breaking semantic relations in flow data using random distribution affects the detection results.

3.2   Scattering Based on Network Topology

Scattering based on network topology is another logical way of distributing the flow data. Since the computer networks are designed using hierarchical model that usually respects geographical and logical division into subnets and network lines.

Figure 2 shows a high level topology of CESNET2 National Research and Education Network (NREN), which is a backbone academic network and it is also used as a transit network. It is inter-connected with other networks via several lines that are being monitored. The data taken from the monitoring probes contain a line identification—the line number. Flow scatter can easily distribute the data using these line numbers.

Standard monitoring infrastructure collects flow records from monitoring probes onto one central collector. In case of scattering based on network topology, this concept can be changed and it would be more efficient to send exported flow records directly to computational nodes.

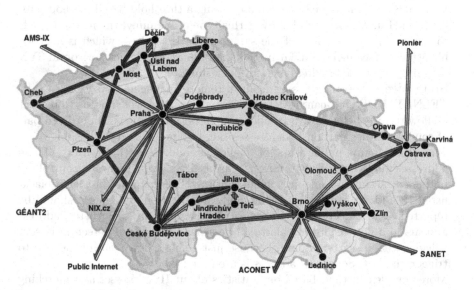

Fig. 2. Topology of Czech national research and education network (NREN) CES-NET2, network traffic on the perimeter is analyzed.

3.3   Hash-Based Scattering

Hash functions are used to transform an input data into an output form with a fixed length. Cryptography expects that the output of an ideal hash function meets requirements such as uniform distribution and missing relation between output and input. In our case, the hash function can be used in the flow scatter to select an appropriate computational node number uniformly. Information from the incoming flow records can be used as an input for the hash function.

The dependency of selected node number on the input data of the hash function leads to divison of flow records into subsets with the same characteristics. The subsets with the same characteristics are then processed together on the same computational node and this can be used to preserve the detection results. For instance, if we use only the source IP address for hashing, all flow records having the same source IP address ends up on the same node. Meanwhile, flow records with different source IP addresses have a high probability to be processed with different nodes.

Let some set of flow records contain a security incident that can be detected using some detection method. Then, there exists a minimal subset of flow records with semantic relations that must be processed by this detection method together to get a correct result. In order to find the semantic relations in flow data, a set of detection methods was studied. The aim is to find a suitable set of information that is used as an input for hash function.

Studied Detection Methods

- Vertical SYN scanning can be detected using a threshold-based method published in [14]. To successfully detect this type of scanning, the method needs to receive all flow records of the same source IP address which is a possible attacker (scanner). Similar method can be used to detect horizontal SYN scanning. Source IP address is used for hashing.
- Brute-force password guessing against remote management services (SSH, TELNET, RDP etc.) can be detected using a method which needs to inspect all flow records between two IP addresses in both directions. An ordered pair of source and destination IP addresses (i.e. bi-flow) is used for hashing.
- There are many public lists of malicious addresses (black-lists). These addresses were abused due to various reasons like sharing malware, controlling botnets or acting in some anomalous evil way. Communication with a black-listed IP address can indicate some malware infection and thus it should be reported. The detection is quite easy—every time any blacklisted address appears in a flow record, an alert can be sent. This type of detection is very efficient with a scattered data, because just a single flow record is needed to trigger an alert. Source IP address is used for hashing.
- More complex method based on statistics about IP addresses and matching the rules describing malicious traffic is able to detect DoS, DNS amplification, SSH brute-force password guessing and horizontal scanning. It needs to receive all flow records with the same IP address regardless of whether it is a source or a destination IP. Therefore, hashing both source and destination IP

addresses separately is needed in this case, which can result in duplication. The flow record can be forwarded to two different computational nodes. The duplication effect will be discussed later in this section.

– One of the detection methods based on application layer can detect brute-force attacks and scanning of user accounts on a Session Initiation Protocol (SIP) device. The detection method analyzes SIP responses from the server so all flows with the same source IP address must be delivered to the same node. Source IP address is used for hashing.

In general, we have recognized three groups of detection algorithms, whereas each group has to process all flow data with the same characteristic (e.g. same source IP address) on a single computation node. Therefore, we have a group of detection algorithms expecting all flow records with the same **source** address, a group expecting flow records with the same **destination** address and a group expecting flow records with the same **ordered pair of source and destination** addresses. Figure 3 shows all three hash functions of the flow scatter where each hash function has the same color as the corresponding group of detection algorithms.

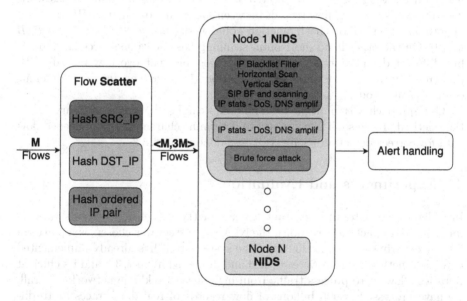

Fig. 3. Flow scatter contains three hash functions, each uses a specific information from flow records. The result of a hash function determines the computational node that processes the flow record with corresponding group of detection methods. (Color figure online)

Since we want to run all detection algorithms in parallel, all three hash functions must be computed for every flow record. Naturally, results of the three hash functions can be different. Therefore, one flow record can be sent to at least one and, in the worst case, up to three computational nodes. This duplication is caused by the number of different groups of algorithms and it is needed to provide all flow records that should be processed together to the algorithms (to preserve correct detection results).

In fact, the number of duplicates does not affect overall scaling of the parallel processing i.e. higher number of computational nodes does not increase the duplicates. Moreover, each hashing function determines a computational node, which processes the flow record with corresponding group of detection methods. Therefore, each group processes the flow record only on one computational node and every flow record is processed by all groups of detection methods. For example, if the selected nodes are 2 (for the SRC IP red hash) and 5 (for the DST IP yellow hash and for the IP pair green hash), it is processed by red group on `node` 2, yellow and green group on `node` 5. It means, that flow record may be duplicated, but only on a communication level between flow scatter and computational nodes.

To compare our approach with a single hashing function e.g. NIDS cluster [7] uses $hash = md5(srcIP + dstIP)$, we can show, that it would not work for us. Let's take methods for detection of horizontal port scanning and brute-force password guessing discussed in Sect. 3.3. The method for brute-force password guessing needs to see all flow records between source and destination IP addresses in both directions, so this hash function would work ($md5(A + B)$ is equal $md5(B + A)$). On the other hand, horizontal scanning has the same source IP address but different destination addresses, so it is possible that two flow records with the same source IP but different destination IP could end up on a different computational node.

Our approach with multiple hash functions can be applied on arbitrary detection method. To do so, it is necessary to determine characteristics of needed flow data for correct detection result, as it was done in Sect. 3.3.

4   Experiments and Evaluation

In order to evaluate all important aspects of the scattering methods (uniformity, speed, impact on detection), the NEMEA system was chosen as a platform for our experiments and evaluation. The system itself has already implemented detection methods, which were studied and discussed in Sect. 3.3 and its efficient libraries allow us to process traffic from high speed backbone network. Overall, we have processed over 5 billions of flow records of real data traces in 10 different (pseudonymised) data sets captured in CESNET2 NREN during August and September 2016 with on average of 60,000 flows/s.

4.1   Testing Environment

For our experiments we used a virtual machine with 64b Scientific Linux 7 OS, with the following hardware specification: 16 CPU cores, 24 GB RAM, 2 TB free disk capacity.

Figure 4 shows the configuration of our testing environment. `IPFIXsend` and `IPFIXcol` [15] were used for replaying the IPFIX data in real-time. The flow data were received by the `flow scatter` and also directly by the `node 0` which was used as a reference single instance (it processes all flow data without any splitting). The `node 0` was a ground truth for us to evaluate an impact of data splitting on detection results. The flow scatter distributes flow data between nodes 1–8 as it was described earlier. All nodes contain exactly the same set of detection methods. During the experiments, we have collected data from 8 exporting probes that monitor different lines.

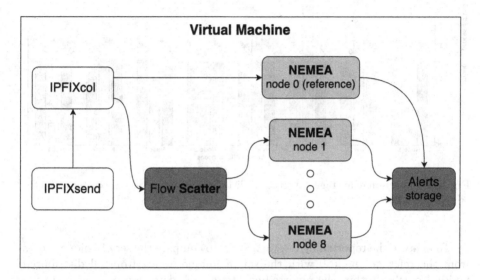

Fig. 4. Testing environment for experiments and evaluation of various methods of flow data distribution between computational nodes running flow-based NIDS NEMEA.

4.2 Results

The detection results from all nodes were stored and the analysis is described in this section.

Figure 5 shows a comparison of an average distribution of flow records based on various scattering methods. The optimal value (red dashed line) is 12.5% for 8 nodes. Random scattering achieves optimal results because of the used statistical uniform distribution. However, hash-based scattering is not significantly worse than the random (i.e. optimal) one. On the other hand, link-wise scattering is unbalanced because of different speeds of the monitored lines and the volume of traffic[1]. Node 1 even processed no data because there were no data exported

---

[1] We expect that such unbalanced distribution based on observation points can be observed in every network with lines of different bandwidth.

from the first line. For hash-based scattering, we have compared data distribution using two different hashing algorithms—CRC32 and Jenkins. On average, CRC32 had better results and therefore it was chosen as a final solution.

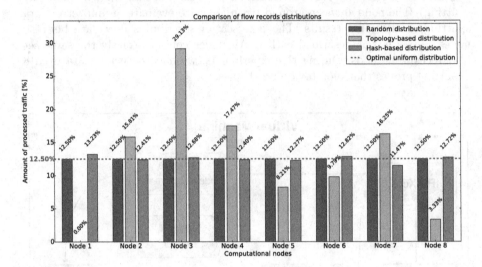

Fig. 5. Comparison of average flow records distributions using various scattering methods. (Color figure online)

To analyze the reported alerts, we needed to compare the set of unique events from the reference node 0 with the set of unique events from all distributed nodes. To achieve this, the reported events of each detection method and each node were analyzed separately at first. Subsequently, the unique events were merged together. For example, in the case of horizontal scanning, if an attacker probes 50 or more computers in two different subnets, where 50 is a threshold of the detection algorithm, 2 events should be reported. Hash-based scattering delivers all flow records representing this traffic to the same node due to the source IP address hashing. Using link-wise scattering, the flow records could end up on different nodes because the traffic can go through different lines. Random scattering will split the flow records randomly.

Figure 6 shows a comparison of the detection results after applying various scattering methods. Note, that *Hoststatsnemea* in the figure legend stands for the method based on statistics about IP addresses, which was discussed in Sect. 3.3. The first column represents the reference instance with 100% reported events, whereas each type of events has a different color and it is normalized so that the number of different event types are represented equally. Random distribution (the second column) has a huge impact on the detection results because of breaking the semantic relations between flow records. This was an expected result, however, the random distribution is a reference of optimal flow data distribution. Scattering based on the network topology (the third column) caused

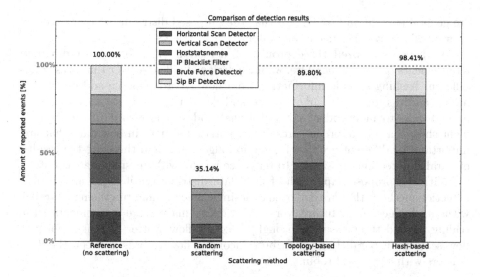

Fig. 6. Comparison of the detection results after applying various scattering methods. Each part of column with different color stands for normalized number of unique events reported by different detection method. (Color figure online)

that some of distributed attacks and, in general, N:1 or 1:N attacks (DDoS, horizontal scanning etc.) were not detected. The last column shows that scattering based on hashing specific information from flow data has the best results. The reason of undetected events is probably a periodic clean-up of structures containing information and timing of stream-wise detection algorithms.

After the evaluation of the uniformity and the impact on the detection, we tested a maximal throughput of the hash-based flow scatter as the best method for distribution. A simple NEMEA module was created to generate and send 100 million flow records at full speed to the flow scatter. Measured computation time was focused on the main cycle receiving the flow record, hashing, making decision about number of computational nodes the flow belongs to according to the computed hashes and sending the flow record. The maximal throughput was on average 1.8 million flow records per second.

5   Conclusion

This paper presented the results of practical experiments with different approaches of splitting a stream of network flow data for the purposes of parallel anomaly detection. The aim of our work was to compare not only a uniformity of distribution but also an impact of data splitting on the detection results. Our experiments were performed using real traffic traces from Czech national research and education network (NREN). For simulation of parallel processing, we used an open source detection system NEMEA, however, the analysis results are general enough and we believe that the proposed distribution approach can be used with any other detection system.

We have recognized three groups of detection algorithms with different requirements on data. Therefore, we have designed a flow scatter that uses three different hashing specific information from flow records (source address, destination address, ordered pair of source and destination address) to provide all needed data to independent computational nodes. The results of our experiment show that our approach preserves semantic relations in flow data that are important for different groups of detection algorithms and therefore the results of parallel detection are similar to reference results without splitting the data.

With the proposed approach of flow data distribution, it is possible to use detection methods that are deployed on a single machine and run them in parallel without changes. As a future work, we want to make more experiments with scaling beyond the measured throughput of the flow scatter by using multiple flow scatters in parallel and distribute incoming flow records between the flow scatters with e.g. round robin.

Acknowledgment. This work was supported by the Technology Agency of the Czech Republic under No. TA04010062 *Technology for processing and analysis of network data in big data concept*, grant No. SGS17/212/OHK3/3T/18 funded by MEYS and the project Reg. No. CZ.02.1.01/0.0/0.0/16_013/0001797 co-funded by the MEYS and ERDF.

References

1. Munz, G., Carle, G.: Real-time analysis of flow data for network attack detection. In: 2007 10th IFIP/IEEE International Symposium on Integrated Network Management, pp. 100–108, May 2007. doi:10.1109/INM.2007.374774
2. Cejka, T., Bartos, V., Svepes, M., Rosa, Z., Kubatova, H.: NEMEA: a framework for network traffic analysis. In: 2016 12th International Conference on Network and Service Management (CNSM), pp. 195–201, October 2016. doi:10.1109/CNSM.2016.7818417
3. Xinidis, K., Charitakis, I., Antonatos, S., Anagnostakis, K.G., Markatos, E.P.: An active splitter architecture for intrusion detection and prevention. IEEE Trans. Dependable Secure Comput. **3**(1), 31–44 (2006). doi:10.1109/TDSC.2006.6
4. Roesch, M.: Snort - lightweight intrusion detection for networks. In: Proceedings of the 13th USENIX Conference on System Administration, LISA 1999, Berkeley, CA, USA, pp. 229–238. USENIX Association (1999)
5. Sallay, H., Alshalfan, K.A., Fred, O.B., Words, K.: A scalable distributed IDS architecture for high speed networks. IJCSNS Int. J. Comput. SciNetw. Secur. **9**(8), 9–16 (2009)
6. Kim, N.-U., Jung, S.-M., Chung, T.-M.: An efficient hash-based load balancing scheme to support parallel NIDS. In: Murgante, B., Gervasi, O., Iglesias, A., Taniar, D., Apduhan, B.O. (eds.) ICCSA 2011. LNCS, vol. 6782, pp. 537–549. Springer, Heidelberg (2011). doi:10.1007/978-3-642-21928-3_39

7. Vallentin, M., Sommer, R., Lee, J., Leres, C., Paxson, V., Tierney, B.: The NIDS cluster: scalable, stateful network intrusion detection on commodity hardware. In: Kruegel, C., Lippmann, R., Clark, A. (eds.) RAID 2007. LNCS, vol. 4637, pp. 107–126. Springer, Heidelberg (2007). doi:10.1007/978-3-540-74320-0_6

8. Paxson, V.: Bro: a system for detecting network intruders in real-time. Comput. Netw. **31**(23–24), 2435–2463 (1999). doi:10.1016/S1389-1286(99)00112-7

9. Apache: Hadoop. http://hadoop.apache.org

10. Apache: Spark. http://spark.apache.org

11. Fontugne, R., Mazel, J., Fukuda, K.: Hashdoop: a MapReduce framework for network anomaly detection. In: IEEE Conference on Computer Communications Workshops (INFOCOM) (2014). doi:10.1109/INFCOMW.2014.6849281

12. Mai, J., Sridharan, A., Chuah, C.N., Zang, H., Ye, T.: Impact of packet sampling on portscan detection. IEEE J. Sel. Areas Commun. **24**(12), 2285–2298 (2006). doi:10.1109/JSAC.2006.884027

13. Bartos, K., Rehak, M.: Towards efficient flow sampling technique for anomaly detection. In: Pescapè, A., Salgarelli, L., Dimitropoulos, X. (eds.) TMA 2012. LNCS, vol. 7189, pp. 93–106. Springer, Heidelberg (2012). doi:10.1007/978-3-642-28534-9_11

14. Cejka, T., Svepes, M.: Analysis of vertical scans discovered by naive detection. In: Badonnel, R., Koch, R., Pras, A., Drašar, M., Stiller, B. (eds.) AIMS 2016. LNCS, vol. 9701, pp. 165–169. Springer, Cham (2016). doi:10.1007/978-3-319-39814-3_19

15. Velan, P., Krejčí, R.: Flow information storage assessment using IPFIXcol. In: Sadre, R., Novotný, J., Čeleda, P., Waldburger, M., Stiller, B. (eds.) AIMS 2012. LNCS, vol. 7279, pp. 155–158. Springer, Heidelberg (2012). doi:10.1007/978-3-642-30633-4_21

A Blockchain-Based Architecture for Collaborative DDoS Mitigation with Smart Contracts

Bruno Rodrigues[1]([✉]), Thomas Bocek[1], Andri Lareida[1], David Hausheer[2], Sina Rafati[1], and Burkhard Stiller[1]

[1] Communication Systems Group (CSG), Department of Informatics (IfI), University of Zürich (UZH), Zürich, Switzerland
{rodrigues,bocek,lareida,rafati,stiller}@ifi.uzh.ch
[2] P2P Systems Engineering Lab, Department of Electrical Engineering and Information Technology, TU Darmstadt, Darmstadt, Germany
hausheer@ps.tu-darmstadt.de

Abstract. The rapid growth in the number of insecure portable and stationary devices and the exponential increase of traffic volume makes Distributed Denial-of-Service (DDoS) attacks a top security threat to services provisioning. Existing defense mechanisms lack resources and flexibility to cope with attacks by themselves, and by utilizing other's companies resources, the burden of the mitigation can be shared. Emerging technologies such as blockchain and smart contracts allows for the sharing of attack information in a fully distributed and automated fashion. In this paper, the design of a novel architecture is proposed by combining these technologies introducing new opportunities for flexible and efficient DDoS mitigation solutions across multiple domains. Main advantages are the deployment of an already existing public and distributed infrastructure to advertise white or blacklisted IP addresses, and the usage of such infrastructure as an additional security mechanism to existing DDoS defense systems, without the need to build specialized registries or other distribution mechanisms, which enables the enforcement of rules across multiple domains.

Keywords: Distributed Denial-of-Service (DDoS) · Security · Blockchain · Software-defined Networks (SDN) · Network management

1 Introduction

In the past years, a rise in DDoS attacks could be observed [1]. DDoS attacks have the simple goal of interrupting or suspending services available on the Internet and its motivations range from personal grudges over blackmail to political reasons [10]. A recent example is an attack conducted against Domain Name System (DNS) servers responsible for domains such as Twitter, PayPal, and

© The Author(s) 2017
D. Tuncer et al. (Eds.): AIMS 2017, LNCS 10356, pp. 16–29, 2017.
DOI: 10.1007/978-3-319-60774-0_2

Spotify [20] in October 2016. As a consequence, those services became unavailable to many US (United States) users for several hours. Besides the frequency, also the strength and duration of DDoS attacks are growing making them more efficient and dangerous. One reason for the increasing size of attacks is the availability of many reflectors, and *i.e.*, weakly secured or configured IoT (Internet of Things) devices or home gateways [20].

By exploiting legal services on those devices, *e.g.*, the Simple Service Discovery Protocol, the power of a DDoS attack is amplified, and the problem of defense is made more complicated. Thus, the impact of DDoS varies from minor inconvenience to severe financial losses for enterprises that rely on their online availability [14]. Various mitigation techniques have been proposed. However, only a few have been considered for widespread deployment because of their effectiveness and implementation complexities. An ongoing IETF (Internet Engineering Task Force) proposal discusses the development of a collaborative protocol called DOTS (DDoS Open Threat Signaling) to advertise DDoS attacks [13]. However, this paper proposes an infrastructure of blockchains and smart contracts, which provide the required instrumentation without the need to maintain design and development complexities of such a new protocol.

As with a different direction, the adoption of DDoS protection services, offered by companies such as Akamai [1] or CloudFlare [3], is increasing [7]. Those cloud-based solutions can absorb DDoS attacks by increasing capacity and taking the burden of detection away from the device under attack by exporting flow records from edge routers and switches. Additional analysis is performed in the cloud and packet filtering is used to balance, reroute, or drop the traffic inside the cloud. However, those solutions requires a third party DDoS Protection Service (DPS) provider, which is implying in additional costs and a decrease in service performance.

This paper presents the architecture and design of a collaborative mechanism using smart contracts and investigates the possibility of mitigating a DDoS attack in a fully decentralized manner. Thus, service providers interested in shared protection, can not only signal the occurrence of attacks but also share detection and mitigation mechanisms. The objective is to create an automated, and easy-to-manage DDoS mitigation. Three major building blocks are identified to build such a mechanism.

Blockchains and Smart Contracts. This approach proposes an architecture and an implementation of an approach to signaling white or blacklisted IP addresses across multiple domains based on blockchains and smart contracts. The advantage of using smart contracts in a blockchain is: (a) to make use of an already existing infrastructure to distribute rules without the need to build specialized registries or other distribution mechanisms/protocols, (b) to apply rules across multiple domains, which means that even if the AS (Autonomous System) of the victim is not applying these rules, some traffic can still be filtered, and (c) the victim or its AS can control which customers get blocked. The only central element remaining is to show proof of IP ownership.

Software-defined Network (SDN) is an effective solution to enable customizable security policies and services in a dynamic fashion. The centralized network control and its deployment based on the OpenFlow [11] protocol facilitates the enforcement of high-level security policies moving away from current approaches based on SNMP (Simple Network Management Protocol) and CLI (Command Line Interface). With SDN, flow-rules can be applied to block DDoS attacks, and the closer these rules are applied, and those malicious packets can be dropped, the less DDoS traffic occurs. This work uses SDN-based networks as a use case to perform in a more rapid fashion in ASes the definition and verification of flows to mitigate DDoS attacks. However, the presented solution is not limited to the usage of an SDN-based network, being compatible with detection/monitoring tools able to export attack information to be published in the blockchain.

This paper is structured as follows. Section 2 introduces basic concepts and related work on blockchain and smart contracts. Section 3 presents related collaborative DDoS mitigation strategies. Section 4 presents the architecture detailing its components and basic functioning, as well as describing the implementation details of the proposed solution. Section 5 provides a discussion on the development and results obtained so far. The work is concluded in Sect. 6 highlighting the significant contributions and discussing future work.

2   Background

Smart contracts are a piece of software made to facilitate the negotiation or performance of a contract, being able to be executed, verified or enforced on its own. A smart contract alone is not "smart" as it needs an infrastructure that can implement, verify, and enforce the negotiation or performance of a contract by particular computer protocols. It has gained attention in the context of blockchains that provide a fully decentralized infrastructure to run, execute, and verify such smart contracts [2]. Therefore, smart contracts need to run on a blockchain to ensure (a) its permanent storage and (b) obstacles to manipulate the contract?s content. A node participating in the blockchain runs a smart contract by executing its script, validating the result of the script, and storing the contract and its result in a block.

Although the Bitcoin [12] blockchain was the first fully decentralized distributed ledger, it is primarily designed for transfer of digital assets, and it is not Turing-complete (*e.g.*, it does not support loops). Such a Turing-complete contract language allows defining rules to allow or block IP addresses that can be interpreted by an SDN controller. While several projects try to address these issues, the Ethereum [23] blockchain is the most popular that supports a Turing-complete contract language, empowering more sophisticated smart contracts. In Ethereum, smart contracts run in a sand-boxed Ethereum Virtual Machine (EVM) and every operation executed in the EVM has to be paid for to prevent Denial-of-Service (DoS) attacks.

SDN characteristics provide better network visibility by decoupling the control plane from the data plane and by the centralized management to perform tasks such as network diagnosis and troubleshooting [9]. In addition to SDN, the OpenFlow protocol [11] leverages network management by providing a programmable and standardized interface between the data plane and the control plane. It has been recognized that the decoupling of the data plane and the control plane makes SDN a promising solution to enable the enforcement of customizable security services and policies. Various SDN-based solutions have been proposed to deal with DDoS attacks [24]. A survey on these issues is provided in [17]. However, each security/concern category can be sub-divided in fine-grained aspects *e.g.*, authentication, integrity, network communications. In the following are presented mainly research efforts addressing DDoS attacks in SDN networks.

To analyze the impact of DDoS attacks on network performance, the works in [18] and [8] have shown how such attacks may impact on several parameters like the control plane bandwidth (*i.e.*, controller-switch channel), latency, switches flow tables and the controller performance. Other works as [22] and [4] use the SDN capabilities to implement schemes that allow to detect and mitigate DDoS attacks through packet analysis and filtering. These solutions reduce the impact of attacks, but they may cause an overhead in the flow-tables and the SDN controller. Also, they do not provide any solution to address these particular SDN performance issues as proposed in [5] (*e.g.*, flow-tables, and controller overloading). Furthermore, they also do not consider DDoS attacks and the collaboration with AS customers as [16].

SDN-based solutions allow greater agility to enforce decisions that require a global network view. Therefore, intra-domain security policies and mechanisms to prevent and react to DDoS attacks can be made agiler. By combining the intra-domain capabilities provided by SDN and the inter-domain advantages provided by blockchains and smart contracts, the efficiency to mitigate DDoS attacks in both inter- and intra-domains can be improved.

3   Related Work

There are four broad categories of defense against DDoS attacks according to [14]: (1) attack prevention, (2) attack detection, (3) attack source identification, and (4) attack reaction.

(1) Tries to prevent attacks before they become a problem, *i.e.* as close to the sources as possible. The obvious method to achieve this for amplified or reflected attacks is for the access provider to filter spoofed packets;
(2) Can be a difficult task since certain attacks mask themselves as legitimate user traffic or use various traffic types. Due to this complexity, it can be hard to make a confident decision if traffic is part of an attack or special user behavior, *e.g.* a flash crowd;
(3) Is applied after an attack was detected. This step is important to efficiently contain or re-route the attack as close to its source as possible;
(4) The final step involves taking concrete measures against the attack. The better the result from (3) the more efficiently this can be done.

Among the collaborative DDoS mitigation techniques, there are two main approaches using resource management to react against bandwidth attacks [14]. The first takes effect within the victim's domain and the second within the domain of the victims ISP, *i.e.* the AS. Both techniques apply traffic classification and define specific actions for those classes. Both customer and AS resource management schemes need to classify traffic into several types, and then treat them differently. However, it is rather difficult to give an accurate classification as DDoS attacks can mimic any legitimate traffic. In this regard, some sophisticated techniques can be implemented to classify traffic, but a unified reaction strategies implemented both at the AS and the customer can be more efficient than applying just one.

Other works exist for cooperative defense against DDoS attacks. However, it is still an open issue since DDoS attacks are growing in scale, sophistication, duration and frequency [10]. The IETF is currently proposing a protocol [13] called DOTS (DDoS Open Threat Signaling) covering both intra-organization and inter-organization communications to advertise attacks. The protocol requires servers and clients DOTS agents, which can be organized in both centralized and distributed architectures to advertise black or whitelisted addresses. A DOTS client should register to a DOTS server in advance sending provision and capacity protection information and be advertised of attacks. Then, the DOTS protocol is used among the agents to facilitate and coordinate the DDoS protection service as a whole. Also, a similar approach to the IETF proposal is presented in [19]. The authors use a similar architecture but using an advertising protocol based on FLEX (FLow-based Event eXchange) format, which is used to simplify the integration and deployment of the solution and facilitate the communication process between the involved domains.

The proposed standard advertises the need for defensive measures in anticipation of or response to attack. The main drawback compared to the approach presented herein is the requirement of additional infrastructure requiring trust and collaboration between ISPs. A collaborative defense approach using VNF (Virtual Network Functions) is presented in [15]. The authors propose a cooperation between domains that implements VNFs to alleviate DDoS attacks by redirecting and reshaping excessive traffic to other collaborating domains for filtering. In [24], a gossip-based communication mechanism is proposed to exchange information about attacks between independent detection points to aggregate information about the overall observed attacks. The system is built as a peer-to-peer overlay network to disseminate attack information to other listening users or systems rapidly.

A similar approach was presented in [21], formalizing a gossip-based protocol to exchange information in overlay network using intermediate network routers. A different approach is presented in [16], which proposes a collaborative framework that allows the customers to request DDoS mitigation from ASes. However, the solution requires an SDN controller implemented at customer side interfaced with the AS, which can change the label of the anomalous traffic and redirect them to security middle-boxes. In the approach presented in this paper customers and ISPs can take action to mitigate an attack by interfacing directly with a blockchain providing the necessary trust.

Instead of making use of an existing infrastructure such as the blockchain and smart contracts, approaches mentioned above proposes the development of specific gossip-based protocols. In this sense, the deployment and integration of such solutions become complex since existing solutions need to be modified to support these protocols. The IETF proposal focuses on standardizing a protocol to facilitate its deployment. However, its implementation complexity still exists in distributed and centralized architectures to support the different types of communication. Instead, some of the requirements can be inherited from the natural characteristics of blockchains, smart contracts, and SDN, avoiding the complexities of development and adoption of new protocols.

4   Proposed System Architecture

This section presents the design principles considered in the architectural design. First, Sect. 4.1 exemplifies a deployment scenario. Section 4.2 provides a detailed description of its main components. Implementation details are presented in Sect. 4.3.

4.1   Application Scenario

A scenario is presented in Fig. 1 illustrating the system architecture. A web server hosted at AS C is under a DDoS attack from devices hosted at various domains (ASes A, B, and C). With a non-collaborative DDoS mitigation approach, the web server relies on defense mechanisms that are implemented at the AS where it is allocated, which in many cases may be distant from the origin of the attack traffic and therefore overloading several domains with attack traffic.

Participants of the collaborative defense (ASes and customers) first need to create a smart contract, that is promptly linked with a registry-based type of smart contracts. Therefore, when attackers overload web server, the customer or the AS under attack stores the IP addresses of attackers in the smart contract. In an Ethereum blockchain a new block is created every 14 s, so subscribed ASes will receive updated lists of addresses to be blocked and confirm the authenticity of the attack by analyzing the traffic statistics and verifying the authenticity of the target's address.

Once other ASes retrieve the list of attackers and confirm the attack, different mitigation strategies can be triggered according to the security policies and mechanisms available in the domain. Also, it can block malicious traffic near of its origin. Near-source, defense is ideal for the health of the Internet because it can reduce the total cost of forwarding packets which, in the case of DDoS attacks mostly consist of useless massive attack traffic [13].

In scenarios involving multiple domains, once collaborative defense nodes receive information about attacks, these can apply mitigation actions in agreement with their security policies. In this sense, an incentive mechanism is necessary to prevent domains from abusing cooperative defense.

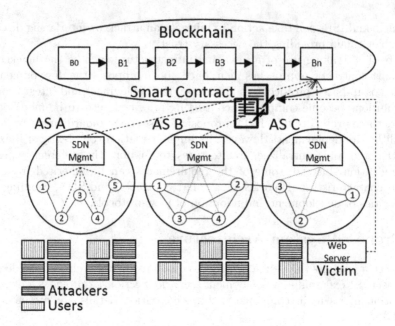

Fig. 1. Application scenario

4.2   Architectural Design

As DDoS attacks continue to increase and vary in their patterns, the need for coordinated responses also increases to detour the attacks efficiently. However, it is important to note that only the collaboration between customers and ASes is an additional approach to existing defense mechanisms. The architecture depicted in Fig. 2 is composed of three components:

- **Customers**: may report white or blacklisted IP addresses to the Ethereum blockchain via smart contracts;
- **ASes**: may publish white or blacklisted IP addresses and retrieve lists containing the published IP addresses, and may implement their DDoS mitigation mechanisms;
- **Blockchain/Smart Contract**: the public Ethereum blockchain (Ethereum Virtual Machine nodes) running Solidity smart contracts, which comprises the logic to report IP addresses in the blockchain.

The architecture is built considering the following principles:

(1) DDoS detection and mitigation countermeasures are provided as on-demand services by either the ASes or third-party services;
(2) To report/receive attack information, it is necessary for the domain to dedicate a node connected to the blockchain. This can be dedicated hardware exclusively for this purpose or virtualized to minimize resource consumption;

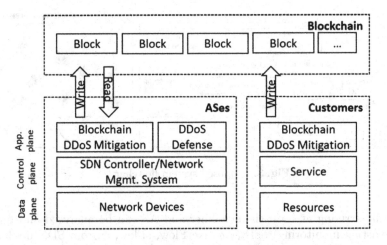

Fig. 2. Proposed system architecture

(**3**) To efficiently aid coordinated attack responses, Blockchain DDoS Mitigation modules are running on the entities (customers or ASes) reporting IP addresses and listening to the blockchain;

(**4**) Only customers or ASes with proof of ownership of their IP may report addresses to the smart contract;

(**5**) Different domains implement different security policies as well as different underlying management systems. Once notified of a DDoS attack in which the customer has its authenticity confirmed, countermeasures are defined according to the domain security policies and available actions.

To mitigate DDoS attacks (1) different techniques can be used upon the detection by ASes or customers, which typically involves analyzing Internet traffic with sophisticated attack detection algorithms, followed by filtering. In this regard, a collaborative approach decreases the overhead of such algorithm in the detection phase using information from other domains. Blockchain DDoS Mitigation appliances (2) both on the customer and ASes are simpler as Ethereum is public and already available technology, which can be used to perform rapid and widespread DDoS advertisement using smart contracts. Services with challenge/response authentication can be utilized by an AS to ensure that the IP address (3) of the customer reporting the attack is the customer under attack, and to enforce the necessary countermeasures (4) by the security policies implemented in the domain.

The smart contract logic illustrated in Fig. 3 is deployed as a complementary solution to existing DDoS mitigation mechanisms. However, domains implementing the system should consider the principles mentioned above in its design. First, any domain (*e.g.*, customers or ASes) participating must create a smart contract identified with an IP address or range of addresses certified by an authority. Then, the smart contract is registered in a registry-based type of smart contract so that participation can be easily tracked and thus relevant smart contracts can be identified.

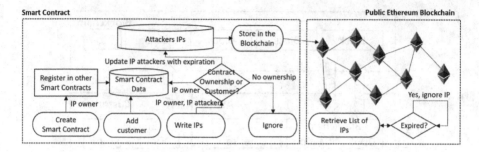

Fig. 3. Proposed system flowchart

Traffic arriving at both the customer and AS can be analyzed and filtered using existing monitoring tools (*e.g.*, NetFlow, sFlow, custom SDN implementations). The Blockchain appliance can be deployed as an additional security feature to any system that implements an apparatus to advertise black or whitelisted IP addresses to the blockchain. The analysis of traffic in a gateway is facilitated by SDN, and therefore the approach is intended to use a monitoring framework based on the OpenFlow protocol.

4.3   Implementation Details

Listing 1.1 and 1.2 outlines current implemented features of the smart contract to store source IP addresses that should be blocked or allowed. For simplicity, only IPv4 addresses are shown here. Either the customer or the AS can create the smart contract. In any case, a certificate of IP ownership is required. For the customer, the certificate can be created with an automated challenge-response system, while the AS requires a certificate matching their entry in the AS registration.

The one that created the smart contract (owner of the account that created the contract) can add other addresses that are also allowed to add IPs to block. Before such address is added, it is checked if the address matches its parent subnet. Both AS and the customer can store src IP with an expiration time. The time is measured in blocks, and the access to the stored data is public and can be viewed by anyone.

Before retrieving a list of IP pairs (source/destination), the verifyIP() function needs to be called to make sure that the target IP address has a proof of ownership. The issuing of a certificate (certOwnerIPv4) is the only remaining central entity in the architecture. After that, any AS (does not need to be the customers AS) can use these IPs to block traffic on its network.

The smart contract needs first to register itself in another smart contract Registry, which stores all relevant smart contracts that should be watched. Thus an AS listens for these changes, and any addition can be monitored and assessed against the network properties of the AS and apply a blocking rule if necessary.

```
1  contract SDNRulesAS {
2    struct ReportIPv4 {
3      uint32 expiringBlock;
4      uint32 src_ip;
5      DstIPv4 dst_ip;
6    } ReportIPv4[] report_src_ipv4;
7
8    struct DstIPv4 {
9      uint32 dst_ipv4;
10     uint8 dst_mask;
11   } DstIPv4 dstIPv4;
12   bytes certOwnerIPv4; address owner;
13   mapping (address => DstIPv4) customerIPv4;
14   bool flag; //Indicate black or whitelisted addresses
15   function SDNRulesAS(uint32 dst_ipv4, uint8 dst_ipv4_mask,
          bytes _certOwnerIPv4, bool _flag) {
16     owner = msg.sender;
17     certOwnerIPv4 = _certOwnerIPv4;
18     dstIPv4 = DstIPv4(dst_ipv4, dst_ipv4_mask);
19     flag = _flag;
20     //TODO: register in a registry contract
21   }
22   //suicide and deregistering function here
23   function createCustomerIPv4(address customer, uint32 dst_ipv4,
          uint8 dst_ipv4_mask) {
24     if(msg.sender == owner &&
25        isInSameIPv4Subnet(dst_ipv4, dst_ipv4_mask)) {
26       customerIPv4[customer] =
27         DstIPv4(dst_ipv4, dst_ipv4_mask);
28     }
29   }
30   function isInSameIPv4Subnet(uint32 dst_ipv4, uint8 dst_mask)
          constant returns (bool) {
31     // true if customer IP is in same subnet
32   }
33 }
```

Listing 1.1. Smart contract structures and core functionality

```
1  function reportIPv4(uint32[] src, uint32 expiringBlock) {
2    if (msg.sender == owner) {
3      for (uint i = 0; i < src.length; i++) {
4        drop_src_ipv4.push(ReportIPv4(
5          expiringBlock, src[i], dstIPv4));
6      }
7    }
8    DstIPv4 customer = customerIPv4[msg.sender];
9    if(customer.dst_ipv4 != 0) {
10     for (i = 0; i < src.length; i++) {
11       report_src_ipv4.push(ReportIPv4(
12         expiringBlock, src[i], customer));
13     }
14   }
15 }
16
```

```
17  function verifyIP(bytes pubKey) constant returns (bool) {
18    //check if signature in certOwnerIPv4 is correct
19  }
20
21  function reportedIPv4() constant returns (uint32[] src_ipv4,
22  uint32[] dst_ipv4, uint8[] mask) {
23    uint32[] memory src; uint32[] memory dst; uint8[] memory msk;
24    for (uint i = 0; i < report_src_ipv4.length; i++) {
25      if(drop_src_ipv4[i].expiringBlock > block.number) {
26        src[src.length] = report_src_ipv4[i].src_ip;
27        dst[dst.length] = report_src_ipv4[i].dst_ip.dst_ipv4;
28        msk[msk.length] = report_src_ipv4[i].dst_ip.dst_mask;
29      }
30    }
31    return (src, dst, msk);
32  }
```

Listing 1.2. Smart contract IP reporting functions

5   Discussion

The use of the Ethereum Virtual Machine (EVM) allows the multiple domains involved in an attack scenario to invoke functions in a smart contract reporting attacks or maintaining a list of trusted addresses to be operating in case of attack. The support of white or blacklisted IP addresses is a decision that depends on the policies and security mechanisms available in each domain. Therefore, the smart contract was developed to support both lists using a flag indicating which type of address is being reported. The existing and distributed storage infrastructure reduces the complexity in the development and adoption of the approach as it supersedes the design and standardization process of a gossip-based protocol, which needs to be embraced by the various ASes and customers. Also, the EVM smart contracts support in a decentralized and native way the logic to control who is reporting an attack and who are the attackers.

Through a high-level comparison with the ongoing IETF proposal (the DOTS protocol) [13], instead of making use of an existing infrastructure such as the blockchain and smart contracts, the IETF proposes from scratch the development of such protocol with several requirements (*e.g.*, extensibility, resilience) to be deployed in a distributed architecture. In this sense, the protocol development becomes complex since it must be deployed in distributed and centralized architectures to support different types of communication (inter and intra domain, *i.e*, inside the domain of an AS and between ASes). Instead, it is argued that some of the requirements can be inherited from the natural characteristics of blockchains, smart contracts and SDN, avoiding the complexities of development and adoption of new protocols.

However, this smart contract works well for a small number of attacks, while for large-scale attacks, the approach is currently costly the contract size, but will be addressed this issue in a future work to make reference to a larger list of IP addresses. Therefore, to keep the complexity of the architecture low, only the data (*e.g.*, IP addresses) should be stored in the contract, and it may become necessary to add a reference as shown in Listing 1.3, where the full list of addresses can be retrieved. The cost of adding 50 source IPs directly in a freshly deployed contract is 2.5 mio gas (gas is the internal pricing for running a transaction or contract in Ethereum) at the current gas price [6] of 20 gwei, which is 0.05 ETH at the current market price of 9.3 USD is in total 0.46 USD, while 100 source IPs cannot be mined in one contract and multiple contracts have to be used as it exceeds the 4 mio gas limit.

```
1  struct ReportIPv4 {
2  uint32 expiringBlock;
3  uint32 src_ip;
4  //e.g. https://example.com/blockedips.txt
5  string src_ipv4_ref;
6  DstIPv4 dst_ip;}
7  ReportIPv4[] report_src_ipv4;
```

Listing 1.3. Storing references

6   Summary and Future Work

This paper proposes a collaborative architecture using smart contracts and blockchain to enable DDoS mitigation across multiple domains. As a distributed and primarily public storage, the blockchain determines a straightforward and efficient structure to develop a collaborative approach toward DDoS attacks mitigation. The proposed architecture can be deployed as an additional security mechanism to existing DDoS protection schemes. Therefore, it is not intended to dictate how security mechanisms and policies should be implemented in a particular domain. Instead, it can be combined with existing solutions to reduce the DDoS detection and mitigation overhead by involving multiple domains in the process. Coupled with current solutions, the DDoS detection and mitigation overhead process comprising multiple domains can be reduced.

The architecture enables ASes to deploy their DPS and generate added value for their customers without transferring control of their network to a third party. The main contributions of this new approach are summarized as (a) the design and development of an architecture based on blockchains to advertise DDoS attacks across multiple domains, (b) the adoption and integration of the approach is facilitated since Ethereum and smart contracts are publicly available, and the ability to enforce rules on the ASes-side by the use of SDN, (c) can be utilized as an additional security mechanism without modifying existing ones.

Future work will investigate ways to compress the list, *e.g.*, with a bloom filter, and its advantages and disadvantages. Another limitation is that blocking of destination IPs should be possible only for static IPs. Thus, automated services issuing these certificates of IP ownership need to check for dynamic IPs first, *e.g.*, using services such as SORBS (dul.dnsbl.sorbs.net). Also, the current smart contract supports only one hierarchy. Thus, createCustomerCertIPv4() in Listing 1.1 needs to be extended to allow more hierarchies to map subnets accordingly.

Another major factor towards the practicability of the approach is the fairness among the cooperative domains. If an AS is targeted more times than others, means that one would be using resources of others to protect themselves. Therefore, this relevant aspect will be detailed in a future work to propose a reputation scheme based on the participation of the domains in the cooperative architecture.

References

1. Akamai: How to Protect Against DDoS Attacks - Stop Denial of Service (2016). https://www.akamai.com/us/en/resources/protect-against-ddos-attacks. jsp. Accessed 10 Jan 2017
2. Bocek, T., Stiller, B.: Smart Contracts - Blockchains in the Wings, pp. 1–16. Springer, Heidelberg. Tiergartenstr. 17, 69121, January 2017
3. CloudFare: Cloudflare advanced DDoS protection (2016). https://www.cloudflare. com/static/media/pdf/cloudflare-whitepaper-ddos.pdf
4. Dao, N.N., Park, J., Park, M., Cho, S.: A feasible method to combat against DDOS attack in SDN network. In: 2015 International Conference on Information Networking (ICOIN), pp. 309–311, January 2015
5. Dridi, L., Zhani, M.F.: SDN-guard: Dos attacks mitigation in SDN networks. In: 2016 5th IEEE International Conference on Cloud Networking (Cloudnet), pp. 212–217, October 2016
6. Fund, E: Ether unit converter. http://ether.fund/tool/converter
7. Jonker, M., Sperotto, A., van Rijswijk-Deij, R., Sadre, R., Pras, A.: Measuring the adoption of DDoS protection services. In: Proceedings of the 2016 ACM on Internet Measurement Conference, IMC 2016, Santa Monica, California, USA (2016)
8. Kandoi, R., Antikainen, M.: Denial-of-service attacks in openflow SDN networks. In: 2015 IFIP/IEEE International Symposium on Integrated Network Management (IM), pp. 1322–1326. IEEE (2015)
9. Kreutz, D., Ramos, F.M., Verissimo, P.E., Rothenberg, C.E., Azodolmolky, S., Uhlig, S.: Software-defined networking: a comprehensive survey. Proc. IEEE **103**(1), 14–76 (2015)
10. Mansfield-Devine, S.: The growth and evolution of DDoS. Netw. Secur. **10**, 13–20 (2015)
11. McKeown, N., Anderson, T., Balakrishnan, H., Parulkar, G., Peterson, L., Rexford, J., Shenker, S., Turner, J.: Openflow: enabling innovation in campus networks. ACM SIGCOMM Comput. Communi. Rev. **38**(2), 69–74 (2008)
12. Nakamoto, S.: Bitcoin: a peer-to-peer electronic cash system (2008)
13. Nishizuka, K., Xia, L., Xia, J., Zhang, D., Fang, L., Gray, C.: Inter-organization cooperative DDOS protection mechanism. Draft. https://tools.ietf.org/html/ draft-nishizuka-dots-inter-domain-mechanism-02
14. Peng, T., Leckie, C., Ramamohanarao, K.: Survey of network-based defense mechanisms countering the DoS and DDOS problems. ACM Comput. Surv. (CSUR) **39**(1), 3 (2007)
15. Rashidi, B., Fung, C.: CoFence: a collaborative DDOS defence using network function virtualization. In: 12th International Conference on Network and Service Management (CNSM 16), October 2016
16. Sahay, R., Blanc, G., Zhang, Z., Debar, H.: Towards autonomic DDOS mitigation using software defined networking. In: SENT 2015: NDSS Workshop on Security of Emerging Networking Technologies. Internet society (2015)

17. Scott-Hayward, S., O'Callaghan, G., Sezer, S.: SDN security: a survey. In: 2013 IEEE SDN for Future Networks and Services (SDN4FNS), pp. 1–7. IEEE (2013)
18. Shin, S., Gu, G.: Attacking software-defined networks: a first feasibility study. In: Proceedings of the Second ACM SIGCOMM Workshop on Hot Topics in Software Defined Networking, pp. 165–166. ACM (2013)
19. Steinberger, J., Kuhnert, B., Sperotto, A., Baier, H., Pras, A.: Collaborative DDOS defense using flow-based security event information. In: NOMS 2016–2016 IEEE/IFIP Network Operations and Management Symposium, pp. 516–522, April 2016
20. The Associated Press: Hackers Used 'Internet of Things' Devices to Cause Friday's Massive DDoS Cyberattack. http://www.cbc.ca/news/technology/hackers-ddos-attacks-1.3817392. Accessed 10 Jan 2017
21. Velauthapillai, T., Harwood, A., Karunasekera, S.: Global detection of flooding-based DDOS attacks using a cooperative overlay network. In: Network and System Security (NSS), pp. 357–364. IEEE (2010)
22. Wei, L., Fung, C.: Flowranger: a request prioritizing algorithm for controller dos attacks in software defined networks. In: 2015 IEEE International Conference on Communications (ICC), pp. 5254–5259. IEEE (2015)
23. Wood, G.: Ethereum: a secure decentralised generalised transaction ledger. https://goo.gl/LG7adX
24. Zhang, G., Parashar, M.: Cooperative defence against DDoS attacks. J. Res. Pract. Inf. Technol. 38(1), 69–84 (2006)

Achieving Reproducible Network Environments with INSALATA

Nadine Herold, Matthias Wachs, Marko Dorfhuber, Christoph Rudolf,
Stefan Liebald[✉], and Georg Carle

Department of Informatics, Chair of Network Architectures and Services,
Technical University of Munich (TUM), Munich, Germany
{herold,wachs,liebald,carle}@net.in.tum.de,
{marko.dorfhuber,christoph.rudolf}@tum.de

Abstract. Analyzing network environments for security flaws and
assessing new service and infrastructure configurations in general are
dangerous and error-prone when done in operational networks. Therefore, *cloning* such networks into a dedicated test environment is beneficial
for comprehensive testing and analysis without impacting the operational
network. To automate this reproduction of a network environment in a
physical or virtualized testbed, several key features are required: (a) a
suitable network model to describe network environments, (b) an automated acquisition process to instantiate this model for the respective
network environment, and (c) an automated setup process to deploy the
instance to the testbed.

With this work, we present INSALATA, an automated and extensible framework to reproduce physical or virtualized network environments in network testbeds. INSALATA employs a modular approach for
data acquisition and deployment, resolves interdependencies in the setup
process, and supports just-in-time reproduction of network environments. INSALATA is open source and available on Github. To highlight
its applicability, we present a real world case study utilizing INSALATA.

Keywords: Infrastructure Information Collection · Automated Testbed
Setup and Configuration · Testbed Management

1 Introduction

The increasing number of attack vectors and the growing complexity of attacks
on computer networks force operators to continuously assess and improve their
networks, services, and configurations. Analyzing, testing, and deploying new
security features and configuration improvements is time-consuming, challenging, and error-prone. The same holds for general software upgrades or network
infrastructure changes. Performing this on an operational network is often not
suitable, as service continuity has to be ensured and outages cannot be tolerated.

Therefore, reproducing a network environment into a self-contained test environment is beneficial as the operational network is not influenced. Testing and

© The Author(s) 2017
D. Tuncer et al. (Eds.): AIMS 2017, LNCS 10356, pp. 30–44, 2017.
DOI: 10.1007/978-3-319-60774-0_3

analyzing different options to improve the network and its security can be evaluated and tested sufficiently before deployment. With large and complex network environments, reproducing such network environments cannot be done manually as information about the environment and its elements may be unknown, incomplete, or not available in a formal description. Hence, an automated process to reproduce network environments in a physical or virtualized testbed is required.

In this work, we present *INSALATA*, the *IT NetworkS AnaLysis And deploymenT Application*. INSALATA enables network operators and researchers to automate reproduction of arbitrary network environments in physical or virtualized testbeds. To represent network environments, we provide a network model comprising layer-2 network segments, IP networks, connectivity information (routing and firewalling), network nodes (routers, hosts), network services (DNS, DHCP), and host information (network interfaces, memory, disks, operating system). INSALATA can analyze network environments to obtain a formal *description* of the network to track the state continuously or in discrete intervals. Here, INSALATA uses *information fusing* to provide a comprehensive view on the network by aggregating information from multiple *collector modules*. Using descriptions decouples analysis and deployment and enables re-using, archiving, and distributing these descriptions. INSALATA can instantiate descriptions on physical or virtualized testbeds employing a PDDL planner to structure the setup process and resolve inter-dependencies between setup steps. To minimize setup steps and reuse existing testbed setups, we support *incremental setups* by determining the delta between current and target testbed state.

The key contributions of our work are (a) INSALATA, a fully automated, modular, and extensible framework to reproduce network environments on testbeds, (b) the open source implementation of INSALATA available on GitHub, and (c) a case study showing INSALATA's applicability to real world scenarios using exemplary module implementations.

The remainder of this paper is structured as follows: First, we describe our goals and requirements for INSALATA in Sect. 2. Afterwards, we analyze if related work can fulfill these in Sect. 3. In Sect. 4, we present INSALATA's design and introduce its components. Next, we present the main components of INSALATA in detail, in particular the underlying information model in Sect. 5, the *Collector Component* in Sect. 6, and the *Deployment Component* in Sect. 7. In Sect. 8, we summarize important implementation details. In Sect. 9, we present a case study to show the applicability of our proposed system. Finally, we give a conclusion and present future work in Sect. 10.

2   Goals and Requirements

The overall goal is to reproduce arbitrary network environments into physical or virtualized testbeds. Therefore, we need (a) a suitable information model reflecting required information, (b) an automated information acquisition process, and (c) an automated deployment process.

(a) Information Model: The information model abstracts from the network environment. The goal is to reflect network environments up to application layer of the TCP/IP reference model. The information model has to be extensible to allow to add use case specific services and additional information elements. Therefore, we require the following information to be present: (a) basic network nodes, like hosts and routers, (b) networks on layer 2 and 3, including appropriate addressing schemes, (c) connectivity information like routing and firewalling, (d) basic network services like DNS and DHCP, and (e) host information, including network interfaces, disks, memory, CPUs, or operating system.

(b) Information Acquisition: The goal is to provide information acquisition that supports different types of information collection techniques, supports continuous monitoring of the network environment, and is fully automated. We identified that the following information collection techniques, differing in terms of intrusiveness and quality of information they provide, have to be supported:

Manually specified information is not intrusive, but rarely up-to-date. Including such information is required if other techniques are not applicable.
Passive scanning has no direct impact on networks, but collected information is limited and access to all network segments is required.
Active scanning creates load in a network and on components, but provides more detailed information about entities and services in the network.
Network management protocols need to be available on investigated nodes, but reduce system's load and information requests are standardized.
Direct access to components, e.g. with *SSH*, delivers rich information, but requires appropriate access, to invoke applications, and interpret the output.
Agent-based information collection collects information just-in-time, but agents need to be deployed and run on the components.

(c) Deployment Process: The deployment process has to be *incremental*, so that the delta between the current and the target state is computed during setup and only required configuration steps are executed. Additionally, the deployment process has to be modular and extensible in order to cope with use case specific requirements. Therefore, the setup process has to be divided into small, self-contained steps. To be able to use the deployment process on different testbed architectures, the process itself needs to be independent from the underlying architecture as much as possible.

3 Related Work

To the best of our knowledge, no application to reproduce network environments exists. Therefore, we examine the two main components of INSALATA, namely information acquisition and testbed setup for deployment, separately. Next, we investigate network description languages as we need a suitable network model for INSALATA. Finally, we discuss network management protocols and frameworks to investigate appropriate implementation mechanisms to deploy the description of the network environment on the testbed.

Data Acquisition Applications are needed to obtain information about the network environment. Here, continuous monitoring is required and information from different sources needs to be fused. Additionally, tracking changes is a requirement. *IO-Framework* [6,19] does not support continuous monitoring and only supports intrusive collection methods. The *common Network Information Service (cNIS)* [1] utilizes static information and higher level services (SSH or SNMP) but does not include less invasive information collection techniques. *MonALISA* [7,11] and *PerfSONAR* [29] are not capable of continuously monitoring the network and detect changes. *OpenVAS* [23] is used to identify vulnerabilities within an infrastructure but has limited scanning capabilities. Single purpose tools like *Nmap* [20], *Traceroute* [2], or *xprobe2* [35] can be used to collect single aspects of the network environment but do not provide a holistic view. Dedicated network management protocols, like *SNMP* [8,21] or *Netconf* [27] can only be used to retrieve dedicated information from single network components, but do also not provide a complete view on the network.

Testbed Management Frameworks are used to orchestrate and control testbeds. All presented frameworks do not provide incremental setups but rebuild the designated network from scratch leading to higher effort within the setup process and manually configured changes get lost. Additionally, testbed orchestration and experiment execution are often tightly coupled. *vBET* [18] and *Laas-NetExp* [24] are both closed source, preventing to extend those frameworks. *VNEXT* [25] and *NEPTUNE* [5] do not provide the automated setup of basic network services, like DNS or DHCP. *Emulab* [34] or *DETER* [4] tightly couple the infrastructure setup and the experiment execution. This requires to rebuild the network after each experiment.

Network Description Languages and Ontologies can be used as information model. The related work within this field lacks in providing the information elements needed for a proper mirroring of network environments, especially in terms of reflecting the connectivity due to routing and the usage of firewalls. *IF-MAP* [3,30,31] is not capable of reflecting interfaces or routing information. The *target-centric ontology for intrusion detection* [32] does not provide a sufficient addressing scheme for elements nor reflect routing or firewalls. The *Network Markup Language (NML)* [14,15] provides a schema for exchanging network descriptions on a generic level, but does not provide concepts like network routing. The *Infrastructure and Network Description Language (INDL)* [13,17,28] extends NML, but is not capable of reflecting routes or firewall rules. Tcl-based format in *Emulab* and *ns-2* [34] is not capable of modeling networks explicitly resulting in verbose definitions for large networks.

Network Management Protocols and Frameworks can be used to setup and configure the descriptions in testbeds. To do so, the virtualized testbed has to be setup, e.g. router and hosts as virtual machines, and those components need to be configured appropriately afterwards, e.g. using adequate routing tables. Dedicated network management protocols, like *SNMP* [8,21] or *Netconf* [27] can be used to configure components and request dedicated information in a standardized way. Both protocols do not provide built-in mechanisms to manage larger infrastructures as a whole. *Ansible* [9] is a push-based framework to configure larger infrastructures using so-called *playbooks*. Those playbooks need to be written or adapted for each configuration. Ansible can not be used directly for our approach, but is suitable as an important building block. *Puppet* [26] is a pull-based framework for infrastructure configurations. As the testbed is reconfigured in irregular intervals, a pull-based mechanism is not suitable.

4   Approach and System Design

INSALATA consists of the Collector and the Deployment Component as its two main components:

The **Collector Component** is responsible for collecting and fusing information of the network environment and the current state of the testbed into a descriptions (see Sect. 6).
The **Deployment Component** manages configuration changes and the automated setup process on the testbed (see Sect. 7).

Both components utilize the same *information model* to structure the information about the network environment (see Sect. 5) and are managed and orchestrated by a central controller, the *Management Unit*. The system architecture of INSALATA showing these basic components and their interaction is depicted in Fig. 1.

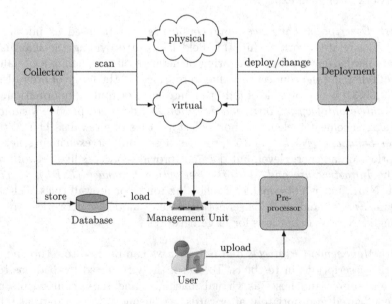

Fig. 1. System overview of INSALATA showing basic components

The Collector acquires information about the network environment and is used to generate a description for the testbed. It maintains the current state of the monitored network. Here, the collection process can be done continuously whereas configuration changes can be tracked and stored with a timestamp in a database. This approach allows to rebuild a network at each point in time.

The Deployment Component utilizes a description that is either obtained by the Collector or provided by the user. Based on this, the Deployment Component configures the testbed to reproduce a network environment. To ease writing descriptions, a *Preprocessor* is utilized, replacing missing but calculable values in the description and checking the it for its validity.

5 Description of the Information Model

To be able to reflect a network environment in a testbed, a formal description of this network is required. This description needs to contain *information elements* discussed in Sect. 2. Each information element needs to be leviable from the network environment in an automated manner and has a unique *identifier*. The proposed information model is shown in Fig. 2. An information element is represented as box, the identifier of each element is underlined and additional attributes describing the information element are listed. For FirewalRules and Routes a combination of attributes is used as identifier. Relations between information elements are denoted as arrows in between and additionally denote their cardinality.

The main information element is the *Network Component* representing a node in the network environment, e.g. hosts, routers or switches, and are further specified by the *Template* attribute. A Network Component is equipped with certain *Disks* and *Interfaces*. Interfaces are needed to interconnect Network Components in different kinds of networks, e.g. *Layer 2 Networks* or *Layer 3 Networks*.

Depending on its functionality, a Network Component can maintain *Routes* or *Firewall Rules*. Those express the connectivity between Network Components. The latter can be represented as raw dumps (*Firewall Raw*) or in a simplified format (*Firewall Rule*) to ease transformation between different firewall applications as proposed in [10]. As a simplification is not free of information loss, the raw information is stored additionally.

To support large-scale test environments consisting of multiple servers, a Network Element is associated with a *Location* specifying the testbed server the Network Component is emulated on. In case of a description reflecting the network environment, the Location is set to *physical*.

Another important concept of the information model is the *Service* element. This information element is used to reflect basic network services, like *DNS* or *DHCP*. A Service can be further specified by adding a *Product* and a *Version* to allow a high accuracy. Additionally needed services can be added to the information model using inheritance, allowing use case specific applications.

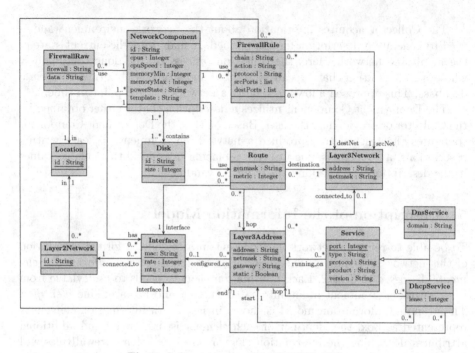

Fig. 2. Information model of INSALATA

6   Information Collector Component

The Collector Component is capable of managing multiple *Environments* describing multiple networks to be monitored. The overview of INSALATA's information *Collector Component* is depicted in Fig. 3.

For each Environment, multiple *Collector Modules*, employing a particular information collection technique as described in Sect. 2, can be configured to collect the required information. A Collector Module obtains information about at least one information element and possible relations between information elements. Therefore, modules have to obtain the unique identifier of an information element. The collected information elements are handed over to the Environment fusing all obtained information into a comprehensive graph describing the network. Here, we assume that a module delivers no false, but potentially incomplete information. This modular approach has the advantage that different, specialized information collection techniques can be combined resulting in a more detailed and more precise view on the network environment.

To fuse information, the Collector utilizes the identifier of each object and the type of the information element. Objects with the same identifier and of the same type are treated as the same object. Each Collector Module passes discovered objects to the Collector. Attributes and relations are fused together in case multiple modules report the same objects.

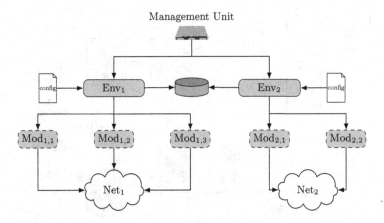

Fig. 3. Information Collector Component of INSALATA

Another challenge is to manage existing information elements in the model becoming obsolete. Therefore, a deletion scheme needs to be implemented within an Environment. Each information element in an Environment is equipped with timers for each Collector module. Each time, an information element is delivered by a module, the module specific timer is updated. If all timers in the list expire, the information element and its relations are deleted from the Environment. In addition, each module can actively set its own timer to zero, if it is capable to determine the non-existence of an element.

To be able to recreate an environment at any (observed) point in time, we track the network environment's state over time. Whenever an information element or relation is modified, i.e., is added, deleted, or updated, we save this delta as an event to the database. Such events contain the type of change, the information element and its properties. Within an Environment, only the current state of the network description is maintained.

7 Infrastructure Deployment Component

The Deployment Component executes the following steps: (a) determine required configuration steps using the current testbed state and the given description, (b) determine a correct *execution plan* how to achieve the given description, and (c) deploy the changes on the testbed following the computed execution plan. The overview of the execution flow of INSALATA's Deployment Component is depicted in Fig. 4.

First, the Deployment Component has to determine *what* needs to be changed. Therefore, we need the current state of the testbed in the form a description as *Description D_2* that can be determined using the Collector Component. Additionally, we need the target state in the form a description as *Description D_1* provided from the Collector or the user. The Deployment

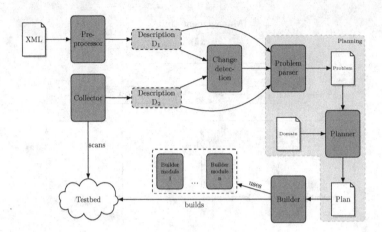

Fig. 4. Execution flow of INSALATA's Deployment Component

Component uses a *Change Detection Module* to detect added, removed, and updated information elements in the delta between these states.

To determine *how* to change the testbed, we use *automated planning and scheduling* from the domain of artificial intelligence [16]. A planning problem is described using a dedicated planning language such as the *Planning Domain Definition Language (PDDL)*. PDDL separates the planning problem into a *domain* description, describing the problem domain, and a *problem* description, describing an instance of the problem [12]. A PDDL domain description describes the *objects' types*, *predicates* (i.e., properties), and *actions*. Each action has a definition of objects it is applicable to, *preconditions* that have to be fulfilled, and an *effect* altering the predicates of objects. With INSALATA, we provide a domain description for our information model and steps as PDDL actions necessary to setup a testbed. A detailed overview on the steps we defined and their interdependencies can be found in the domain description provided with the implementation. The PDDL problem description describes all objects, their type and their *initial state*. The problem specifies the *goal state* of all objects by giving their desired predicates [22] inside a goal section. While the domain file is static, the problem file depends on the current and target state and is computed each time a description is deployed on the testbed.

The computed changes, the current testbed state, and the target state are given to the *Problem Parser Module* computing a PDDL problem description. This description is given to the *Planner Module*, an automated planning and scheduling solver computing an execution plan containing the correct order of actions that will bring the testbed from the current into the target state. The execution plan is passed to the *Builder* to execute the steps on the designated testbed. Implementations of these steps are provided by architecture-specific *Builder Modules* since the implementation of such steps is different for different testbed architectures and objects. The Builder uses meta-data associated with the Builder Modules and the objects to identify the correct implementation.

This allows us to dynamically add new implementations, e.g. for new operating systems or services, without changing the Deployment Component.

8 Implementation

INSALATA is written in Python 3 and is available in INSALATA's GitHub repository[1]. A detailed code documentation is available on[2].

The *Management Unit* can be controlled using a XML-RPC client communicating with INSALATA. The presented information model is reflected using object-oriented Python classes.

Besides the *Collector Component* itself, we provide the following *Collector Modules*: (1) a *XEN module* using to collect information from environments using XEN virtualization, (2) an *XML module* for manually provided information, (3) a *Tcpdump module* for passive network scanning using Tcpdump, (4) an *Nmap module* for active network scanning using Nmap, (5) an *SNMP module* to retrieve information from nodes using SNMP, (6) an *SSH module* to retrieve information from nodes via SSH, and (7) a *Zabbix module* for agent-based information collection with the Zabbix network monitoring system. Some modules have limited functionality, meaning that not all information possible to collect is implemented, e.g. the SSH module does not collect firewall rules. New collector modules can be added to INSALATA to cover the desired scanning environment.

We integrate *fast-forward*[3] as a planner into INSALATA's *Deployment Component*. The domain file describing the setup process of a testbed we provide, is given in PDDL. The required problem files are generated for each setup individually in an automated manner. We provide a framework allowing to add new *Builder Modules* in an easy way. Here, we utilize Python annotations to determine the most suitable Builder Module for a given step within the determined plan and the configured object. Besides provided Builder Modules to setup the basic topology on XEN (hosts, routers, layer 2 networks), we utilize Ansible for additional configurations (routing, firewalling, DNS, and DHCP).

9 Case Study: Chair's Teaching Infrastructure – iLab

To show INSALATA's applicability in practical scenarios, we assesed INSALATA in a case study. For this case study, we use a setup adapted from the lab course *iLab*[4] offered by the TUM's Chair of Network Architectures and Services. The iLab is a course to teach student's practical skills in administering network setups and configurations for different scenarios using real hardware. A typical setup students have to work with during an iLab course is shown in Fig. 5. This setup consists of two Cisco and a Linux router, and four host residing in different private networks. In our case study, our goal is to reproduce this network environment in a network testbed using XEN virtualization.

---

[1] https://github.com/tumi8/INSALATA.

[2] https://insalata.readthedocs.io/en/latest/index.html.

[3] http://www.fast-downward.org/ObtainingAndRunningFastDownward.

[4] https://ilab.net.in.tum.de.

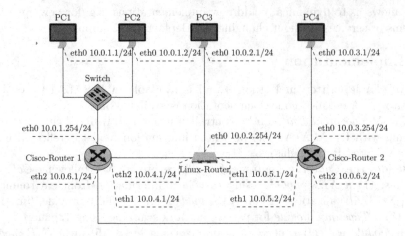

Fig. 5. Typical infrastructure setup within the iLab course

We provide the IP addresses of all routers to the INSALATA system as a starting point using manual input in form of XML files. All routers and hosts are configured to allow INSALATA to access the systems using SSH and SNMP.

In the first phase, we obtain the required description of the network environment using our Collector Component. To expand our infrastructure information using our passive *Tcpdump* Collector Module, we generate traffic on the involved hosts. Using the *SNMP* and *SSH* Collector Modules, missing interfaces, MAC addresses, and routing information is obtained from routers and hosts. Using theses Modules, we are able to reflect the network environment shown in Fig. 5 as description.

In the second phase, we use our Deployment Component to reproduce the obtained description into our virtualized testbed using XEN with the *xapi* toolstack. INSALATA computes an execution plan to setup the testbed from scratch in 0.252 s. The resulting execution plan consists of 92 steps, including setting up virtual machines and networks, configuring interfaces and deploying routes. Each step is executed in sequence and no parallelization is done. The total time required to setup the testbed and configure it is 42 min 32 s. Figure 6 visualizes the setup and configuration process in regard to its execution time.

The most time-consuming tasks during the setup process are the creation of new virtual machines, which happens at the beginning. The reason for this is that here new virtual machines have to be cloned from the respective template, including copying hard disk images and required reboot operations. Configuration steps like creation of virtual networks and interfaces are done nearly instantaneously. After the setup of our description, we validated the correctness of our setup using manual inspection, *Ping* and *Traceroute*.

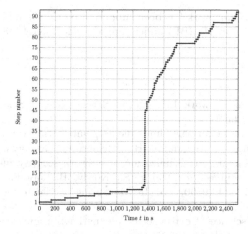

Fig. 6. Time distribution of setup steps in the iLab case study

10   Conclusions and Future Work

In this work we present INSALATA, a system capable of reproducing network environments in network testbeds. INSALATA enables network operators and researchers to test and analyze new security features and general configuration changes in a separated test environment before deployment in operational networks. To be able to formalize network environments, INSALATA utilizes an information model particularly crafted for representing network topologies, entities, and services in *descriptions*. To obtain the required information from network environments, we support a modular *Collector Component* automatically assessing networks and fusing information from different *Collector Modules*. The *Deployment Component* provides automated planning and scheduling to instantiate descriptions onto a physical or virtualized testbeds. Within our case study, we show the applicability of our approach reproducing a real world network environment with several routers and hosts onto a virtualized testbed.

To further improve INSALATA, we will continue our work in this field and on INSALATA and highly appreciate feedback, improvements, and extensions from the community. To extended INSALATA's capabilities, additional Collector and *Builder Modules* can help to obtain additional properties from the network environment, such as user information or generic service configurations from hosts. Existing Collector Modules can be extended to obtain more information using existing assessment techniques, such as firewall information using SSH. To reproduce network environments more realistically, Builder Modules to support Microsoft Windows and additional network services, like mail or ftp are beneficial. One of our main goals is to make the deployment process more efficient by parallelizing the execution of the setup plan. Since INSALATA only provides mechanisms to setup and orchestrate a testbed, we aim to integrate our experiment execution framework GPLMT [33] into the INSALATA system.

Acknowledgments. This work has been supported by the German Federal Ministry of Education and Research (BMBF) under support code 16KIS0538 (DecADe).

References

1. GEANT2 common Network Information Service (cNIS) Schema Specification. http://www.geant2.net
2. traceroute(8) - Linux man page. linux.die.net/man/8/traceroute
3. Ahlers, V., Heine, F., Hellmann, B., Kleiner, C., Renners, L., Rossow, T., Steuerwald, R.: Integrated visualization of network security metadata from heterogeneous data sources. In: Mauw, S., Kordy, B., Jajodia, S. (eds.) GraMSec 2015. LNCS, vol. 9390, pp. 18–34. Springer, Cham (2016). doi:10.1007/978-3-319-29968-6_2
4. Benzel, T.: The science of cyber security experimentation: the DETER project. In: Proceedings of 27th Annual Computer Security Applications Conference, pp. 137–148 (2011)
5. Bifulco, R., Stasi, G.D., Canonico, R.: NEPTUNE for fast and easy deployment of OMF virtual network testbeds [Poster Abstract] (2010)
6. Birkholz, H., Sieverdingbeck, I., Sohr, K., Bormann, C.: IO: an interconnected asset ontology in support of risk management processes. In: 7th International Conference on Availability, Reliability and Security (ARES), pp. 534–541 (2012)
7. Carpen-Amarie, A., Cai, J., Costan, A., Antoniu, G., Boug, L.: Bringing introspection into the BlobSeer data-management system using the MonALISA distributed monitoring framework. In: International Conference on Complex, Intelligent and Software Intensive Systems (CISIS), pp. 508–513 (2010)
8. Case, J.D., Fedor, M., Schoffstall, M.L., Davin, J.R.: Simple network management protocol (SNMP). RFC 1157, IETF, May 1990
9. DeHaan, M.: Ansible (2012–2016). https://www.ansible.com/
10. Diekmann, C., Hupel, L., Carle, G.: Semantics-preserving simplification of real-world firewall rule sets. In: 20th International Symposium on Formal Methods, pp. 195–212 (2015)
11. Dobre, C., Voicu, R., Legrand, I.: Monitoring large scale network topologies. In: IEEE 6th International Conference on Intelligent Data Acquisition and Advanced Computing Systems (IDAACS), vol. 1, pp. 218–222 (2011)
12. Fox, M., Long, D.: PDDL2.1: an extension to PDDL for expressing temporal planning domains. J. Artif. Int. Res. **20**(1), 61–124 (2003)
13. Ghijsen, M., van der Ham, J., Grosso, P., Dumitru, C., Zhu, H., Zhao, Z., de Laat, C.: A semantic-web approach for modeling computing infrastructures. Comput. Electr. Eng. **39**(8), 2553–2565 (2013)
14. van der Ham, J., Dijkstra, F., Apacz, R., Zurawski, J.: Network Markup Language Base Schema version 1 (2013)
15. van der Ham, J., Dijkstra, F., Lapacz, R., Brown, A.: The Network Markup Language (NML): A Standardized Network Topology Abstraction for Inter-domain and Cross-layer Network Applications (2013)
16. Hoffmann, J.: Everything you always wanted to know about *Planning*. In: Bach, J., Edelkamp, S. (eds.) KI 2011. LNCS, vol. 7006, pp. 1–13. Springer, Heidelberg (2011). doi:10.1007/978-3-642-24455-1_1
17. van der Ham, J.J.: A semantic model for complex computer networks: the network description language. Ph.D. thesis, University of Amsterdam (2010)

18. Jiang, X., Xu, D.: vBET: A VM-based emulation testbed. In: Proceedings of ACM SIGCOMM Workshop on Models, Methods and Tools for Reproducible Network Research, pp. 95–104 (2003)
19. Lorenzin, L., Cam-Winget, N.: Security automation and continuous monitoring (SACM) requirements. Internet-Draft draft-ietf-sacm-requirements-15, Internet Engineering Task Force (2016)
20. Lyon, G.: nmap(1) - Linux man page (2015)
21. McCloghrie, K., Rose, M.: Management information base for network management of TCP/IP-based internets. RFC 1156, IETF, May 1990
22. McDermott, D., Ghallab, M., Howe, A., Knoblock, C., Ram, A., Veloso, M., Weld, D., Wilkins, D.: PDDL - the planning domain definition language (1998)
23. OpenVAS: Project Homepage. http://www.openvas.org/
24. Owezarski, P., Berthou, P., Labit, Y., Gauchard, D.: LaasNetExp: a generic polymorphic platform for network emulation and experiments. In: Proceedings of 4th International Conference on Testbeds and Research Infrastructures for the Development of Networks & Communities, no. 24, pp. 1–9 (2008)
25. Pisa, P.S., Couto, R.S., Carvalho, H.E.T., Neto, D.J.S., Fernandes, N.C., Campista, M.E.M., Costa, L., Duarte, O., Pujolle, G.: VNEXT: Virtual network management for Xen-based testbeds. In: International Conference on the Network of the Future (NOF 2011), pp. 41–45 (2011)
26. Puppet Labs: Puppet (2005–2016). https://puppet.com/
27. Enns, R., Bjorklund, M., Schoenwaelder, J., Bierman, A.: Network configuration protocol (NETCONF). RFC 6241, IETF, June 2011
28. Taketa, T., Hiranaka, Y.: Network design assistant system based on network description language. In: 15th International Conference on Advanced Communication Technology (ICACT), pp. 515–518 (2013)
29. Tierney, B., Metzger, J., Boote, J., Boyd, E., Brown, A., Carlson, R., Zekauskas, M., Zurawski, J., Swany, M., Grigoriev, M.: perfSONAR: instantiating a global network measurement framework. In: SOSP Workshop on Real Overlays and Distributed Systems (ROADS 2009). ACM (2009)
30. Trusted Network Connect Work Group: TNC IF-MAP Bindings for SOAP, Version 2.2, Revision 10 (2014)
31. Trusted Network Connect Work Group: TNC MAP Content Authorization, Version 1.0, Revision 36 (2014)
32. Undercoffer, J., Pinkston, J., Joshi, A., Finin, T.: A target-centric ontology for intrusion detection. In: Proceeding of 9th Workshop on Ontologies and Distributed Systems, pp. 47–58 (2004)
33. Wachs, M., Herold, N., Posselt, S.-A., Dold, F., Carle, G.: GPLMT: a lightweight experimentation and testbed management framework. In: Karagiannis, T., Dimitropoulos, X. (eds.) PAM 2016. LNCS, vol. 9631, pp. 165–176. Springer, Cham (2016). doi:10.1007/978-3-319-30505-9_13
34. White, B., Lepreau, J., Stoller, L., Ricci, R., Guruprasad, S., Newbold, M., Hibler, M., Barb, C., Joglekar, A.: An integrated experimental environment for distributed systems and networks. pp. 255–270 (2002)
35. Yarochkin, F., Arkin, O., Kydyraliev, M.: xprobe2(1) - Linux man page

Management of Cloud Environments and Services

Towards a Software-Defined Security Framework for Supporting Distributed Cloud

Maxime Compastié[1,2]([☒]), Rémi Badonnel[1], Olivier Festor[1], Ruan He[2], and Mohamed Kassi-Lahlou[2]

[1] LORIA - Inria, Campus Scientifique, 54600 Villers, France
{maxime.compastie,remi.badonnel,olivier.festor}@loria.fr
[2] Orange Labs, 44 Avenue de la République, 92320 Chatillon, France
{ruan.he,mohamed.kassilahlou}@orange.com

Abstract. Cloud computing provides new facilities for building elaborated services hosted through various infrastructures over the Internet. In the meantime, these ones pose new important challenges in terms of security due to their intrinsic nature. We propose in this paper to detail a software-defined security framework supporting the protection of these services, in the context of distributed cloud. These ones require security mechanisms able to cope with their multi-tenancy and multi-cloud properties. The foundations of this framework rely on the software-defined logic to express and propagate security policies to the considered cloud resources, and on the autonomic paradigm to dynamically configure and adjust these mechanisms to distributed cloud constraints. In particular, we describe the main components and protocols of this software-defined security framework, evaluate this one and discuss implementation considerations, through the analysis of different realistic scenarios.

1 Introduction

The cloud computing architectural model permits to build elaborated services and applications based on multiple computing resources, such as virtual machines, network devices, software components, themselves provided as a service that can be easily deployed through the Internet. Based on the NIST Institute [1] definition, this model is mainly characterized by the following features: *on-demand self-service*, *broad network access*, *resource pooling*, *rapid elasticity*, and *measured service*. It supports an as a service scheme that permits a transparent access to resources and the outsourcing of part of the management to the cloud provider. This separation enables optimizing the resource allocation and usage, but may also introduce management complexity due to its distributed nature. In particular, the cloud infrastructure and its applications may typically be divided into isolated sets of resources called *tenants*, corresponding to different ownerships and requirements, defining the *multi-tenancy* property. Another property comes to the facts that the resources may be distributed among several infrastructures, as each of them may be specialized in a dedicated

D. Tuncer et al. (Eds.): AIMS 2017, LNCS 10356, pp. 47–61, 2017.
DOI: 10.1007/978-3-319-60774-0_4

processing. Distributed cloud can be defined by the conjunction of the *multi-tenancy* and *multi-cloud* properties. In this context, security management has become a major challenge. The dynamics of cloud infrastructures induced by their *on-demand self-service, rapid elasticity* and distribution has outrun traditional security management, while the ubiquity and high availability of cloud resources make them attractive targets for attackers [2].

Exploiting autonomic and programmability mechanisms opens new perspectives for enabling such a security management. Autonomic computing permits to address the scalability issues induced by large and distributed cloud infrastructure resources, by delegating part of the management tasks to the environment itself. In our context, this concerns more particularly the management tasks related to self-protection and self-configuration, and aims at maintaining the security level of a distributed cloud and its services in an adequate manner with the security threats, based on the activation or deactivation of available countermeasures in a proactive and/or reactive manner. In addition, network programmability has already shown its advantage for software-defined networking by separating the network infrastructure into two separate planes, i.e. the data plane and the control plane, and contributing to its dynamic configuration and adaptation. Similarly, there is an important need for supporting *software-defined security* in the context of distributed cloud.

We have already highlighted the benefits of software-defined security for distributed cloud environments in [3]. We detail in this paper the different components and protocols of our security framework relying on software-defined and autonomic paradigms, and provides a critical analysis of the proposed solution considering a set of validation scenarios based on a realistic use case. The framework permits to specify security policies, and enables their autonomic enforcement in a multi-tenant and multi-cloud environment. Security mechanisms should be dynamically aligned and adjusted based on changes that may occur in the distributed cloud. The rest of this paper is organized as follow: Sect. 2 gives an overview of existing work related to our software-defined security solution. The proposed framework, its components and their interactions are detailed in Sect. 3. We evaluate it and give a critical analysis as well as implementation considerations in Sect. 4. Finally, we conclude the paper and point out future research efforts in Sect. 5.

2   Related Work

The security of cloud infrastructures has already been largely explored in the literature. In particular [4] highlights several challenges related to policy-based security management, such as the specification of a cloud security policy, the assurance of the security decisions, as well as the certification of security components in that context. In the same manner, the *TCloud* framework [5] proposes to enforce a security policy with a hardened cloud stack. This one provides infrastructure-level and platform-level security components, that might be compatible with multi-cloud environments, with a hardened build of OpenStack environments. However, these solutions do not specifically address self-configuration mechanisms, nor the management issues generated by multi-cloud and multi-tenancy properties. The *Iceman* architecture [6] enables secure federated inter-cloud identity management. The author of [7] proposes a cloud management framework able to deal with multi-tenancy, but this one is limited to access control policies and cannot support other security mechanisms. The proposed architecture is independent from the available security mechanisms and addresses their self-configuration in a distributed cloud.

In the area of programmability, *software-defined networking (SDN)* permits to separate the *control plane* making decisions about where the traffic should be sent from the *data plane* forwarding of packets. This paradigm enables a dynamic and adaptive policy enforcement. It may also serve as a support for chaining security functions. For instance, the *Flowtags* framework described in [8] enables the integration of middleboxes whose composition is supported by SDN controller. [9] proposes a framework for enforcing a network security policy through a set of middleboxes. But, this solution only considers middleboxes for instantiating security mechanisms. We have also shown in [10] how to exploit the SDN paradigm to build a chain of security functions, including intrusion detection systems and firewalls, to protect smart devices. IETF is also working on SDN-based security services using interface to network security functions [11]. Such approaches take advantage of SDN with respect to security policy enforcement.

Important efforts have also focused on the verification of security chains. For instance, *VeriCon* [12] combines a language for specifying SDN policies with an approach to check whether a policy verifies invariants expressed in predicate logic. In the same manner, *FlowChecker* [13] represents the network as a binary decision diagram (BDD), whereas properties are expressed in computation tree logic (CTL). However, the model based on BDDs requires a certain expertise of formal methods, which cannot be generally expected from network operators. In our context, we are focusing on a software-defined security framework to protect distributed cloud, in line with software-defined networking, but not limited to network enforcement considerations.

The autonomic computing paradigm gives a framework for self-management activities, and relies on several main areas: self-configuration, self-optimization, self-protection and self-healing [14]. Although it does not bring a formal distributed cloud support, it may introduce the negotiation among independent components. This approach may deal with exhaustive enforcement issues, as autonomic components can continuously enforce the security policy and adapt to the changes in their action perimeters. Even if the two previous paradigms do not directly deal with distributed cloud issues, they provide important building blocks for supporting security policy enforcement and defining a security management architecture in that context and in our framework.

With respect to security policies, the OASIS consortium introduces two standardized languages: *XACML (eXtensible Access Control Markup Language)* for representing and exchanging security policies [15] and SAML (*Security Assertion Markup Language*) for specifying security statements [16]. However, they do not handle any modifications of cloud policies nor its evolution propagation to enforcers. This approach remains relevant as the XACML defines modular components for security enforcement. Besides, an architecture and use-cases featuring XACML and SAML in distributed environment have been detailed in [17]. The latter validates the usability of XACML in distributed systems, underlining some limitations such as the need for a high granularity of sub-policies and the difficulty of maintaining an encoded security policy. The languages and formats introduced by SCAP protocol constitutes also an interesting support, as they cover many complementary specifications, such as vulnerability descriptions and scorings, that are exploitable for automating security in distributed cloud [18]. These standards are usable in our solution.

In accordance with [3] where we give the basement of our software-defined security approach, the autonomic paradigm is tied to endorse the continuous security policy enforcement able to cope with the changes occurring on the security policy, the tenant configuration and the protected resource state. We extend our previous work by detailing each components and protocols supporting our framework, and giving a critical analysis and implementation considerations based on realistic scenarios.

3   Software-Defined Security Framework

We propose a software-defined security (SDSec) framework for protecting distributed cloud. These one is composed of two main layers, called respectively security control plane and security data plane (as depicted on Fig. 1). It relies on a *software-defined* scheme to provide a global security policy specification interface and exploit autonomic mechanisms within distributed cloud infrastructures to enable cloud resources to be dynamically and exhaustively protected according to this policy. More precisely, it first consists in a *global security policy (GSP)* which formally defines at a business level the security objectives of cloud resources and is then translated into several *tenant-level security policies (TLSP)*, providing security statements that must be verified by specified resources at the tenant level within the distributed cloud.

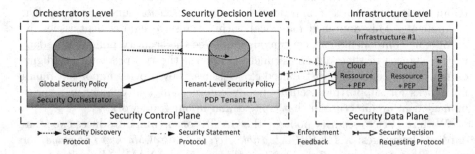

Fig. 1. SDSec framework in a single-infrastructure single-tenant scenario

These *security statements* are then enforced on cloud resources, i.e. virtualized infrastructures and software products. They aim at altering the behavior of these components and protecting them based on countermeasures available with distributed cloud. This application can be active if its application requires negotiation with a decisional instance. The enforcement should be performed dynamically, more precisely in an adaptive (it adapts to any change in the enforced resource state or in the infrastructure), automatic (no operator interventions are needed for it), and self-configured manner (policy decisions for it are automatically made according to several criteria including the security requirements).

The components of the framework part of the security control plane include the *security orchestrator* hosting a GSP specified by the system administrator, exposing through a dedicated interface the TLSPs, and receiving enforcement feedbacks from the *policy decision point* (PDP) to adapt them. These interactions are supported by the *security discovery protocol* enabling the PDP to identify the security orchestrator and fetch its security policy. The components part of the security data plane correspond to the *policy enforcement points* (PEP) executing the security statements (using the *security statement protocol*) and dedicated to the policy enforcement on one type of cloud resources. It may also solicit the PDP for taking a needed security decision for an active enforcement (using the *security decision requesting protocol*).

This framework follows a software-defined paradigm to specify security constraints, and relies on self-configuration mechanisms to enable a dynamic and local management. Self-configuration enables a lower coupling with respect to orchestration. Instead of the regular orchestration model addressing requests and expecting feedbacks, the security orchestrator adopts a passive approach by exposing security requirements, and letting the PDP to interpret them, according to their enforcement contexts. In addition, the framework has been designed to fit with distributed cloud constraints, in particular the following ones:

- *multi-tenancy*, corresponding to the characteristic for a cloud infrastructure to be subdivided into different sets of isolated cloud resources called *tenants*. With that isolation comes the need of regulated access control between each tenant of the infrastructure,
- *multi-cloud*, corresponding to the capability for cloud infrastructures to collaborate to enable communications and common treatments on their resources. With a security-oriented point of view, these treatments come with a security coordination over potentially heterogeneous infrastructures.

In doing so, we detail the role and functioning of its different components, considering a multi-cloud and multi-tenant context, as depicted on Fig. 2. This figure makes the assumption that each PDP is dedicated to a tenant, which is a simple interpretation of software-defined security in this multi-tenant context. We consider the existence of a cloud orchestrator in charge of managing cloud resources. Even though this component is not meant to be a part of the proposed security framework, its supposed existence allows taking into account the changes on cloud resources, which can be done manually by a system administrator or automatically by one or several potential orchestrators.

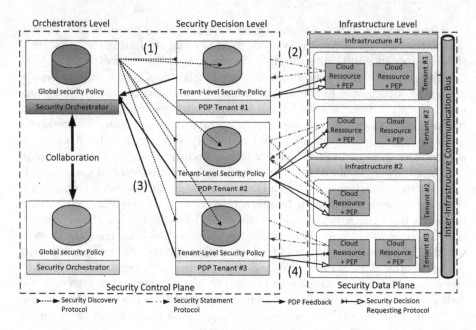

Fig. 2. SDSec framework interacting with a cloud orchestrator, in a multi-cloud multi-tenant scenario. (1) accounts for the TLSP fetching, (2) for the security statement, (3) for the enforcement feedback and (4) for the policy decision request.

3.1 Security Orchestrator

Amongst the framework components, the security orchestrator is responsible for the management of the GSP, its interpretation (TLSPs) and distribution. This policy is meant to be enforced on the distributed cloud, and so, on multiple collaborating cloud infrastructures with different tenants. The interpretation is influenced by feedbacks provided by the enforcement. In line with the XACML terminology [15], the security orchestrator can be seen as a Policy Administration Point (PAP) allowing the storage of the global policy and generating TLSPs. The changes operated on the global security policy must be propagated to the whole enforcement perimeter. Contrary to the cloud orchestrator, the security orchestrator is not meant to manage cloud resources. Consequently, the instantiation, the removal or the reconfiguration of cloud resources is not endorsed by the security orchestrator.

However, this highlights the need for the security orchestrator and the cloud orchestrator to collaborate. For instance, the security orchestrator requires to be noticed in case of deployments of new cloud resources, in order to enforce the security policy on them. In the same manner, the cloud orchestrator must remove a cloud resource and reconfigure its workflow, when the security orchestrator requests its removal for security purpose. This collaboration is modeled on Fig. 2 by the double arrow between the two orchestrators on the leftmost plane. An overview of the activity diagram of the security orchestrator is given

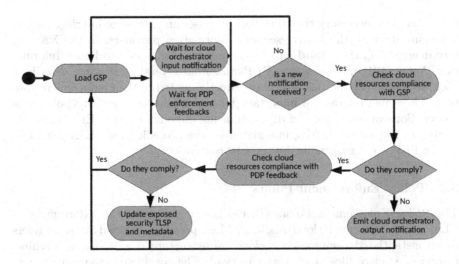

Fig. 3. Overview of the security orchestrator activity diagram

on Fig. 3. The orchestrator does not push the TLSPs to the PDPs for privacy purposes, the multi-tenancy property implying the isolation of tenants amongst each others and with the cloud administrator. These TLSPs must be attached to meta-datas to enable PDPs to fetch only the policies they are concerned to, by discriminating each TLSP according to enforcement context criteria. The policy must be exposed through a dedicated interface accepting incoming connections from PDPs (with the use of the security discovery protocol). Another interface assumes the reception of all PDP enforcement feedbacks. The determination of the exposed TLSPs (as well as the notification sent to the cloud orchestrator) is correlated to the GSP, the PDP feedbacks and the notifications potentially sent by cloud orchestrator.

3.2 Policy Decision Points

The Policy Decision Point (PDPs) play a central role in this software-defined security framework, serving as intermediates between the security orchestrator and the PEPs enforcing policies on resources. More precisely, the PDPs are in charge of fetching and hosting the TLSPs using the policy security discovery protocol, and locating their PEPs by invoking the enforcement discovery protocol. Moreover, they support the interactions with PEPs by collecting their feedbacks and responding to security requests in according to the hosted TLSPs. According to the XACML terminology [15], the PDPs assume different roles: the role of PDPs providing authorization decisions, but also the role of PAPs with respect to TLSPs, and the role of PRPs (Policy Retrieval Points). PDPs must take into account external informations modulating the interpretation of their TLSPs. For instance, time-regulated access control policy requires an access point to a system clock, as this parameter cannot be generalized to all PDPs of the enforced perimeter, it is necessary that the PDP proposes an extensible interface able to communicate with third-party security information providers. In the XACML terminology [15], these third-party resources are assimilated to Policy Information Points (PIPs). Besides, the PDPs maintain several meta-datas describing their decisional capabilities, which are directly related to their enforcement context. These meta-datas are important for the tenant-level security policy discovery. Consequently, the security statements intended to the PEPs is directly related to the stored TLSPs, modulated by the preceding feedbacks generated by the PEPs, and eventually, by the PIP contents.

3.3   Policy Enforcement Points

The Policy Enforcement Points (PEPs) are in charge of the enforcement of TLSPs for a dedicated cloud resource. More precisely, a cloud resource refers to an instantiated resource on a cloud infrastructure (i.e. a virtual machine, a service, a set of files, a network function). The considered enforcement consists in (1) the control and modification of security parameters on the resource according to security statements and (2) the insertion of security event hooks to handle with state changes and prepare associated security decisional requests. Besides, these objectives correspond the ones defined by the XACML for PEPs. Consequently, the PEPs must expose an interface to the PDP for receiving security statements, and be able to contact the PDPs to return feedbacks (after the execution of a security statement or after an event hook) and to transmit a security decisional request. The configuration of security parameters is directly dependent on received security statements. The feedbacks are defined based on received security statements, states of considered security parameters and event hook states. Security decisional requests are emitted by PEPs based on event hook states.

3.4   Interactions Amongst Components

The interactions amongst the software-defined security framework components is supported by different protocols. The *Security Policy Discovery Protocol* is a discovery protocol invoked by a PDP to discover the security orchestrator and fetch a TLSP. The discovery process takes as inputs the PDP meta-data, and gives back the required TLSPs. Because of the criticality of this protocol, its specification must integrate technical measures to protect the integrity of information and remain tamper-proof. In addition, the *Enforcement Discovery Protocol* enables a PDP to discover available PEPs in its enforcement perimeter, and so, to quantify its enforcement capabilities. More precisely, these capabilities are expressed by available PEPs through their enforcement meta-datas, and brought back to the PDP which determines their potential contributions to the security enforcement. To prevent security policy information leaks to an intruder or to prevent an intruder to weaken the security enforcement by providing false security assessment feedbacks, the protocol must enable the PDP to verify the authenticity of the discovered PEPs. The *Security Statement Protocol* enables the PDPs to generate security statements, and send them to PEPs in their enforcement perimeters. The feedback must be emitted asynchronously, in case of enforcement statement execution time-out. Hence, to provide a reactive enforcement, it must be able to emit new feedbacks, when a correctness of a previously executed security statement changes. Finally, the *Security Decision Requesting Protocol* offers to the framework its dynamic enforcement properties. Indeed, this protocol enables the PEPs to solicit the PDPs for handling a security decision. This security decision request occurs when a security hook of a PEP is triggered and verification of the issued security statement cannot be handled by the PEP itself. The security of these different protocols is out of the scope of this paper, but is of course a mandatory to guarantee the security of the whole framework.

4 Framework Evaluation

In order to analyze and validate our proposed framework, we have confronted it to a set of scenarios based on a realistic use case, corresponding to a Cloud Service Provider (CSP) proposing a *Platform-as-a-Service (PaaS)* solution to customers, based on world-wide infrastructures. The multi-tenancy corresponds to the use of the same infrastructure by several independent customers, while the multi-cloud property comes from the world-wide location of cloud infrastructures. To protect its solution, the CSP enforces a security policy on its own infrastructure, and on its client instantiated cloud resources. In that context, we will consider the case of a customer, deploying two virtual machines (VM) for hosting two web applications: one for the European version of his application and one for the American one.

4.1 Validation Scenarios

The scenarios make the following assumptions: the CSP has implemented every business process in the cloud orchestrator, each customer request is endorsed by the cloud orchestrator, the customers are unable to remove the PEPs of its cloud resources, no connection error occurs between PEPs and PDPs, the deployment of software stacks in the PaaS resources is governed by the cloud orchestrator and embeds the related PEPs, the cloud resource manager comes with its own PEP which is managed by the tenant PDP. We have analyzed a set of five scenarios: the deployment of a new system instance for a customer, the security policy update by a CSP, a DDoS attack to an instantiated cloud VM, an inter-resource access request, and the removal of a VM instance.

Resource Instantiation Scenario. The customer sets up a dedicated server associated to his tenant to synchronize and back up the informations of the instances of his web application. The virtual machines hosting its web applications are Linux-powered, embeds a SSH server for administrative tasks and a web server. The chosen technical solution consists in using a SQL server and a

FTP server in a dedicated VM stored in the European infrastructure, which will accept connections from the two web application servers. The cloud orchestrator processes the deployment of these two services with their respective PEPs and notifies the security orchestrator. As FTP and SQL are newly deployed services in the tenant, the security orchestrator assumes that the TLSP of the tenant PDP is not adapted anymore, and modifies the exposed TLSP to this PDP. The PDP discovers the two new PEPs, fetches the newly available TLSPs from the security orchestrator, and sends the security statements to the PEPs. Finally, the PDP transmits a positive enforcement feedback to the security orchestrator. This prevents the security orchestrator to request the cloud orchestrator to take counter-measures against the tenant.

Security Policy Update Scenario. The CSP security administrator enforces the security of its infrastructure, by restricting the access of critical services only to the local network and the CSP VPN. The criticality of a service is not defined in the GSP, but is delegated to the PDP. After the update of the GSP, the PDP of each tenant detects and collects updated TLSPs. All the PDPs interpret their TLSPs into security statements restricting the critical service access. The PDP associated to the consider customer has deduced that all SSH and SQL servers were critical. It requests their PEPs to restrict their access and notifies the security orchestrator of the effective enforcement. If one of the PDPs receives a PEP negative feedback and has no other counter-measure to apply, it notifies the security orchestrator which will in turn notify the cloud orchestrator to disable vulnerable services.

Resource Evolution Scenario. The virtual machine in charge of the European version of the web application hosting is targeted by a Distributed Denial of Service (DDoS) attack. An alert is generated by the PEP to the PDP, indicating the resource consumption is higher than a threshold (initially specified by the PDP). Consequently, the PDP activates a counter-measure by temporarily increasing the resources allocated to the customer. As this counter-measure is not efficient, the PDP informs the security orchestrator of its inability to enforce the GSP. The security orchestrator then relies on the security enforcement stack dedicated to the network infrastructure to perform investigation and block attacker IP addresses. It requests the tenant PDP to switch the affected VM into a fail-safe mode. Once the DDoS attack has been countered, the security orchestrator reverts back the TLSP exposed to the customer in order to restore the attacked VM state.

Access Request Scenario. The cloud service provider has defined in its GSP that the used credentials for the connections amongst cloud resources have a limited lifetime, and have to be regularly changed. The verification of the validity is committed by the PDP using a third-party module. Meanwhile, the client has set-up an automatic back-up process between the backup server hosted in the

European infrastructure and the production server located in the USA, by using SQL and FTP transactions: the production server authenticates to the backup server using a dedicated password. When the production server connects to the back-up server, the connection attempts trigger the connection hooks of PEPs related to SQL and FTP servers. Both of them block temporarily the connection attempts, and make decision requests to the PDP, providing hashes of used credentials. As the TLSP imposes the verification of the credential lifetime, it uses its third party module to check it. As this module has no precedent records of hashes, it concludes that the transmitted credentials are newly created and are allowed to be used. The PDP responses to both security decision requests are positive, and incoming connections are authorized by respective PEPs.

Resource Removal Scenario. The client wants to update the virtual machine supporting the American web application by proceeding to a fresh installation. To meet this objective, the client wants to completely remove it and reconfigure a new virtual machine. He uses the cloud orchestrator to remove this virtual machine, which is notified to the security orchestrator. The security orchestrator updates its GSP, to take into account the removal of the cloud resource and checks its consequences on the enforcement: the TLSP is updated. The PDP of the customer fetches the new TLSP, and stores it. Through the Business Orchestrator, the security orchestrator starts deallocating resources to the American VM and the PEP addresses a security decisional request to its PDP for allowing the removal. According to its TLSP, the PDP grants the request. The PEP lets the cloud orchestrator to complete the resource removal.

This analysis shows that all the presented scenarios can be addressed by our proposed software-defined security framework. However, some limitations with respect to the considered use case should be highlighted. First, the use case has dealt with a GSP set by one security orchestrator. The case of multiple security administrators, with different enforcement parameters is an addressable issue as well although we still can abstract it through the single security orchestrator case. Second, the use case assumes that one PDP is allocated to one tenant, corresponding to one customer. This is however only one possible interpretation of the multi-tenancy notion, but other ones would have made the use case unnecessarily more complex.

4.2 Implementation Considerations

After reviewing validation scenarios to evaluate the consistency of our framework, we are discussing in this subsection implementation considerations.

Cloud Environment. Before considering a software-defined security stack for our framework, we focus on the environment and the resources we want to enforce. We address distributed cloud infrastructure security. The retained technical solution should be a proven solution in the multi-tenancy area as well as the multi-cloud one. Moreover, as arisen in the third validation scenario, some of the countermeasures are likely to rely on infrastructure configuration. This highlights the need for an extensible cloud stack embedding add-on mechanisms. In both cases, the OpenStack cloud suite is an attractive solution, as it supports multi-tenancy through the users and region management, and the main components of this suite provide plug-in managers.

Considering the orchestration, we have to distinguish the need of a security orchestrator based on a security policy ruling, and a regular cloud one whose actions are driven by customer solicitation or CSP management tasks. The first one will be further analyzed in the next subsection. The second has no specific security expectation except its capability to handle cloud orchestration notifications, and reciprocally emits notification to it. These two requirements are related to common orchestrator features as both are linkable to basic messaging between cloud appliances, each one issuing a request to the other and waiting for a feedback. Therefore, no more prerequisite other than distributed cloud support is expected from them.

In the cloud resource area, our framework is designed to be resource agnostic in the sense that the PEPs are the only agents of the architecture depending on cloud resources. Their interactions are based on resources programmability, inspection and event handling. Those common features could arise particular interests the more they are related to dynamic and complex resources. In this context, virtual machines operating systems and applications are well-suited for exploring this kind of enforcement, but cannot be generalized as the only type of resources to be protected. Besides, their nature directly influences the way PEPs are implemented: an executable cloud resource opens the debate about whether the PEP should be totally, partially or not at all included in it while a non-executable one excludes it.

Framework Components. Considerations are also raised by the implementation of the framework itself. The security orchestration is the component responsible for the coordination of the PDPs with each others and the cloud infrastructure (through the cloud orchestrator). As such, it is a highly critical single point of failure in charge of supervising several tenants and infrastructures. Such a criticality raises technical issues about redundancy or distribution among the infrastructure, but also policy concerns such as handling enforcement state transition due to GSP modification: if the modification process is not properly handled, as cloud tenant-level security policy and cloud-resource statement are not instantly propagated (due to network or processing overhead), we can conceive that a subset of resources of the cloud infrastructure managed by the security orchestrator to be trapped into a inconsistent security state. This eventuality must urge the orchestrator to check the consistency of intermediate enforcement stated, at the infrastructure level (resource enforcement state can conflicts) and at the policy-decision level (concurrent low-level security policy can as well conflicts).

Moreover, the privacy concerns is risen with the PDP. Indeed, it can access all the PEPs it is in charge of, and any data leak may allow an attacker to collect resource data or metadata. Incidentally, the confidentiality of the communication between PEPs and PDPs is as critical as the isolation between PDPs is. This statement decides the question of the relation between PDPs and tenants. To enforce a correct isolation between PDPs, it is necessary that none of them address several tenants. Otherwise, one tenant could compromise a multi-tenant PDP, and use-it to fetch data from the other tenant resources.

Finally, the variability of the resources this security framework addresses the enforcement leads to the question of PEP design. Building one PEP for each type of resource to enforce a TLSP in a cloud is not a sustainable approach as the workload for a sufficient enforcement coverage would go too far. Thus, we should consider a more generic approach allowing an automatic adaptation to cloud resource. A *model-driven* design and instantiation of PEP is a interesting response element as the core logic of the PEP could be specified in the model, before being compiled and adapted on-the-fly to the specificities of the resource to protect. Moreover, such an approach could eventually take advantage of the cloud resource build environment: if this PEP design and integration process is able to extract the required information from cloud resources being constructed, it would lead to an automatic and adaptive design of PEPs tied to cloud resource dynamics.

5 Conclusions

We have proposed in this paper a software-defined security framework for protecting distributed cloud. It relies on the programmability of software-defined security, and exploits the autonomic paradigm for addressing the constraints induced by multi-tenancy and multi-cloud properties. We have detailed the different components of this framework, including a security orchestrator, policy decision points (PDPs) and policy enforcement points (PEPs) interacting according to a dedicated set of protocols. Based on the specification of a security policy, our framework supports the dynamic configuration of security mechanisms to adjust to contextual changes, based on available resources and counter-measures. Autonomic methods also enable a lower coupling with respect to orchestration. We have evaluated the proposed solution and discussed implementation considerations, through a set of validation scenarios corresponding to a realistic use case. The proposed solution has raised several challenges with respect to the design of the considered components, and the specification of security policies in a multi-cloud and multi-tenant context. The PEPs will apply model-driven scheme to facilitate the interoperability of heterogeneous enforcements. In the longer term, the security policy specification of distributed cloud, and the dedicated access mode will be investigated to complement the security orchestration.

References

1. Mell, P., Grance, T.: The NIST Definition of Cloud Computing (2011)
2. Cloud Security Alliance: Top Threats to Cloud Computing v1. White Paper (2010)

3. Compastié, M., Badonnel, R., Festor, O. He, R., Kassi-Lahlou, M.: A software-defined security strategy for supporting autonomic security enforcement in distributed cloud. In: Proceedings of the 2016 IEEE International Conference on Cloud Computing Technology and Science (CloudCom), PhD Track, Short Paper, pp. 464–467, December 2016

4. Waller, A., Sandy, I., Power, E., Aivaloglou, E., Skianis, C., Muñoz, A., Maña, A.: Policy based management for security in cloud computing. In: Lee, C., Seigneur, J.-M., Park, J.J., Wagner, R.R. (eds.) STA 2011. CCIS, vol. 187, pp. 130–137. Springer, Heidelberg (2011). doi:10.1007/978-3-642-22365-5_16

5. Bessani, A., Cutillo, L.A., Ramunno, G., Schirmer, N., Smiraglia, P.: The TClouds platform: from the concept to the implementation of benchmark scenarios. ACM SIGOPS Oper. Syst. Rev. **48**(2), 13–22 (2014)

6. Dreo, G., Golling, M., Hommel, W., Tietze, F.: ICEMAN: an architecture for secure federated inter-cloud identity management. In: Proceedings of the IFIP/IEEE International Symposium on Integrated Network Management (IM 2013), May 2013

7. Runsewe, O.A.: A policy-based management framework for cloud computing security. Master's thesis, University of Ottawa (2014)

8. Fayazbakhsh, S.K., Sekar, V., Yu, M., Mogul, J.C.: Flowtags: enforcing network-wide policies in the presence of dynamic middlebox actions. In: Proceedings of the Second ACM SIGCOMM Workshop on Hot Topics in Software Defined Networking, pp. 19–24. ACM (2013)

9. Koorevaar, T.: Dynamic enforcement of security policies in multi-tenant cloud networks. Master's thesis, École Polytechnique de Montréal (2012)

10. Hurel, G., Badonnel, R., Lahmadi, A., Festor, O.: Behavioral and dynamic security functions chaining for android devices. In: Proceedings of the 11th IFIP/IEEE/In Assoc. with ACM SIGCOMM International Conference on Network and Service Management (CNSM 2015) (2015)

11. Park, J., Jeong, J., Kim, H.: Software-Defined Networking Based Security Services using Interface to Network Security Functions, October 2015

12. Ball, T., et al.: Vericon: towards verifying controller programs in software-defined networks. In: Proceedings of 35th ACM SIGPLAN International Conference Programming Language Design (PLDI 2014), Edinburgh, UK, pp. 282–293 (2014)

13. Al-Shaer, E., Al-Haj, S.: FlowChecker, configuration analysis and verification of federated OpenFlow infrastructures. In: Proceedings of the 3rd ACM Workshop on Assurable and Usable Security Configuration (CCS 2010) (2010)

14. Kephart, J.O., Chess, D.M.: The vision of autonomic computing. Computer **36**(1), 41–50 (2003)

15. Godik, S., Moses, T., Anderson, A., Parducci, B., Adams, C., Flinn, D., Brose, G., Lockhart, H., Beznosov, K., Kudo, M., et al.: EXtensible Access Control Markup Language (XACML) version 1.0 (2003)

16. Maler, E., et al.: Assertions and Protocols for the OASIS Security Assertion Markup Language (SAML). OASIS, September 2003

17. Golbeck, J.: Trust on the World Wide Web: a survey. Found. Trends Web Sci. **1**(2), 131–197 (2006)

18. Waltermire, D., Quinn, S., Scarfone, K., Halbardier, A.: The technical specification for the security content automation protocol (SCAP): SCAP version 1.2. NIST Spec. Publ. **800**, 126 (2011)

Optimal Service Function Chain Composition in Network Functions Virtualization

Andrés F. Ocampo[1], Juliver Gil-Herrera[1], Pedro H. Isolani[2], Miguel C. Neves[3],
Juan F. Botero[1(✉)], Steven Latré[2], Lisandro Zambenedetti[3],
Marinho P. Barcellos[3], and Luciano P. Gaspary[3]

[1] University of Antioquia, Cl. 67 #53 - 108, Medellín, Colombia
{andres.ocampop,juliver.gil,juanf.botero}@udea.edu.co
[2] University of Antwerp - imec, Middelheimlaan 1, 2020 Antwerp, Belgium
{pedro.isolani,steven.latre}@uantwerpen.be
[3] Federal University of Rio Grande do Sul, Paulo Gama, 110, Porto Alegre, Brazil
{mcneves,granville,marinho,paschoal}@inf.ufrgs.br

Abstract. Network Functions Virtualization (NFV) is an emerging initiative where virtualization is used to consolidate Network Functions (NFs) onto high volume servers (HVS), switches, and storage. In addition, NFV provides flexibility as Virtual Network Functions (VNFs) can be moved to different locations in the network. One of the major challenges of NFV is the allocation of demanded network services in the network infrastructures, commonly referred to as the Network Functions Virtualization - Resource Allocation (NFV-RA) problem. NFV-RA is divided into three stages: (i) Service Function Chain (SFC) composition, (ii) SFC embedding and (iii) SFC scheduling. Up to now, existing NFV-RA approaches have mostly tackled the SFC embedding stage taking the SFC composition as an assumption. Few approaches have faced the composition of the SFCs using heuristic approaches that do not guarantee optimal solutions. In this paper, we solve the first stage of the problem by characterizing the service requests in terms of NFs and optimally building the SFC using an Integer Linear Programming (ILP) approach.

Keywords: Network Function Virtualization · Virtual Network Functions · Service Function Chain · VNFs chain composition

1 Introduction

Network Functions Virtualization is an emerging network management framework for service deployment, which allows Network Functions to be allocated onto general purpose servers [2]. It enables to dynamically compose chains of Virtual Network Functions and embed them anywhere in the network according to a predefined objective. For instance, network functions such as firewalls, load balancers, and deep packet inspection systems can be placed at the most appropriate location in the network to support users demand, Quality of Service (QoS) requirements, or management needs. NFV has grabbed the attention from industry because it has

© The Author(s) 2017
D. Tuncer et al. (Eds.): AIMS 2017, LNCS 10356, pp. 62–76, 2017.
DOI: 10.1007/978-3-319-60774-0_5

the potential to reduce both CAPEX and OPEX, by the dynamic deployment of VNFs to commodity hardware, avoiding vertically integrated solutions. In academia, NFV has been a hot topic because there are interesting technical challenges to be overcome [1–3], such as the NFV allocation problem [4,5].

To better understand our proposed model in later sections, we introduce the most important terms used throughout this paper.

Network Service (NS): It is an offering provided by an operator that is delivered using one or more network functions. Network service is a complete, end-to-end functionality provided by the network operator, such as network protection. A network service may comprise one or more VNFs, for example, a firewall, a deep packet inspector (DPI), and a data monitor, as in the case of a network protection system.

Virtual Network Function (VNF): It is a function responsible for a specific treatment of data flows. A VNF can act at various network layers of the protocol stack. As a logical component, a VNF can be realized as a virtual element or be embedded in a physical network appliance. One or more VNFs can be embedded in the same physical element.

Service Function Chain (SFC): It is an ordered or partially ordered set of VNFs. The implied order may not be a straight line, since the architecture allows SFCs that send traffic to more than one branch, and also allows cases where there is flexibility in the order in which VNFs need to be applied. SFCs may be unidirectional or bidirectional, depending on the state requirements of the network functions. Many common functions such as DPI and firewalls often require bidirectional chaining in order to ensure that the flow state is consistent. An SFC, in ETSI's terminology, is called VNF Forwarding Graph (VNF-FG)[1].

Efficient network services require the optimal allocation of resources in NFV (NFV-RA), a challenging problem [5]. A chain of VNFs must be intelligently composed and allocated to the infrastructure to provide end-to-end QoS guarantees for the applications. However, given the VNFs dependencies, the allocation is extremely challenging.

The above mentioned NFV-RA problem can be sub-divided into three subproblems: (i) SFC composition, (ii) SFC embedding and (iii) SFC scheduling. Due to the fact that several chains can fulfill the same NS, the order of VNFs is often flexible; that is, some VNFs have to be placed in a specific order (e.g., the network flow first has to be decrypted before it can be further processed), while others are flexible in that regard (i.e. they don't depend from one another). Therefore, the composition of the best possible chain (SFC composition) for each NS is very important for the operator. However, SFC composition has been so far overlooked by the scientific community, typically taken as an assumption. Besides, to the best of our knowledge, previous solutions are heuristic in nature and, therefore, do not guarantee optimal solutions.

In this paper, our contributions are twofold: (1) we propose a way to formally describe network services as a set of VNFs considering the dependences among

---

[1] http://www.etsi.org/deliver/etsi_gs/NFV/001_099/003/01.02.01_60/gs_NFV003v010201p.pdf.

them and how they can be concatenated in SFCs and (2) we propose an ILP-based approach to optimally solve this sub-problem by characterizing the service requests in terms of virtual network functions and solving the SFC composition problem.

The remainder of this paper is organized as follows. In Sect. 2, we describe the main approaches tackling the NFV-RA problem. In Sect. 3, we define the SFC composition problem. Section 4 specifies our ILP formulation in detail. Section 5 presents the performance evaluation of our proposed approach. Finally, in Sect. 6, we conclude the paper with final remarks and perspectives for future work.

2   Related Work

The majority of current NFV-RA approaches starts from the assumption that the chain of VNFs has been already composed, *i.e.*, the important stage of SFC composition is taken for granted. Few approaches have been proposed to solve the SFC composition stage so far. Mehraghdam *et al.* [7] formulate a context-free language for formalizing chaining requests. They propose a greedy heuristic that tries to minimize the total data rate of the resulting chain by composing first the VNF that reduces the data rate of the flows in each step. Recently, Beck and Botero [1] proposed a scalable recursive heuristic that, at each step, composes a VNF in the service chain and, at the same time, embeds it in the substrate network (SN) trying to rapidly find a feasible solution.

Most of the existing NFV-RA approaches deal just with the embedding stage as they consider the VNF-FG as a given input of the problem [5]. For instance, Bari *et al.* [4] propose exact Integer Linear Programming (ILP) and heuristic based approaches trying to minimize the OPEX caused by the SFC embedding. Also, Elias *et al.* [3] formulate the SFC embedding as a non-linear integer optimization model where the objective function is to minimize the network congestion.

The aforementioned review shows that, up to now, little research has been performed in the composition stage of the SFC problem. Current solutions are heuristic-based and no optimal solution for the problem has been proposed so far. An optimal solution results in the best possible composition of the service chain with regard to a predefined objective. In this paper, we propose an optimal approach to solve the problem based on Integer Linear Programming.

3   The SFC Composition Problem

When allocating resources for a given NS, service providers receive a chain of VNFs and apply an embedding strategy for placing and linking these functions on the physical substrate. Despite being automatic, this process is rigid for clients and service providers, respectively. While clients must deal with complex function dependencies when specifying services, providers are not able to structure the chains in order to find the best fit for their infrastructure. The result is the

allocation of suboptimal chains, which may require many more VNF instances
or network bandwidth than necessary, leading to high costs and expenditures.

Although some dependencies and connections among VNFs in a service must
be considered, the order of the VNFs (*i.e.*, the structure of the chain) is often
flexible. For example, normally there is no explicit dependency between a leakage
prevention system and a traffic shaper or between a proxy server and a WAN
optimizer. As a consequence, it is possible for several different chains to fulfill the
same service. We call the problem of finding the most appropriate VNF chain,
given a network service specification and a set of resource constraints, the *SFC
composition problem*.

Figure 1(a) shows our proposal on how a network service specification (*i.e.*, a
Virtual Network Functions Request - VNFR) looks like. Instead of providing the
VNF chain structure as a whole, clients have to inform only the necessary information for allowing network service providers to derive the best chain according
to some predefined goal (*e.g.*, to minimize the number of NF instances or the
bandwidth demand).

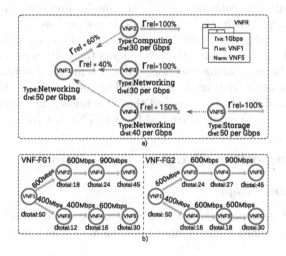

Fig. 1. VNF chain composition (Color figure online)

Essentially, a VNFR has five elements: *(i)* the initial data rate of the network
flow (r_{init}), *(ii)* the set of VNFs that compose the service, each one with their
respective processing requirement (d_{rel}), *(iii)* the VNFs where the flow initiates
(n_{init}) and terminates (n_{term}), *(iv)* a number of outgoing links (solid purple
arrows) at each VNF, and *(v)* mandatory dependencies (dotted blue arrows).

Outgoing links can be used to represent scenarios where traffic is split (*e.g.*,
bifurcations). If a VNF has more than one outgoing link, then it splits the traffic
flow into the same number of sub-flows. For example, consider a load balancer or
a DPI server separating TCP and non-TCP traffic. Each sub-flow has a relative

traffic rate (r_{rel}), which can be higher than 100% if the function replicates or encodes traffic.

Dependencies, in turn, may be of two different types: between a VNF and an outgoing link, or between two distinct VNFs. Outgoing link dependencies represent VNFs that should selectively be placed on one of the sub-flows (e.g., a firewall that succeeds an anomaly-based IDS only for suspicious traffic). Dependencies between VNFs, on the other hand, indicate that the dependent function must be present in each and every sub-flow in the chain (e.g., the cache servers succeeding a load balancer).

In Fig. 1(b), we represent two possible chains for the service described in Fig. 1(a). Notice that VNFs 2 and 3 selectively appear in the sub-flows of VNF 1, while VNF 4 is present in both subpaths. Moreover, bandwidth and processing demands are determined according to the relative traffic of each outgoing link. Although structurally similar, the left chain (i.e., VNF-FG 1) requires less network and computing resources, which at the end results in lower costs for both clients and providers. As an outcome of the SFC composition problem, VNF-FG 1 would be sent for embedding in the provider infrastructure.

Table 1 details the notation used in the model proposed in the following section. The first part of the table introduces the parameters of a Network Service Request. The second part explains the sets of nodes of an augmented graph used to build the ILP model. Finally, the table shows the ILP variables.

Before jumping into the next section, it is worth mentioning that the outcome of the chain composition stage is one complete service chain (VNF-FG) with regard to one predefined objective and that the amount of required capacities depends on the amount of data handled by that VNF instance.

4   SFC Composition Problem Formulation

4.1   Augmented Graph

To solve the SFC composition problem, we propose an ILP model that is built based on an augmented graph created from the VNFR as follows:

- For the first VNF (n_{init}) of the VNFR, one node is placed in the augmented directed graph $G^{ext} = (V^{ext}, L^{ext})$;
- For each of the remaining VNFs, we create as many nodes as the maximum number of instances that a VNF may have. For example, in Fig. 2, the maximum number of instances is 2, as the VNF 1 splits the traffic in two sub-flows. To ease the notation, the node $i^m \in V^{ext}$ denotes the m-th instance of the node $i \in V$;
- Then, we place directed links between each pair of nodes of the graph except for:
  - Instances of the same VNFs: $(i^m, j^n) \in L^{ext}, \forall i^m \in V^{ext}, j^n \in V^{ext} \iff i \neq j$;
  - Links directed to n_{init}: $(i^m, j^n) \in L^{ext}, \forall i^m \in V^{ext}, j^n \in V^{ext} \iff j \neq n_{init}$.

Table 1. SFC composition inputs and variables

	Symbol	Description
Virtual Network Functions Request (VNFR) — *Sets*	$VNFR(V, L)$	Is the service request formed by V VNFs and L VNF links
	V	Set of VNFs
	L	Set of VNF links; this is the set of all links coming out the different VNFs belonging to the VNFR
	$L_{out}^i \subset L$	Determines the (outgoing) VNF links of the VNF $i \in V$; a VNF with multiple links splits the network flow into several sub-flows
	$N_{term} \subset V$	VNFs where the service terminates
Parameters	$r_{init} : \mathbf{Z}$	Initial data rate of the VNFR
	$r_{rel}(i) : V \to \mathbf{Z}$	Total traffic (in percentage) departing from node $i \in V$
	$n_{init} \in V$	Initial VNF of the service
	$d_{rel}(i) : V \to \mathbf{R}$	Relative processing capacity demands of the VNF $i \in V$
	$r_{rel}(i, b) : L \to \mathbf{Z}$	Relative link traffic rate of link $(i, b) \in L$, here $i \in V$ identifies the link source VNF and b is the link number of i
	$req(i) : V \to L^*$	Dependencies of the VNF $i \in V$; defined as the incoming edges of a VNF and refer to outgoing links of other VNFs. This allows the specification of VNFs that get selectively deployed on specific sub-flows. An assignment of a VNF instance is only valid if traffic has first been routed through instances of all the required VNFs.
	$MI(i)$	Minimum number of instances of the VNF $i \in V$ in the VNF-FG
Augmented Graph — *Sets*	$G^{ext} = (V^{ext}, L^{ext})$	This augmented graph is created from the VNFR. The final service chain (VNF-FG) will be a subgraph of G^a
	V^{ext}	Set of nodes of the augmented graph, each node in V may have one or more instances in V^{ext}
	L^{ext}	Set of links of the augmented graph
	P	Set of paths from the node in V^{ext} that correspond to the instance of $n_{init} \in V$ to the set of instances of the terminating nodes N_{term} in the augmented graph $i^m \in V^{ext}$: $i \in N_{term}$
Parameters	$Pos_{i^m}^p$	Position of the augmented node $i^m \in V^{ext}$ in path $p \in P$, if i^m is not part of the path, then 0
	δ_{i^m, j^n}^p	Binary parameter that indicates if augmented link $(i^m, j^n) \in L^{ext}$ is part of path p
Variables	$y_{i^m, j^n}^{i, b}$	Binary variable that says whether the link $(i, b) \in L$ is mapped in the link $(i^m, j^n) \in L^{ext}$ of the augmented network
	y_{i^m, j^n}	Binary variable that says whether the link $(i^m, j^n) \in L^{ext}$ of the augmented network is chosen as a part of the resulting VNF-FG
	x_i^m	Binary variable that says whether the instance $i^m \in V^{ext}$ of the augmented network is part of the resulting VNF-FG
	$LD_{i^m, j^n}^{i, b}(BW)$	Bandwidth required by link $(i, b) \in L$ assigned to $(i^m, j^n) \in L^{ext}$ in the augmented network
	$LD_{i^m, j^n}(BW)$	Total bandwidth required by $(i^m, j^n) \in L^{ext}$ in the augmented network
	$TD_{i^m}(BW)$	Total bandwidth arriving to node (i^m) in the augmented network
	$z_{i^m, j^n}^{i, b}$	Auxiliary variable to perform the following product between variables $z_{i^m, j^n}^{i, b} = TD_{i^m}(BW) \cdot y_{i^m, j^n}^{i, b}$
	$v_{i^m, j^n}^{i, b, p}$	Binary variable that says whether the link $(i, b) \in \mathbf{L} : i \in V^k$ is mapped in the link (i^m, j^n) belonging to the path p of the augmented network
	u^p	Binary variable that says whether the path $p \in P$ is used in the augmented network

Figure 2, where $n_{init} =$ VNF1, shows how an augmented graph (see Fig. 2b[2]) is created from a VNFR (see Fig. 2a).

Our ILP model is based on the fact that any possible chaining is a subgraph of the augmented graph, so the ILP variables (cf. Table 1) mainly denote which nodes and links of the augmented graph are considered to be parts of the chain, and the demands they will have due to the chosen chaining. Figure 3a shows two possible chains that can be created out of VNFR in Fig. 2a, and how they are present in the augmented graph (see Fig. 3b).

---

[2] For the sake of clarity, directed links are drawn with arrows, so a link with arrows in its extremes a and b represents a pair of directed links; one from a to b, and the other from b to a.

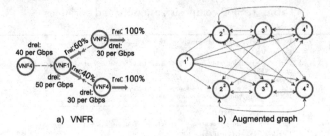

Fig. 2. VNFR and augmented graph

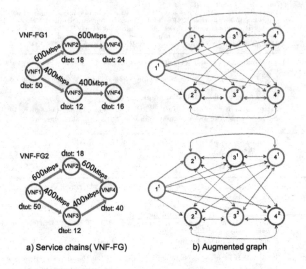

Fig. 3. VNFR and augmented graph

4.2   ILP Formulation

The following is the ILP formulation of the chain composition problem. That is to say, the ILP that models how to insert a VNFR in the augmented graph with respect to a predefined objective (*e.g.* minimize the number of VNF instances of the resulting VNF-FG).

Constraints:

Link Mapping Constraints:

$$y_{i^m,j^n}^{i,b} \leq \sum_{p\in P} y_{i^m,j^n}^{i,b,p} : (i^m, j^n) \in L_{ext}, (i,b) \in L \tag{1}$$

$$H \cdot y_{i^m,j^n}^{i,b} \geq \sum_{p\in P} y_{i^m,j^n}^{i,b,p} : (i^m, j^n) \in L_{ext}, (i,b) \in L \tag{2}$$

$$y_{i^m,j^n}^{i,b,p} \leq \delta_{i^m,j^n}^p : (i^m, j^n) \in L_{ext}, (i,b) \in L, p \in P \tag{3}$$

Equations 1, 2, and 3 indicate the relationship between variables $y_{i^m,j^n}^{i,b}$ and $y_{i^m,j^n}^{i,b,p}$ (here H is a big number that enforces the binary constraint). They indicate that the augmented link $(i^m, j^n) \in L^{ext}$ can map the outgoing link $(i,b) \in L$ when it is mapped using a predefined path $p \in P$. Remember that the same outgoing link $(i,b) \in L$ may be mapped in several links $(i^m, j^n) \in L^{ext}$. For example, in Fig. 1a, in the VNFR, the outgoing link of VNF 4 is mapped in two different links between VNF 4 and VNF 5 in the VNF-FG 1 (see Fig. 1b).

Equations to ensure that if a path p is mapped to the augmented graph, all its links have to be assigned.

$$\sum_{(i^m,j^n)\in L_{ext}} \sum_{(i,b)\in L} y_{i^m,j^n}^{i,b,p} \leq H \cdot u^p : p \in P \tag{4}$$

$$\sum_{(i,b)\in L} y_{i^m,j^n}^{i,b,p} \geq \delta_{i^m,j^n}^p \cdot u^p : (i^m, j^n) \in L_{ext}, p \in P \tag{5}$$

Equation 4 ensures that if a path is not mapped in the augmented graph, then variable $y_{i^m,j^n}^{i,b,p}$ should be zero for all links belonging to that path. Equation 5 ensures that if path is mapped in the augmented graph, then the variable $y_{i^m,j^n}^{i,b,p}$ should be one for all links belonging to that path.

Equation 6 ensures that an outgoing link $(i,b) \in L$ of the VNFR should be mapped in an augmented link of the augmented graph just for one path:

$$\sum_{p\in P} y_{i^m,j^n}^{i,b,p} \leq 1 : (i^m, j^n) \in L_{ext}, (i,b) \in L \tag{6}$$

Establishment of y_{i^m,j^n}:

$$y_{i^m,j^n} = \sum_{(i,b)\in L} y_{i^m,j^n}^{i,b} \leq 1 : (i^m, j^n) \in L_{ext} \tag{7}$$

$$y_{i^m,j^n} \leq x_i^m : (i^m, j^n) \in L_{ext} \tag{8}$$

$$y_{i^m,j^n} \leq x_j^n : (i^m, j^n) \in L_{ext} \tag{9}$$

Constraints 7, 8, and 9 establish the belonging of a link of the augmented graph $(i^m, j^n) \in L^{ext}$ to the resulting service chain (VNF-FG).

Node Mapping Constraints:

Establishment of x_i^m:

$$x_i^m = \sum_{(i^m,j^n)\in L_{ext}} y_{i^m,j^n}^{i,b} : i \in V^k, 1 \leq m \leq M^i, (i,b) \in L_{out}^i \tag{10}$$

Lower bound in the possible number of instances for i:

$$\sum_{m=1}^{M_i} x_i^m \geq MI(i) : i \in V^k \tag{11}$$

Constraints 10 and 11 establish the belonging of a node $i^m \in V^{ext}$ in the resulting service chain (VNF-FG).

Dependencies fulfillment constraints:

$$\sum_{(i^m, j, n) \in L_{ext}} y_{i^m, j^n}^{i,b} \geq 1 : l \in V^k, l \neq n_{init}, (i, b) \in req(l) \tag{12}$$

Constraint 12 ensures that for each node $l \in V$, all the dependencies are mapped.

Position constraints:

$$y_{i^m, j^n}^{i,b,p} \cdot Pos_{i^m}^p \leq Pos_{l^r}^p : l \in V^k, l \neq n_{init}, (i, b) \in req(l),$$
$$l^r \in V_{ext}, (i^m, j^n) \in L_{ext}, p \in P, \delta_{i^m, j^n}^p \neq 0 \tag{13}$$

$$\sum_{l^r \in V_{ext}} \sum_{p \in P : l^r \in P} \sum_{(i^m, j^n) \in L_{ext}} y_{i^m, j^n}^{i,b,p} \geq 1 : l \in V^k, l \neq n_{init}, (i, b) \in req(l) \tag{14}$$

Constraint 13 ensures the precedence of the dependencies. If one VNF instance $l \in V$ is mapped in the augmented graph, then the set of its dependent links should be mapped in a prior position in the path going from n_{init} to l. Constraint 14 ensures that the path being used to map the VNF's dependencies also contains an instance of the VNF.

Incoming links for each x_i^m:

$$\sum_{(j^n, i^m) \in L_{ext}} y_{j^n, i^m} \geq x_i^m : i \in V^k, 1 \leq m \leq M^i, i \neq n_{init} \tag{15}$$

$$\sum_{(j^n, i^m) \in L_{ext}} y_{j^n, i^m} \leq H \cdot x_i^m : i \in V^k, 1 \leq m \leq M^i \tag{16}$$

Equations 15 and 16 state that if a link of the augmented graph is part of the resulting service chain (VNF-FG) then the end nodes of this link should be part of the chain too.

The following Equations to establish $z_{i^m, j^n}^{i,b}$ linearize the following product $z_{i^m, j^n}^{i,b} = TD_{i^m}(BW) \cdot y_{i^m, j^n}^{i,b}$.

$$z_{i^m, j^n}^{i,b} \leq y_{i^m, j^n}^{i,b} \cdot H : (i^m, j^n) \in L_{ext}, (i, b) \in L \tag{17}$$

$$z_{i^m,j^n}^{i,b} \leq TD_{i^m}(BW) : (i^m, j^n) \in L_{ext}, (i, b) \in L \tag{18}$$

$$z_{i^m,j^n}^{i,b} \geq TD_{i^m}(BW) - (1 - y_{i^m,j^n}^{i,b}) \cdot H : (i^m, j^n) \in L_{ext}, (i, b) \in L \tag{19}$$

Constraints to set demands:

$$LD_{i^m,j^n}^{i,b}(BW) = r_{rel}(i, b) z_{i^m,j^n}^{i,b} : (i^m, j^n) \in L_{ext}, (i, b) \in L \tag{20}$$

$$LD_{i^m,j^n}(BW) = \sum_{(i,b)\in L} LD_{i^m,j^n}^{i,b}(BW) : (i^m, j^n) \in L_{ext} \tag{21}$$

$$TD_{j^n}(BW) = \sum_{(i^m,j^n)\in L_{ext}} LD_{i^m,j^n}(BW) : j^n \neq n_{init} \in V_{ext} \tag{22}$$

$$TD_{n_{init}^1}(BW) = r_{init} \cdot x_{n_{init}^1} \tag{23}$$

$$\sum_{(i^m,j^n)\in L_{ext}} LD_{i^m,j^n}(BW) = TD_{i^m}(BW) \cdot r_{rel}(i) : i^m \in V_{ext}, i \notin N_{term} \tag{24}$$

These set of equations simply set the bandwidth demand of each link in the augmented graph and also the complete load received by each node in the augmented graph. Here, H is just a big number to force binary variables to take 0 or 1 values.

5 Performance Evaluation

In this section, a performance evaluation of the ILP is presented. Our evaluation focuses primarily on minimizing the total bandwidth demanded by the constructed service chain (VNF-FG). Three scenarios are configured in order to analyze our ILP model following typical cases for service chaining [8].

5.1 Simulation Scenario

The ILP model for SFC composition presented in the previous section was implemented in the Gurobi solver [6] which provides an exact solution. To the best of our knowledge, just one work [7] has dealt separately with the composition phase of NFV-RA. This work heuristically tries to allocate those VNFs with flexible order following an ascending order according to their ratio of outgoing to incoming data rate. Here, we compare our ILP-based exact model with this heuristic proposal.

Simulations are performed for three VNFRs based on typical use cases of networks chains [8]. Figure 4 illustrates the simulation settings for each scenario. The first request VNFR 1 is given for service with NAT64 functions where the

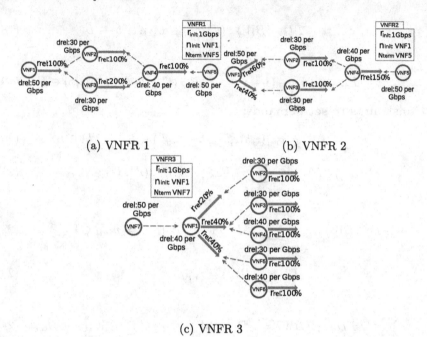

(a) VNFR 1   (b) VNFR 2

(c) VNFR 3

Fig. 4. Virtual network function requests

traffic is processed by a subchain (composed of VNF 1, VNF 2 and VNF 3), then the NAT function (VNF 4) for IP capabilities (e.g., mapping from IPv6 to IPv4), and then processed by another subchain (VNF 5). The first subchain could have VNFs with optional order, so a good planning of such functions in the final VNF-FG would impact the entire network performance.

The second scenario (VNFR 2) follows the structure of a service chain used to split service paths where service providers enable content awareness. VNF 1 splits the traffic into two sub-flows through two outgoing links. On the one hand VNF 2 is disposed at the sub-flow of VNF 1 to process 60% of its outgoing traffic; on the other hand, VNF 3 is located at the second sub-flow of VNF 1 to process 40% of its outgoing traffic. VNF 4 has to be processed by both sub-flows and, subsequently, the final function of the VNFR is VNF 5.

Finally, VFNR 3 is given for scenarios in the Gi Interface for mobile network environments. We define an scenario with seven VNFs disposed as follows: VNF 1 is the initial function to be performed, this function divides the incoming traffic into three sub-flows through three links with relative bandwidth demands of 20%, 40% and 40% respectively. VNF 2 depends on the first sub-flow while VNFs 3 and 4 depend on the second sub-flow and VNFs 5 and VNF 6 depend on the last sub-flow. Finally, Each sub-flow must to be processed by the terminal function VNF 7.

5.2 Results

The solution of our model is given in terms of a VNF-FG to be embedded on the physical network. The main objective is to find a VNF-FG with the minimal bandwidth demand on its links. Therefore, the objective function of our ILP is to minimize:

$$\sum_{(i^m,j^n)\in L_{ext}} LD_{i^m,j^n}(BW) \tag{25}$$

In order to validate the effectiveness of our solution, we compare it with the heuristic mentioned before, in terms of the total bandwidth demanded by VNF-FG, that is, the sum of all bandwidth demands on each link of the VNF-FG.

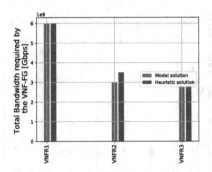

Fig. 5. Total bandwidth demanded by VNF-FG

Figure 5 shows the comparison between the ILP model and the heuristic in the aforementioned scenarios. On the one hand, for scenarios where the traffic is split out into several links (e.g. VNFR 2), our solution yields better results than the VNF-FG of the heuristic, demanding around 5 Mbps less of the total bandwidth. On the other hand, for scenarios such as VNFR 1 as well as on each bifurcation of VNFR 3, where all the possible chains are disposed in a monotonic order, i.e., following and straight concatenation, both solutions yields same results in terms of demanded bandwidth.

For VNFRs splitting the traffic into several bifurcations (e.g., scenarios VNFR 2 and VNFR 3), the ILP model would be able to obtain VNF-FGs with more than one instance of the same VNF for those cases in which such function must be performed by each sub-flow. This is the case of VNFR 2: for instance, where VNF 4 has to be performed by each sub-flow, our solution establishes that it must be implemented in two separately instances (one per sub-flow). Thus, the load of traffic arriving at VNF 4 is divided requiring less processing device capabilities into the physical network before the embedding process. As shown in Fig. 6b, VNF 4 in our ILP solution VNF 4 is created with two instances with incoming traffic loads of 400 Mbps and 600 Mbps respectively whereas the heuristic solution maps VNF 4 to the same instance for both sub-flows processing an

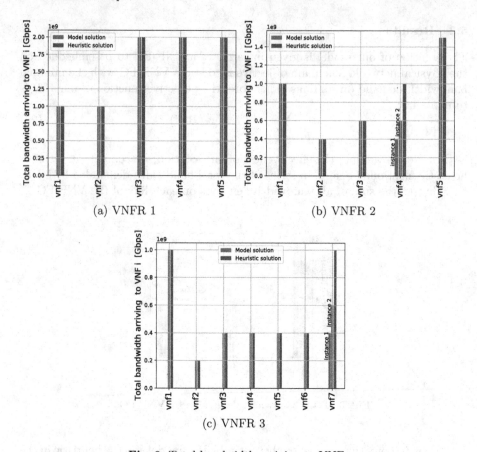

Fig. 6. Total bandwidth arriving to VNFs

incoming load traffic of 1 Gbps. The fact that VNFs are created in more than one instance would facilitate the subsequent embedding phase of NFV-RA.

Similarly, in VNFR 3, VNF 7 has to be located after all three sub-flows. Our ILP solution generates two instances of this function; instance 1 receives a load traffic of 400 Mbps from one sub-flow, while instance 2 receives a traffic load of 600-Mbps from two sub-flows, as shown in Fig. 6c.

In VNFR 1 where the VNF-FG in any combination is a monotonic graph without bifurcations, only one instance of each function is mapped. Figure 6a illustrates the traffic arriving at each VNF; for both solution the results were exactly the same.

Summarizing, results show that, for the simulated scenarios, our ILP model always performs better or equal than the evaluated heuristic proposal [7]. Specifically, the proposed ILP model provides better behavior when VNFRs present traffic bifurcations as it results in less total demanded bandwidth than the heuristic approach. Also, our solution creates several instances per VNF when bifurcation is present in the VNFR which would ease the subsequent embedding phase of NFV-RA as instances with less arriving bandwidth are easier to be embedded in the substrate network. The mean run time of our model considering all performed scenarios was 1.33 s, in comparison to the heuristic with a mean run time of 0.028 s. Also, it is important to note that the objective function of our ILP was restricted here to the minimization of the total link bandwidth in the resulting VNF-FG (to be comparable with the existing heuristic). However, this objective may change depending on the operator's goals to several ones, such as: minimization of the number of created instances, minimization of the total processing capacities, etc.

6   Conclusion and Future Work

This paper introduces a novel approach to optimally solve the SFC composition problem based on Integer Linear Programming. Evaluation results indicate that the proposed approach outperforms existing heuristic-based approaches. Specially, when bifurcation of VNFs is present in the VNFR, the proposed ILP model reduces the total incoming bandwidth and creates lighter instances of VNFs in the VNF-FG in order to facilitate the subsequent embedding phase.

Scalability issues of the proposed approach are still to be tested. Simulation scenarios were based in current IETF drafts that show only small VNFRs. A evaluation on larger scenarios to test the scalability of the approach is left for future work. Also, the extension of the ILP model to include the embedding phase of NFV-RA is an exciting branch of future research. In this way, a coordinated model including SFC composition and embedding may be created to optimally solve the two phases of NFV-RA.

Acknowledgment. This work has been funded by COLCIENCIAS, the University of Antioquia and by the Flemish fund for scientific research (FWO) and the EMD and 5GUARDS project, co-funded by imec and VLAIO.

References

1. Beck, M.T., Botero, J.F.: Coordinated allocation of service function chains. In: 2015 IEEE Global Communications Conference (GLOBECOM), pp. 1–6, December 2015
2. Beck, M.T., Botero, J.F.: Scalable and coordinated allocation of service function chains. Comput. Commun. (2016)
3. Elias, J., Martignon, F., Paris, S., Wang, J.: Efficient orchestration mechanisms for congestion mitigation in NFV: models and algorithms. IEEE Trans. Serv. Comput. **PP**(99) (2015)
4. Bari, M.F., Chowdhury, S., Ahmed, R., Boutaba, R.: On orchestrating virtual network functions. In: 2015 11th International Conference on Network and Service Management (CNSM), pp. 50–56, November 2015
5. Gil-Herrera, J., Botero, J.F.: Resource allocation in NFV: a comprehensive survey. IEEE Trans. Netw. Serv. Manag. **13**(3), 518–532 (2016)
6. Gurobi Optimization, Inc.: Gurobi optimizer reference manual (2016). http://www.gurobi.com

7. Mehraghdam, S., Keller, M., Karl, H.: Specifying and placing chains of virtual net-work functions. In: 2014 IEEE 3rd International Conference on Cloud Networking (CloudNet), pp. 7–13, October 2014
8. Liu, W., Li, H., Huang, O., Boucadair, M., Leymann, N., Qiao, F., Qiong, Q., Pham, C., Huang, C., Zhu, J., He, P.: Service function chaining (sfc) general use cases. Internet-Draft draft-liu-sfc-use-cases-08, IETF Secretariat, September 2014

Evaluation and Experimental Study
of Rich Network Services

An Optimized Resilient Advance Bandwidth Scheduling for Media Delivery Services

Maryam Barshan[✉], Hendrik Moens, Bruno Volckaert, and Filip De Turck

Department of Information Technology, Ghent University – IMEC,
Technologiepark-Zwijnaarde 15, 9052 Gent, Belgium
maryam.barshan@intec.ugent.be

Abstract. In IP-based media delivery services, we often deal with predictable network load and traffic, making it beneficial to use advance reservations even when network failure occurs. In such a network, to offer reliable reservations, fault-tolerance related features should be incorporated in the advance reservation system. In this paper, we propose an optimized protection mechanism in which backup paths are selected in advance to protect the transfers when any failure happens in the network. Using a shared backup path protection, the proposed approach minimizes the backup capacity of the requests while guaranteeing 100% single link failure recovery. We have evaluated the quality and complexity of our proposed solution and the impact of different percentages of backup demands and timeslot sizes have been investigated in depth. The presented approach has been compared to our previously-designed algorithm as a baseline. Our simulation results reveal a noticeable improvement in request acceptance rate, up to 9.2%. Moreover, with fine-grained timeslot sizes and under limited network capacity, the time complexity of the proposed solution is up to 14% lower.

Keywords: Advance bandwidth reservation · Resilient reservation · Fixed timeslot size · Media delivery service

1 Introduction

Currently, in the media-centric industries, the distribution of media content is generally performed by either people transporting the content on a physical storage media or over dedicated point-to-point high-speed optical links. However, these are highly inefficient and costly methods. In order to support decentralized collaboration, reduce capital expenditures and increase network resource utilization, media related environments tend to switch to the cost-effective IP-based WAN approaches. Deploying a shared IP-based WAN solution enables the existing media content owners and their collaborators to work together in a cost effective way, while new actors can more easily find new collaboration opportunities, thus fostering the whole industry's further growth.

As media-centric networks usually offer predictable network traffic, this knowledge of future transmissions can be exploited to use advance reservation

© The Author(s) 2017
D. Tuncer et al. (Eds.): AIMS 2017, LNCS 10356, pp. 79–93, 2017.
DOI: 10.1007/978-3-319-60774-0_6

(AR) services. This makes it easier to offer guarantees in advance, improves the number of admitted requests and increases network utilization. In AR techniques, users submit requests for future data transfers, generally encompassing a start time in the future, a deadline, and total data transfer size or rate. To allocate the necessary resources (more specifically network bandwidth), a scheduling algorithm is needed to ensure that all admitted requests finish before their specified deadline, while admitting as many requests as possible. Clearly, AR has advantages for next generation media related networks: it allows network operators to better plan resource usage, leading to greatly increased resource utilization and guaranteed Quality of Service (QoS).

Reliability of the transport is also of crucial importance in the digital-centric media transfer process, when different media actors are geographically located far apart. Therefore, strategies to deal with network dynamics such as failures should be defined to enable reliable transmission of accepted requests without any loss in QoS upon occurrence of a failure. For example, in media production networks, meeting transfers' deadlines is of crucial importance. Consider a live show or a news program which is broadcasted everyday at a specific time. Clearly, even slight delays in transfer of pre-production contents are intolerable in such a setting.

Media-centric networks impose requirements not supported by existing AR scheduling techniques, such as different types of video or audio transfers, flexible or unspecified start or end times, strict deadlines, interdependent requests, reliability, etc. Addressing these unexplored aspects was the main focus of our previous contributions. First optimal and near optimal AR scheduling algorithms, customized for media production networks, have been proposed [1]. To offer reliable reservations, we have further presented the resilient version of our approach based on a protection mechanism to improve the reliability of the AR systems [2]. The proposed scheme is capable of covering single link failures using pre-reserved disjoint backup paths. Additionally, the resilient solution improves the scheme's availability compared to the non-resilient approach.

Continued research has shown us that the resilient bandwidth allocation algorithm, in [2], can be further improved and this is the main contribution of the work presented in this paper. This algorithm is optimized to reduce network reservation waste by proposing a more efficient solution to finding an optimal allocation of bandwidth for each file transfer request. We have made a tradeoff between the complexity and performance of the resilient bandwidth allocation algorithm for file-based transfers. This results in better network utilization and consequently higher request admittance ratio.

The remainder of this paper is structured as follows. In Sect. 2, we discuss the related work. Section 3, provides brief information about the media delivery services and elaborates on the resilient AR approach. The proposed solution to improve the performance of resilient AR scheduling approach is described in Sect. 4. Designed algorithms are explained in Sect. 5. Section 6 provides simulation results and finally, Sect. 7 concludes the paper.

2   Related Work

The authors in [3] survey the AR algorithms, mostly focusing on Wavelength-Division Multiplexing (WDM) networks, and provide a taxonomy for classifying these algorithms. Advance reservation requests can be classified in 4 individual categories, which are also valid for different types of requests in media related networks. However, based on this survey, only two works offer variable-bandwidth reservation in their scheduling process [4,5]. While both approaches consider a fixed start time for the requests, all four classes for requests with specified or unspecified time and duration are supported in our work. Current research on AR scheduling mostly focuses on rescheduling [6–8], multi-domain reservations [9], and real-life deployments [10–13]. Nevertheless, reliability and fault tolerance properties have not been investigated.

Resilient AR systems can be deployed either through restoration or protection failure recovery mechanisms [14]. In protection approaches, backup resources are reserved in advance before any failure happens in the network, while in case of restoration backup resources are found upon failure detection. The former results in more resource consumption but the recovery time is quite fast. In [15], the authors propose a restoration technique to deal with link failures. In their work, the active requests and the scheduled requests for the future which are affected by a failure are restored. In [16,17], optimal ILP-based solutions were proposed to provide shared and dedicated path protection. Authors in [18,19] also provide resiliency through shared path protection. Since meeting strict deadlines and QoS requirements is of great importance in our approach, we have made use of protection mechanisms.

The work detailed in this paper presents a significant optimization to our previous works on bandwidth reservation approaches [1,2]. In [1], we proposed a theoretical Integer Linear Programming (ILP) based model and heuristic algorithms for advance bandwidth reservation with no support for failure recovery. In [2], the media production reservation system is enhanced by following a protection mechanism and provisioning backup reservations for each request. This resilient solution guarantees 100% recovery against any single link failure. While this approach strives to minimize the needed bandwidth for the backup paths and determination of allocations is fast it does not fully utilize the network capacity. This work aims at optimizing the resilient solution proposed in [2] and improving the request admittance ratio by reducing wasted network capacity and thus improving network utilization.

3   Background

We briefly explain about the specific properties of media delivery networks and provide a summery of the resilient advance bandwidth reservation approach.

3.1   Media Delivery Networks

In the digital-centric media related industries, various actors are connected to a shared wide area network to build a collaboration over IP media contents.

This shared network supports the exchange of different media contents, e.g. raw and encoded video and audio files and streaming transfers. We refer to each transfer as a *request*. A request can have a fixed or unspecified start and end times. Media delivery requests, supported in our work, are of 4 different classes: independent streaming requests, independent file transfers, dependent streams and dependent file based transfers. The requests of independent type can be started at the specified start time but dependent requests have to wait until the requests upon which they are dependent have finished. Dependency among different transfers implies that either all or none of the interdependent requests must be admitted. We refer to a set of interdependent requests as a *scenario*.

We assume that *volume* for file-based requests, and *duration* for streaming requests duration must be specified. The allocated bandwidth for the streams must be equal to their required bandwidth demand, from the start time to the end time, because their demand is fixed. However, for file-based requests, the volume of file is the determinative factor. The file can be transferred whenever possible from the time the file is ready to be transferred till its deadline. The residual demand of file-based transfers is modified whenever a part of the file is transferred.

3.2 Resilient AR Scheduling

In order to have a quick response to sudden changes such as failures in the network, we use a protection mechanism which finds backup paths for connections in advance, before the occurrence of any failure to ensure there is enough capacity left when failures occur. The objective is to minimize the resource usage by the protection paths while full recovery is guaranteed against any single link failure. In this scheme, first the primary paths for a given request are determined using an advance reservation algorithm which we presented in [1]. Then disjoint backup paths are found corresponding to these primary paths [2]. Note that in the proposed schemes, the user can indicate the amount of required backup for each request. This way, the higher priority requests can be fully protected while the ones with lower priority can remain partially protected or unprotected.

Using shared backup path protection (SBPP) [19] and multi-path approaches, to provide full protection against a single link failure, the backups have to provide the maximum bandwidth allocated on the links of the primary paths. In the resilient approach, when bandwidth is allocated to a request, we look for disjoint paths to be reserved as backup paths for that request. In practice, a request may not ask for full recovery of bandwidth demand upon occurrence of a failure and it is sufficient that a portion of the request demand is transmitted to the destination. Therefore, we compare the maximum primary allocation and the amount of requested backup and select the smaller value as the limit to be fulfilled by the backups. If this backup limit can not be found, it backtracks to the initial state and retries the bandwidth allocation with half of the primary bandwidth demand. This division by 2 is repeated until both primary and backup demands are satisfied. If the file can not be accommodated by its deadline, the scenario to which this request belongs, is rejected and all of its reservations have to be sent back to the network resource pool. Full details can be found in [2].

3.3   Resilient AR Scheduling Architecture

In this section, we briefly explain the heuristic-based resilient AR architecture, detailed in [2], for the reliable bandwidth scheduling problem. There are different blocks in this approach, presented in Fig. 1. As can be seen, new scenarios enter the scheduler through an API which can be transformed using the input transformation block. Then the resilient scheduling algorithm is invoked which follows a timeslot-based scheme. A timeslot is defined as a period of time in which reservations remain invariant. The new scenario is admitted and the schedule is updated provided that this algorithm succeeds in allocating bandwidth to all the scenario's requests. Otherwise, the previous scheduling remains unchanged.

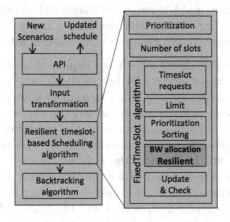

Fig. 1. Components of the resilient advance bandwidth reservation approach.

In the resilient scheduling component, first the requests within the scenario are prioritized and then the *FixedTimeSlot* algorithm is called. In the prioritization algorithm, the requests' priorities are assigned first based on the deadline, and then the request's demand. Requests with sooner deadline and higher demand receive higher priorities.

The *FixedTimeSlot* algorithm iterates over the time slots with 5 sub-modules. (1) TimeSlotRequests: determines the eligible requests which can be served at the current time slot. (2) Limit: defines a limitation for each request. For the streams this limit is equal to their demand which is fixed. For file-based requests the residual demand divided by timeslot size is considered as the limit. (3) Sorting: sorts the requests based on their priorities, assigned by the prioritization algorithm. (4) BWallocationResilient: responsible for resilient bandwidth allocation to the requests depending on their types. (5) Update and check for feasibility: Once the required demands are allocated to the requests, the schedule is updated if all the deadlines are met. Otherwise this schedule is infeasible. Full details can be found in [2].

4   Optimized Resilient AR Scheduling

In this section, we elaborate on how the reliable scheduling approach has been improved to achieve a higher request admittance ratio.

In the resilient approach, if the requested backup can not be found, it retries the primary allocation with fraction of the primary bandwidth demand (50% in our case). Although this is a fast approach, we found that halving the request demand does not always lead to an optimal solution because we may miss the opportunity to transfer a higher volume of the file and the network capacity may not be fully utilized if other concurrent requests can not make use of it. As such, we propose to make better use of leftover capacities by deploying the binary search mechanism [20] for finding the maximum value which satisfies both primary allocation and the requested bandwidth demand. This way, per-step complexity of the reservations increases while a higher amount of allocations will potentially be achieved. We elaborate more on this with two examples.

Example 1: consider Fig. 2 with a file-based request of 300 Gb and timeslot size of 5 min. The limit component sets 1 Gbps (300 Gb/300 s) for the limitation of bandwidth reservations for this request. The resilient approach, first checks if it can fulfill both a 1 Gbps primary allocation and the requested backup demand. The amount of backup allocation depends on the percentage of requested protection and also the way the primary reservations are allocated. If the request's backup demand can not be fulfilled, the limit of the request is divided by 2. Then the same procedure is repeated for the lower limit of 500 Mbps. If both 500 Mbps primary demand and its corresponding backup are available, the primary and backup allocations are reserved and the request demand is updated by reducing reserved network capacity and the rest of the file has to wait for the next timeslots to be processed. Otherwise, this division by 2 is continued until the request limit is fulfilled or the file is finally rejected. However, this division by 2 is not efficient if the network is able to provide e.g. 400 Mbps. Based on this approach the resilient reservation approach can only provide 250 Mbps. This is shown in Fig. 2b following a multi-path allocation approach, i.e. 200 + 50 Mbps for primary and 200 Mbps (to cover single link failure) for shared backup paths. Although the 150 Mbps can be occupied by other requests, this is not optimal and may results in a waste of network resources.

In order to improve the network utilization, we propose to make use of Binary Search to find an optimal value for the amount of reservations. This way if the algorithm recognizes that 500 Mbps is not available but 250 Mbps can be offered, instead of returning 250 Mbps, the algorithm tries to find the maximum available value between 250 Mbps and 500 Mbps. The proposed solution first takes the middle value (375 Mbps) and checks the possibility of reservations again. As this is available, the algorithm again checks for the middle value between 375 Mbps and 500 Mbps which is 437.5 Mbps. This trend is continued with 406.25 and then 390.625, etc. until the difference between the upper and lower bounds is smaller than a given margin, which we refer to as ϵ. Assuming 2 Mbps as this margin the

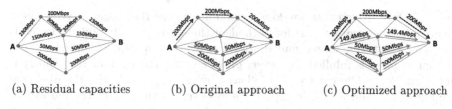

(a) Residual capacities   (b) Original approach   (c) Optimized approach

Fig. 2. An example of primary and backup reservations based on the original and the optimized resilient AR approaches. (Black: network capacity, Blue: Primary reservation, Red and dashed: Backup reservation) (Color figure online)

algorithm stops at 399.4 Mbps. The reservation based on the optimized resilient AR approach is shown in Fig. 2c. This margin can be altered to make a tradeoff between achieving a precise optimal value and solution complexity.

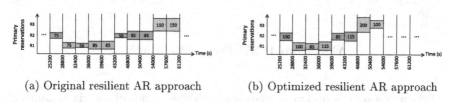

(a) Original resilient AR approach   (b) Optimized resilient AR approach

Fig. 3. Comparing the primary allocations of the original and optimized versions of resilient timeslot-based advance bandwidth reservation approach.

Example 2: Figure 3 shows an example of a schedule for 3 file-based requests, R1, R2 and R3. The timeslot size is 1 h and in both figures only primary reservations are shown. In Fig. 3a and b, the reservations are made using the original and optimized version of the resilient advance bandwidth reservation approaches respectively. Figure 3b reveals how the optimized resilient approach can improve network utilization and increase the probability of admittance for future requests. As can be seen, by allocating a higher volume of a given file, this file can be potentially transferred earlier compared to the original approach. This way, higher capacity is available for requests in future and the request admittance ratio will be potentially increased.

5   Resilient Timeslot-Based AR Algorithms

In this section, we elaborate on the optimized *BWallocationResilient+* algorithm, shown in Algorithm 1, which first assigns a cost to each network link using a cost allocation module. We have previously designed two algorithms for resilient bandwidth allocation depending on the type of the request, which we refereed to as *BWallocationFBResilient* and *BWallocationVSResilient* for file-based and streaming requests respectively. As we have optimized the resilient approach for file transfers, we do not elaborate on the BWallocationVSResilient algorithm. The common part for both algorithms is repeatedly finding the least-cost paths between source and destination of a given request until the limit of that request is fulfilled. However, provided that the limit of the request is not available, a different trend is followed by each approach. For the file-based request, maximum available capacity is reserved as the rest of the file can be processed during the next timeslots. For the streams, if there is not enough capacity to allocate to the request, it can not be served and thus the feasibility is set to false. The next step in the resilient algorithms is to find the backup paths.

Data: sortedReqList
costAllocation(Links);
for *req* ∈ *sortedReqList* **do**
   if *req is FB* **then**
      | reservation← BWallocationFBResilient+(req);
   else
      | reservation← BWallocationVSResilient(req);
   end
end
return reservation;

Algorithm 1: BWallocationResilient+

Depending on the backup demands and primary allocations, the amount of backup demand is first calculated. Both algorithms check if the backup can be fulfilled. In order to cover single failures, the backups have to be disjointed from the primary paths. As such, the links used in the primary paths are removed from the network and the bandwidth allocation algorithms are reused on the residual network to find the backup paths for that request. If the backups can be found, the primary and backup paths can be successfully allocated for the request. Otherwise, the primary paths have to be removed. Again if the backups for the streaming request are not fulfilled, the scheduling is not successful. However, for file transfers if the backup can not be provided, the algorithm tries with a lower primary bandwidth demand. This is repeated until both primary and backup demands of the file are satisfied. If this algorithm is being executed in the timeslot prior to the request deadline, and both primary and backup demands can not be fulfilled, the entire scenarios to which the file belongs, is rejected.

5.1   BWallocationFBResilient+ Algorithm

The main idea behind proposing the *BWallocationFBResilient+* is to improve the performance of the *BWallocationFBResilient* algorithm. In the *BWallocationFBResilient* algorithm, if the backup for a given request can not be provided, the limit of primary allocations is repeatedly halved and the possibility of the reservation is checked with this lower limit. We argue that this halving cycle can be improved by deploying a binary search algorithm. That is, given a file-based request, we seek for maximum available bandwidth which satisfies both primary and backup demands. Therefore, if the *BWallocationFBResilient+* algorithm

Data: an FB request
currentState ← Save the current network state
currentLimit ← Limit(req);
while *currentLimit* > 0.1 **do**
    reservation ← BWallocationFB(req, currentLimit, graph);
    maxBW ← max Bandwidth(reservation);
    graphReduced ← remove the links in reservation from the network graph;
    backupLimit ← min(maxBW, requestedBackup(req));
    backupReservation ← BWallocationFB(req, backupLimit, graphReduced);
    if *!backupReservation* **then**
        set current network state to currentState;
        currentLimit ← currentLimit/2;
    else
        return reservation, backupReservation;
    end
end

Algorithm 2: BWallocationFBResilient for file-based requests

finds that value X can satisfy both primary and backup demands, instead of
returning this value, which was the case in the *BWallocationFBResilient* algorithm, a higher value based on the binary search approach is investigated and
this is repeated until a near-optimal value (within an ϵ margin) is calculated and
returned. This process is shown in Algorithm 3.

Data: an FB request
currentState ← Save the current network state
upperBound ← Limit(req);
optimalLimit ← Limit(req);
lowerBound ← 0;
while *optimalLimit* > 0.1 **do**
    reservation ← BWallocationFB(req, currentLimit, graph);
    maxBW ← max Bandwidth(reservation);
    graphReduced ← remove the links in reservation from the network graph;
    backupLimit ← min(maxBW, requestedBackup(req));
    backupReservation ← BWallocationFB(req, backupLimit, graphReduced);
    if *!backupReservation* **then**
        set current network state to currentState;
        upperBound ← optimalLimit;
        optimalLimit ← lowerBound+upperBound/2;
    else
        if *upperBound − lowerBound* >= ϵ **then**
            set current network state to currentState;
            lowerBound ← optimalLimit;
            optimalLimit ← lowerBound+upperBound/2;
        else
            return reservation, backupReservation;
        end
    end
end

Algorithm 3: BWallocationFBResilient+ for file-based requests

6   Performance Evaluation

This section evaluates the quality and execution time of the proposed solution, compared to our previously designed resilient timeslot-based scheduling

algorithms. For this analysis, SARA (Static Advance Reservation Approach) is evaluated in which all requests are known in advance, before the start of scheduling. The influence of the available network capacity, network load, backup demand, timeslot granularity and execution times are assessed.

6.1   Evaluation Setup

The network topology used for this evaluation contains 8 nodes and 16 bidirectional links. After discussion with our industrial partners in media production industry, 3 scenario types are defined: a soccer after-game discussion program, an infotainment show and a news broadcast program, consisting of 5, 18 and 8 interdependent file-based and video streaming requests respectively. A detailed overview of the randomized variables of requests and network topology can be observed from [1] and [21] respectively. In the fixed size timeslot-based solution, timeslot granularities of 5, 15 and 30 min and backup demand of 50% and 100% are used.

Throughout this section, SARA[XX%, YYmin] denotes that backup demand of XX% and timeslot size of YY minutes is considered in the fixed-size timeslot-based advance reservation algorithm. $SARA+$ refers to the optimized resilient bandwidth reservation approach. In this approach the margin, which we referred to as ϵ, equals 2 Mbps. Each simulation run covers a 24-h period. All results are averaged over 50 runs with different randomized inputs, error bars denote the standard error. All algorithms in this section are implemented in Java 8.

6.2   Evaluation Results

Evaluation of Network Capacity, Backup Demands and Timeslot Sizes: In Figs. 4 and 5, the network infrastructure has been configured for different available bandwidths, respectively for 100% and 50% backup demands to investigate the impact of available network capacity, backup demands and timeslot sizes on the performance of our algorithms in terms of percentage of admitted requests. In both evaluations, 7 scenarios (67 requests) are submitted to the bandwidth reservation system and the network capacities vary from 50 Mbps to 400 Mbps.

What we can observe in these evaluations is as follows: first, the finer the timeslot size, the higher gain achieved by the $SARA+$ approach. As can be observed from Fig. 4, the $SARA+$ approach is able to achieve on average up to 3.6%, 7.3% and 9.2% higher admittance ratio in 30-, 15- and 5-min timeslot sizes, respectively. Second, with higher backup demand, the performance of $SARA+$ is more significant. In Fig. 5, with 50% backup demand, $SARA+$ is able to outperform the $SARA$ approach on average up to 8.5% with 5-min timeslots. Comparing Figs. 4c and 5c, the $SARA+$ with 100% back up demand improves the request admittance ratio on average up to 2.8 times comparing to the 50% backup demand.

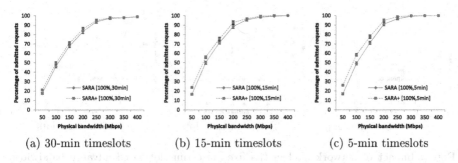

(a) 30-min timeslots   (b) 15-min timeslots   (c) 5-min timeslots

Fig. 4. Impact of timeslot size with 100% backup demand in the timeslot-based advance bandwidth reservation approach.

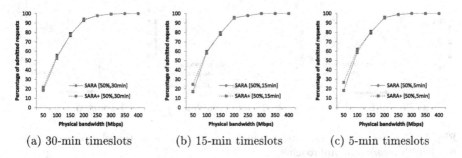

(a) 30-min timeslots   (b) 15-min timeslots   (c) 5-min timeslots

Fig. 5. Impact of timeslot size with 50% backup demand in the timeslot-based advance bandwidth reservation approach.

Evaluation of Network Load, Timeslot Sizes and Execution Times: Figures 6 and 7 compare the influence of the network load and timeslot sizes on the quality and time complexity of our algorithms. Backup demand of 100% and network capacity of 200 Mbps are used.

As can be seen in Fig. 6, by increasing the number of scenarios, the percentage of admitted requests decreases and the $SARA+$ approach performs better with fine-grained timeslot sizes. We notice that the advance bandwidth reservation system gains more by deploying the $SARA+$ approach and with the 5-min timeslot size, shows up to 7.3% higher request admittance ratio.

The time complexity of the approaches are evaluated in Fig. 7 for an increasing range of scenarios. This figure reveals that the granularity of timeslot size impacts the execution times of both approaches differently. While with 30-min timeslot size, the execution time of $SARA+$ is up to 147 milliseconds higher compared to the $SARA$ approach, with 5-min timeslots, this time is up to 4.5 second lower. These results indicate that the quality and complexity of the advance bandwidth reservation system can be improved by deploying the $SARA+$ approach with fine-grained timeslot sizes.

For further investigation of the execution time, we have assessed the impact of network capacity on the execution time, when the timeslot granularity of 5 min is used. This has been shown in Fig. 8. The number of scenarios is 7 and 14

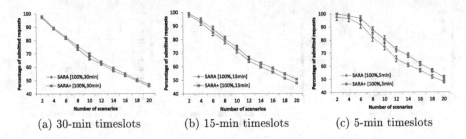

(a) 30-min timeslots   (b) 15-min timeslots   (c) 5-min timeslots

Fig. 6. Impact of network load in the fixed size timeslot-based advance bandwidth reservation approach.

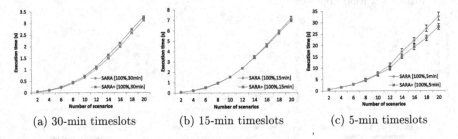

(a) 30-min timeslots   (b) 15-min timeslots   (c) 5-min timeslots

Fig. 7. Comparing the execution times in the fixed size timeslot-based advance bandwidth reservation approach.

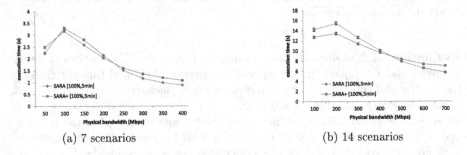

(a) 7 scenarios   (b) 14 scenarios

Fig. 8. Comparing the execution times in the function of network capacity in the fixed size timeslot-based advance bandwidth reservation approach.

in Fig. 8a and b respectively. This evaluation shows that when there is enough bandwidth capacity available, the $SARA$ approach is able to perform faster while $SARA+$ can better manage the time under stressed network conditions, i.e. limited network capacity.

7 Conclusions

In this paper, we have optimized the resilient scheduling algorithms, previously presented for advance bandwidth reservation in media-centric networks. In the original version, for a given file transfer, if both primary and backup demands can not be fulfilled, the algorithm is repeatedly executed with 50% of primary demand until both demands are fulfilled or the request is rejected. We proposed to make use of binary search instead of halving the primary demand and showed that this optimization improves the performance of the timeslot-based advance reservation system in terms of request admittance ratio. The impact of available capacity, network load, timeslot sizes and backup demands is evaluated. Based on the results, we can conclude that the proposed solution specifically performs well under limited network capacity and with fine-grained timeslot sizes. The proposed approach outperform the original one both in terms of the execution time, with 5-min timeslot size, and the percentage of admitted requests, up to 9.2%.

Acknowledgment. This work has been performed within the context of ICON MECaNO, a project co-funded by iMinds, a digital research institute founded by the Flemish Government. Project partners are SDNsquare, Limecraft, VideoHouse, Alcatel-Lucent and VRT, with project support from IWT under grant agreement no. 130646.

References

1. Barshan, M., Moens, H., Famaey, J., De Turck, F.: Deadline-aware advance reservation scheduling algorithms for media production networks. Comput. Commun. **77**, 26–40 (2016)
2. Sahhaf, S., Barshan, M., Tavernier, W., Moens, H., Colle, D., Pickavet, M.: Resilient algorithms for advance bandwidth reservation in media production networks. In: International Conference on the Design of Reliable Communication Networks (DRCN), pp. 130–137. IEEE (2016)
3. Charbonneau, N., Vokkarane, V.M.: A survey of advance reservation routing and wavelength assignment in wavelength-routed WDM networks. IEEE Commun. Surv. Tutor. **14**(4), 1037–1064 (2012)
4. Burchard, L.-O., Heiss, H.-U., De Rose, C.: Performance issues of bandwidth reservations for grid computing. In: Symposium on Computer Architecture and High Performance Computing, pp. 82–90 (2003)
5. Naikstam, S., Figueira, S.: Elastic reservations for efficient bandwidth utilization in lambdagrids. Fut. Gener. Comput. Syst. **23**(1), 1–22 (2007)
6. Rajah, K., Ranka, S., Xia, Y.: Advance reservations and scheduling for bulk transfers in research networks. IEEE Trans. Parallel Distrib. Syst. **20**, 1682–1697 (2009)
7. Xie, C., Alazemi, H., Ghani, N.: Rerouting in advance reservation networks. Comput. Commun. **35**(12), 1411–1421 (2012)
8. Zuo, L., Zhu, M.M., Wu, C.Q.: Fast and efficient bandwidth reservation algorithms for dynamic network provisioning. J. Netw. Syst. Manag. (2013)
9. Alazemi, H., Xu, F., Xie, C., Ghani, N.: Advance reservation in distributed multi-domain networks. IEEE Syst. J. (2013)
10. Guok, C., Engineer, E.N., Robertson, D.: Esnet on-demand secure circuits and advance reservation system (oscars). Internet2 Joint (2006)

11. Gibbard, B., Katramatos, D., Yu, D.: Terapaths: end-to-end network path qos configuration using cross-domain reservation negotiation. In: 3rd International Conference on Broadband Communications, Networks and Systems (BROADNETS), pp. 1–9. IEEE (2006)
12. Gu, J., Katramatos, D., Liu, X., Natarajan, V., Shoshani, A., Sim, A., Yu, D., Bradley, S., McKee, S.: Stornet: integrated dynamic storage and network resource provisioning and management for automated data transfers. J. Phys.: Conf. Ser. **331**, 012002 (2011). IOP Publishing
13. Sharma, S., Katramatos, D., Yu, D., Shi, L.: Design and implementation of an intelligent end-to-end network qos system. In: Proceedings of the International Conference on High Performance Computing, Networking, Storage and Analysis, SC 2012, USA, pp. 68:1–68:11. IEEE Computer Society Press (2012)
14. Watanabe, T., Omizo, T., Akiyama, T., Iida, K.: Resilientflow: deployments of distributed control channel maintenance modules to recover SDN from unexpected failures. In: 11th International Conference on the Design of Reliable Communication Networks (DRCN), pp. 211–218. IEEE (2015)
15. Tanwir, S., Battestilli, L., Perros, H., Karmous-Edwards, G.: Dynamic scheduling of network resources with advance reservations in optical grids. Int. J. Netw. Manag. **18**(2), 79–106 (2008)
16. Li, T., Wang, B., Xin, C., Zhang, X.: On survivable service provisioning in WDM optical networks under a scheduled traffic model. In: IEEE Global Telecommunications Conference, GLOBECOM 2005, vol. 4, p. 5-pp. IEEE (2005)
17. Li, T., Wang, B.: On optimal survivability design in WDM optical networks under a scheduled traffic model. In: 5th International Workshop on Design of Reliable Communication Networks (DRCN), p. 8-pp. IEEE (2005)
18. Cavdar, C., Tornatore, M., Buzluca, F., Mukherjee, B.: Dynamic scheduling of survivable connections with delay tolerance in WDM networks. In: IEEE INFOCOM Workshops 2009, pp. 1–6. IEEE (2009)
19. Cavdar, C., Tornatore, M., Buzluca, F., Mukherjee, B.: Shared-path protection with delay tolerance (SDT) in optical WDM mesh networks. J. Lightwave Technol. **28**(14), 2068–2076 (2010)
20. Lehmer, D.H.: Teaching combinatorial tricks to a computer. In: Proceedings of Symposium in Applied Mathematics Combinatorial Analysis, vol. 10, pp. 179–193 (1960)
21. Barshan, M., Moens, H., Volckaert, B.: Dynamic adaptive advance bandwidth reservation in media production networks. In: IEEE NetSoft Conference and Workshops (NetSoft), pp. 58–62. IEEE (2016)

The Evaluation of the V2VUNet Concept to Improve Inter-vehicle Communications

Lisa Kristiana[1,2(✉)], Corinna Schmitt[1], and Burkhard Stiller[1]

[1] Communication Systems Group CSG, Department of Informatics IfI, University of Zürich, Binzmühlestrasse 14, 8050 Zurich, Switzerland
{kristiana, schmitt, stiller}@ifi.uzh.ch
[2] The Department of Informatics, National Institute of Technology, Bandung 40124, Indonesia
lisa@itenas.ac.id

Abstract. Due to the high mobility behavior in inter-vehicle communications (IVC), packet forwarding among vehicles becomes an important issue. For IVC in a traditional packet forwarding setting, it was observed that the ratio between packets received and the packets transmitted is often very low, sometimes less than 50%. This ratio is highly influenced by the environment, especially by road topologies and obstructions (*e.g.*, buildings or overpasses). Further influences encompass the number of driving vehicles on streets offering burdens for the IVC as well as serving as relay candidates. In order to improve IVC this paper introduces a Vehicular-to-Vehicular Urban Network (V2VUNet) to overcome inevitable obstructions and frequent network changes by selecting the best relay candidate. The V2VUNet implemented was evaluated in an IVC with the focus on three-dimensional road topologies including overpasses with a different number of driving lanes. The result shows that the developed V2VUNet provides about 30% better packet transmission performance compared to traditional packet transmission in IVC.

1 Introduction

Inter-vehicle networks as a part of Vehicular Ad-hoc Network (VANET) are expected to support communications with multiple participating vehicles [3]. Thus, information exchanges in a vehicular network communication require stable and reliable connections. During packet transmissions and receptions the communication path has to be maintained in any cases. For IVC in a traditional packet forwarding setting, it was observed that the Packet Delivery Ratio (PDR) as the indicator of network performance is often less than 50% due to path failures [19]. These path failures are mainly caused by the road topology complexity of the environment, such as overpass constructions and buildings at intersection roads [9].

For inter-vehicle communications, a position-based forwarding scheme is generally used, since it offers an advantage of not relying on packet broadcasting in its routing mechanisms. Since position information is already made available, the approach proposed in this paper, the Vehicular-to-vehicular Urban Network (V2VUNet), emphasizes in filtering unnecessary participant nodes [18] and predicting the routing path based on

D. Tuncer et al. (Eds.): AIMS 2017, LNCS 10356, pp. 94–107, 2017.
DOI: 10.1007/978-3-319-60774-0_7

the position information and on the calculated direction information [17]. Therefore, the packet forwarding scheme is expected to become more efficient. In this research work, the packet forwarding is tested in two types of road environment models. The first type is the cross road model and the second type is the parallel road model. Both types reflect the three-dimensions cases with three coordinate axes x, y, and z. The advance beyond state-of-the-art in this three-dimensional area is determined by the z axis, which in many of VANET scenarios is rarely included. In addition, the three-dimensional case in VANET is significantly influenced by objects placed between signal transmitting devices. These objects can be a building or an overpass. Therefore, it is important to investigate the packet forwarding in these three-dimensional environments. Besides a better performance, the packet forwarding scales best in case of non-safety or non-real-time applications, which can be considered as delay constraint. Thus, delays are evaluated here as a less significant characteristic.

Another relevant aspect today is the use of Multiple Input Multiple Output (MIMO) technology in Inter-vehicle Communication (IVC). MIMO is a method to increase the radio link capacity and becomes a promising solution, since it increases the number of transmitted data by embedding multiple transmitters and receivers [15]. This method is useful to be implemented in a non-safety application, such as for infotainment, since it requires high data rates and large amount of data interchanges. However, as this work in this paper here focuses on the network layer, MIMO is better to be evaluated in the data link layer.

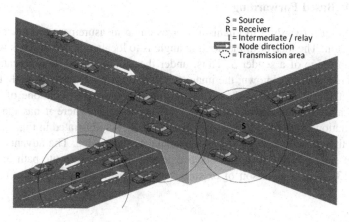

S = Source
R = Receiver
I = Intermediate / relay
= Node direction
= Transmission area

Fig. 1. Inter vehicle communication in a three-dimensional road topology

In previous works as shown in [17, 18], the evaluation of network performance of each approach is compared to a traditional location-based routing. This paper ensues to evaluate both forwarding approaches in V2VUNets by implementing various size of packets, different network densities, and speed of vehicles. The remainder of this paper is organized as follows: Sect. 2 describes related work of the packet forwarding model used. Section 3 introduces the key idea of the vertical angle forwarding scheme being part of a V2VUNet. Additionally, the evaluation of the V2VUNet is discussed in Sect. 4, followed by the summary and future work in Sect. 5.

2   Related Work

Successful communication requires an efficient packet forwarding. Packet forwarding is considered as efficient, when the packet is broadcasted with a smaller probability of errors. Packet forwarding for non-safety applications refers to numerous size of data and is assumed to be distributed at a high rate [1–3]. Therefore, dealing with frequent topology changes in IVC's behavior, the packet forwarding is based on the method of forwarding [2, 5–7]. The first idea is to avoid collision in a dense network [8], thus, the packet forwarding is designed to reduce the number of relay candidates by restricting the area of transmission [18]. The second idea is to predict the direction of relay candidates by calculating the relative direction of a relay and by selecting the candidate that has the same direction with the destination's direction [17]. It is obvious that the relay having the same direction with the destination increases the possibility to prolong the duration of a connection between communicating vehicles. Thus, in a large city environment with its road topology and traffic complexity [5], both approaches will be evaluated to perform a reliable data transmission in VANETs, more specifically in IVC. The two concepts of packet forwarding in IVC are studied in a survey that shows relevant literatures [4–7, 16]. While the first concept follows an angle-based forwarding approach, the second concept is defined as direction-based forwarding approach.

2.1   Angle-Based Forwarding

An angle-based forwarding mechanism utilizes angle measurement to reduce the area of transmission. The idea of implementing angle is to locate relay candidates within the transmission range of a sender S. Thus, under the assumption that the location coordinate of a receiver R is known, the imaginary line is drawn in order to scale the angle as shown in Fig. 2. The angle-based forwarding mechanism selects one of the relay candidates as the intermediate relay based on the location where it has the smallest angle calculation respect to an imaginary line [11, 12]. As illustrated in Fig. 2, S selects node C as the relay node since C has the smallest angle value. The advantage of this mechanism suits on the dense network because of the efficient route path in terms of time [12, 13]. The comparison of existing angle forwarding schemes has been done in [21].

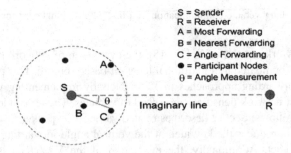

Fig. 2. Angle forwarding scheme

2.2   Direction-Based Forwarding

In IVC, vehicles are assumed to move on a predefined path such a straight or intersection road. Thus, vehicles can have heterogeneous directions depend on the road
types. In order to cover route loss due to the 'free' movement of vehicles, the
direction-based forwarding mechanism involves direction as a weight value to determine the next relay node. The direction has a dynamic value since it depends on the
road topology and time-based factor. The direction value is calculated based on the
sender and receiver position as illustrated in Fig. 3.

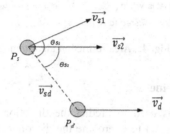

Fig. 3. A relative direction of a vehicle

3   V2VUNet Concept

The concept used in V2VUNet is an enhancement of the selection method in order to
find the best relay node of available candidates [1, 4]. Previous work of V2VUNet
determines the area restriction of transmission [18] and the path prediction [17]. Both
area restriction and path prediction schemes in V2VUNet utilize the angle measurement
on the same road level, *i.e.*, Horizontal Relative Angle (HRA) measurement and different road levels *i.e.*, Vertical Relative Angle (VRA) measurement. The implementation of V2VUNet in this work is performed to compare each algorithm in various
parameters.

3.1   Area Restriction Scheme

In the area restriction scheme, the V2VUNet operates in two steps. The first step is to
define the HRA with value of 30°, which is intuitively based on the width of a road in
two-dimensional area and the closest distance between two vehicles. The second step is
to adjust HRA based on the available relay candidates position. If the number of relay
candidates is more than one, then the V2VUNet algorithm selects the relay based on the
smallest value of HRA. The algorithm for the area restriction scheme is shown as in
Algorithm 1 (cf. Fig. 4). The previously mentioned two steps are also applied in a
three-dimensional area. Similar to HRA, VRA will be first defined as 30°, which is
indicated as the preliminary angle value based on the transmission range. This 30°
value is then increased gradually as part of the searching mechanism.

Algorithm 1
_____

1. $S \leftarrow$ sender node
2. $R \leftarrow$ receiver node
3. I all neighboring nodes of S
4. $\theta_{x,max} \leftarrow$ maximum boundary of the horizontal angle
5. $\theta_{z,min} \leftarrow$ minimum boundary of the vertical angle
6. $\theta_{z,max} \leftarrow$ maximum boundary of the vertical angle
7. $\theta_x \leftarrow$ horizontal angle made by n to s
8. $\theta_z \leftarrow$ vertical angle made by n to s
9. $i_{filtered} \leftarrow$ only i that is within $[-\theta_{x,max}, \theta_{x,max}]$ and $[-\theta_{z,min}, \theta_{z,max}]$
10. $d \leftarrow$ distance from $i_{filtered}$ to R, $nexthop \leftarrow arg_{min}(d)$

Fig. 4. Area restriction algorithm

3.2 Path Prediction Scheme

In this scheme, the HRA is used to predict the direction of relay candidates. The prediction algorithm is designed to overcome the disconnection possibility due to the transmission coverage in two-dimensional area. In case of VRA, the algorithm is designed to encounter the disconnection due to obstruction by the overpass. Furthermore, HRA and VRA in this scheme use the relative direction of each vehicle. This relative direction provides the actual direction in three-dimensional scheme. The path prediction scheme is shown in Algorithm 2 (cf. Fig. 5).

Algorithm 2
_____

1. $s \leftarrow$ sender node, at position of p_s and orientation of v_s
2. $i \leftarrow$ all neighboring nodes of s, at position of p_i and orientation of v_i
3. $\theta_{solid} \leftarrow$ threshold of the solid angle for all i
4. $v_{si} = |p_s - p_i|$
5. $\theta_{si} = $ atan $(\|v_s \times v_{si}\|, \|v_s \cdot v_{si}\|)$
6. $i_{filtered} \leftarrow i$ with θ_{si} within $[-\theta_{solid}, \theta_{solid}]$
7. $d \leftarrow$ distance from $i_{filtered}$ to R
8. next hop $\leftarrow$ argmin (d)

Fig. 5. Path prediction algorithm

For the sake of a precise prediction, the direction that is used in V2VUNet algorithm determines a relative direction since the direction of each vehicle is measured in vehicle's current position. This relative direction is changed whenever a vehicle changes its position as illustrated in Fig. 3. Thus, the traditional direction calculation cannot be implemented in this prediction as it is done in [17]. Those two proposed algorithms are expected to provide a network performance as indicated by high PDR and low end-to-end (E2E) delays. In order to compare all algorithms implemented in this work, Table 1 shows a short description of each scheme and all related factors.

Table 1. Comparison of angle, area restricted, and path prediction forwarding algorithms

Factor	Angle-based forwarding	Area restriction	Path prediction
Coordinate location	x-, and y-axis	x-, y-, and z-axis	x-, y-, and z-axis
Weight value	HRA	HRA and VRA	HRA and VRA
Relative direction	No	No	Yes
Routing based	Greedy	Greedy	Greedy
Road topology	2D intersection, highway	3D intersection, 3D parallel	3D intersection, 3D parallel

As the first factor in this comparison table the coordinate location describes the coordinate axis which is used in measuring the current location of a node. The second factor is the weight value which determines the angle schemes, HRA for two-dimensional area and VRA for three-dimensional area. The third factor is the relative direction which is added in the path prediction algorithm in order to improve the calculation of the location coordinate. This relative direction factor is suitable when nodes move randomly and is useful to indicate the current direction of a node. Greedy routing is used in all algorithms because greedy routing uses the distance factor to do packet forwarding. Basically the greedy approach work best the many routing protocol mechanisms [10]. The last factor that influences all forwarding schemes is the road topology, which becomes the main idea of forwarding packet improvement. The angle-based forwarding scheme is used in two-dimensional intersection, where the direction factor becomes an important value, and in the highway, where the speed of a vehicle is highly considered. However, it is necessary to consider about the complexity of a road topology. Thus, the area restriction and path prediction schemes raise the three-dimensional road topology indicated as three-dimensional intersection (*i.e.*, cross road) and parallel roads.

As previously mentioned in the introduction section, this work evaluates and compares the area restriction and path prediction schemes as the improvement of traditional greedy routing.

4 Performance and Evaluation

The simulation in this work aims to validate the theoretical analysis of the proposed algorithms in IVC. Two simulation scenarios of a road environment with parallel and cross road topology are selected. In parallel road topology, the difference in vehicles' direction is more extreme than in a cross road topology. In a parallel topology, there are less chance that one vehicle can meet another vehicle once they pass each other. In a cross road topology, there is a segment of the road that is under another segment of the road, which could potentially contributes to disconnection at particular moment.

In order to obtain a realistic city environment, typical parameters for the influencing factors are chosen as shown in Table 2. The Network Simulator-3 (NS-3.25) [14] is used to simulate wireless technologies (*i.e.*, IEEE 802.11p), the routing protocol (*i.e.*, Greedy Perimeter Source Routing (GPSR) [10]), the mobility, the road topology, and the network density. The IEEE 802.11p is a well known technology since it is designed to cope the frequent topology changing in IVC. During 200 s of simulation time, each vehicle is expected to run under and on the overpass in the first case, and on the different road level in the second case. S, R, and I are placed randomly both on two different road levels and SUMO [20] is used to generate the realistic mobility of each vehicle. Moreover, the number of S and R are generated equally, which means a 10-vehicle network contains of 5 senders and 5 receivers. The simulation area covers an environment which involves crossing and parallel overpass scenarios (c.f. Fig. 1) in order to show many cases in three-dimensional area.

In previous works, these two algorithms have not been evaluated over various packet sizes, thus, the packet size for the first evaluation is varied from 1–10 kB, especially for non-safety applications: a half page of unformatted email is 1 kB, one typical HTML webpage is 30 kB, 1 min of near-CD quality audio as MP3 or a 2048×1536 (4 megapixel) JPEG photo is 1 MB, to evaluate the size of packet that can be successfully transmitted in two algorithms. However, this simulation focuses only on transmitting email, with the size of the packet from 1 to 10 kB.

The first result (cf. Fig. 6) shows the PDR of all algorithms when different packet sizes are applied. This performed evaluation simulates 40 vehicles that move with an average speed of 40 km/h. The V2VUNet area restriction algorithm gives 20% better PDR compared to the greedy forwarding scheme which in the figure is indicated as No V2VUNet. V2VUNet area restriction also shows 10% better compared to V2VUNet-path prediction scheme. The showed PDR in overall algorithms decreases as the packet size increases, which indicates that more participating vehicles and simulation time are required to successfully complete the packet forwarding mechanism. V2VUNet indicates that HRA and VRA weight values have significant impacts in packet transmission.

Table 2. Parameter Settings

Parameter	Unit
Transmission range IEEE 802.11p	Up to 300 m
Routing protocols	GPSR
Number of vehicles	20–100
Simulation area	500 m $\times$ 500 m
Upper road height	20 m
Vehicle velocity	30–70 km/h
Packet size	1 kB–10 kB
Simulation time	200 s
Number of driving lanes	4
DSRC data rates	6 Mbps

The second result shows the E2E delay of all algorithms (cf. Fig. 7) when different data sizes are applied. The E2E delay increases as the packet size increases. This is because more time are required to transmit packet with bigger size. The E2E delay of 200 ms (highest delay) is indicated by path prediction scheme. This is because the path finding mechanism in the V2VUNet path prediction scheme requires more time

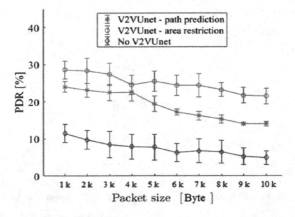

Fig. 6. Evaluation of a packet delivery ratio

compared to the area restriction mechanism. In overall E2E delay results, the traditional forwarding scheme provides lowest delay compared to other two algorithms. This is because the traditional forwarding scheme does not need an additional mechanism to perform packet forwarding.

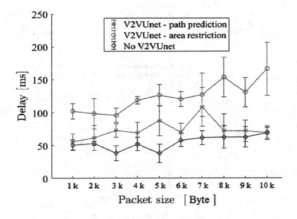

Fig. 7. Evaluation of end-to-end delays

The third set of results shows PDR of all algorithms in various number of partic-ipating vehicles in cross road scenario (cf. Fig. 8). These various number of vehicles are used to evaluate V2VUNet schemes when dealing with the network density and network speed. The V2VUNet-path prediction and V2VUNet-area restriction shows 10% and 20% better PDR, respectively, compared to a greedy forwarding without V2VUNet. As the network density grows, the PDR decreases in all forwarding schemes. From all simulation trials that have been performed, the highest PDR that can be achieved is about 40%. This is due to the path failure that occurs when the com-municating vehicles are under the overpass. This path failure cannot be avoided since

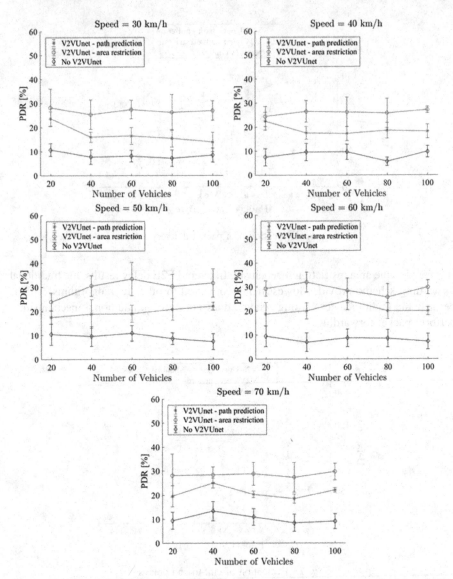

Fig. 8. Evaluation of packet delivery ratios for varying numbers of vehicles and vehicle speeds

the overpass disturbs the transmission, thus it will never reach 100% of PDR. The network density with 60–80 vehicles shows the maximum 40% result at speed 50 km/h. This indicates that 60 vehicles with 30 pairs of S and R are the 'best' condition where the packet transmission is performed.

However, in high speed mobility (*i.e.* 50 km/h–70 km/h), the PDR reaches higher results compared to PDR in low speed mobility (*i.e.*, 30 km/h and 40 km/h). The main reason for this is that in higher speed mobility, the path reconstruction is even more possible than maintaining the old path. In this case, V2VUNet area restriction scheme provides PDR 10% higher compared to V2VUNet path prediction forwarding scheme. This is caused by the overpass construction which blocks the packet transmission, thus, it becomes difficult to complete path finding process.

The fourth set of results shows E2E delays of all algorithms when various number of participating vehicles are involved in a cross road scenario (cf. Fig. 9). This E2E delay reaches 350 ms at 70 km/h speed. The high E2E delay can be caused by two reasons: the first reason is that the intermediate node which moves in the opposite direction (e.g., vehicle that changes its direction or turns back), has impact to the searching mechanism. Thus, the mechanism starts to find a new path and the trans-mission is delayed because of this reason. The second reason is that the connections between two vehicles are interrupted or discontinued, when one of the vehicles is located under the overpass. However, the E2E delays decrease for mobility with higher speeds i.e. 50 km/h–70 km/h. The similar explanation as in the PDR can also be applied to explain the E2E delays. The required period of time to find a new path is less than in the mobility with low speeds (i.e., 30 km/h and 40 km/h). In overall results, the

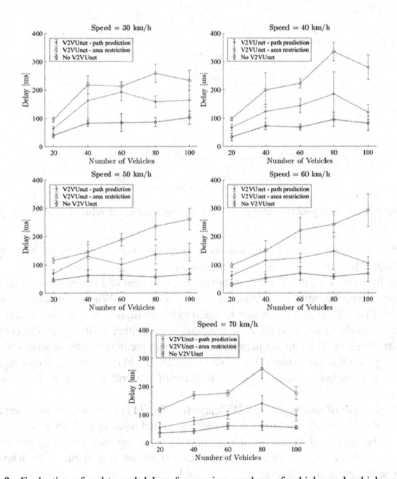

Fig. 9. Evaluation of end-to-end delays for varying numbers of vehicles and vehicle speeds

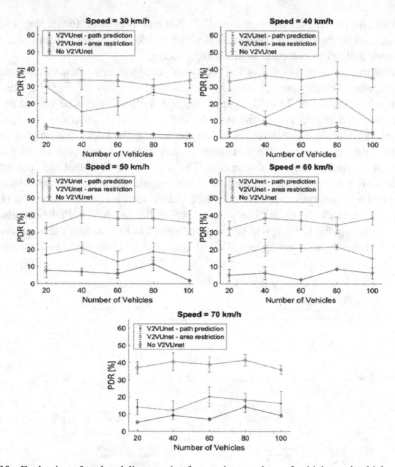

Fig. 10. Evaluation of packet delivery ratios for varying numbers of vehicles and vehicle speeds

E2E delays are considered as drawbacks in order to obtain better PDR by applying V2VUNet. Thus, this becomes an open question.

The fifth set of results in Fig. 10 shows the evaluation of PDR in the parallel road scenario. Here, the path prediction scheme reaches 40%. When compared to other schemes, PDR of the path prediction is found to be the highest because in parallel road scenarios the direction of vehicles is predictable *i.e.*, either in the same direction or opposite direction. Thus, in the parallel scenario, path prediction scheme works well in predicting the relay candidate's direction. In overall, the PDR decreases accordingly to number of participating nodes. This is because of the collision due to the network density.

The sixth set of results shows E2E delays (cf. Fig. 11) in the parallel road scenario. The traditional greedy routing shows the lowest delay compared to other scheme because the scheme does not include additional searching mechanism as previously mentioned. However, the path prediction scheme shows reasonable E2E delays of 50 ms as the prediction mechanism works well in the parallel road scenario.

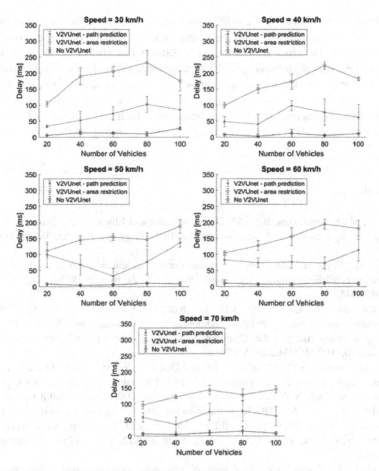

Fig. 11. Evaluation of end-to-end delays for varying numbers of vehicles and vehicle speeds

5 Summary and Future Work

This work covers and ensues the evaluation of V2VUNet through a three-dimensional road topology in a large city. Important parameters of V2VUNet have been evaluated: packet size, speed, and number of vehicles. The V2VUNet takes into account HRA and VRA as additional weight values, which are applied in area restriction and path prediction algorithms. The network performance as indicated by PDR and E2E delay values shows to be reliable in non-safety applications. The PDR in an overall performance shows that V2VUNet provides 20% better result compared to traditional routing algorithms. However, the E2E delays in the overall evaluations are slightly higher than for traditional routing algorithms. Thus, these E2E delays are considered to determine the trade-off in V2VUNet, even though a non-safety application is assumed to be a delay tolerant scheme. Additionally, the path prediction scheme is less suitable to be adopted in the cross scenario, however, it performs better in the parallel scenario. Thus, it can be concluded that the V2VUNet path prediction works better in the parallel scenario, since the direction of vehicles is homogeneous. The V2VUNet area restriction performs better in the cross scenario, since it restricts the number of relay candidates.

Further research in improving V2VUNet, the area restriction, and path prediction concept can be performed for any position-based routing scheme, where the distance and direction indicate the influencing weight value. The combination of these two schemes will be considered as a hybrid scheme, thus, both algorithms in V2VUNet are expected to improve the packet forwarding scheme depending on the use case.

References

1. Mauve, M., Scheuermann, B.: VANET Convenience and Efficiency Applications, VANET Vehicular Applications and Inter-Networking Technology, pp. 81–105. Wiley, Hoboken (2010)
2. Aoki, M., Fujii, H.: Inter-vehicle communication: technical issues on vehicle control application. IEEE Commun. Mag. **34**(10), 90–93 (2002). New York, NY, U.S.A. doi:10.1109/35.544327
3. Papadimitratos, P., La Fortelle, A.D., Paristech, M., Evenssen, K., Asa, Q.: Vehicular communication systems: enabling technologies, applications, and future outlook on intelligent transportation. IEEE Commun. Mag. **47**(11), 84–95 (2009). New York, NY, U.S.A. doi:10.1109/MCOM.2009.5307471
4. Jerbi, M., Senouci, S.M., Meraihi, R., Ghamri-Doudane, Y.: An improved vehicular ad-hoc routing protocol for city environments. In: IEEE International Conference on Communications, New York, N.Y, U.S.A., pp. 3972–3979, June 2007. doi:10.1109/ICC.2007.654
5. Tavakoli, R., Nabi, M.: TIGeR: a traffic-aware intersection-based geographical routing protocol for urban VANETs. In: IEEE 77th Vehicular Technology Conference (VTC Spring), New York, N.Y., U.S.A., pp. 1–5, June 2013. doi:10.1109/VTCSpring.2013.6692786
6. Lin, Q., Li, C., Wang, X., Zu, L.: A three-dimensional scenario oriented routing protocol in vehicular ad-hoc networks. In: IEEE Vehicular Technology Conference (VTC), New York, N.Y., U.S.A., pp. 1–5, June 2013. doi:10.1109/VTCSpring.2013.6691848
7. Wang, H., Tan, G.Z., Yang, J.X.: An improved VANET intelligent forward decision-making routing algorithm. J. Netw. **7**(10), 1546–1553 (2012)
8. Mohimani, G.H., Ashtiani, F., Javanmard, A., Hamdi, M.: Mobility modeling, spatial traffic distribution, and probability of connectivity for sparse and dense vehicular ad-hoc networks. IEEE Trans. Vehicular Technol. **58**(4), 1998–2007 (2009). New York, N.Y., U.S.A. doi:10.1109/TVT.2008.2004266
9. Walfisch, J., Bertoni, H.: Theoretical model of UHF propagation in urban environments. IEEE Trans. Antennas Propag. **36**(12), 1788–1796 (1988). New York, N.Y., U.S.A. doi:10.1109/8.14401
10. Karp, B., Kung, H.T.: GPSR: greedy perimeter stateless routing for wireless network. In: International Conference on Mobile Computing and Networking (MobiCom), pp. 243–254. ACM, New York, August 2000. doi:10.1145/345910.345953
11. Spachos, P., Toumpakaris, D., Hatzinakos, D.: Angle-based dynamic routing scheme for source location privacy in wireless sensor network. In: IEEE Vehicular Technology Conference (VTC), New York, N.Y., U.S.A., pp. 1–5, May 2014. doi:10.1109/VTC-Spring.2014.7022833

12. Banka, R.K., Xue, G.: Angle routing protocol: location aided routing for mobile ad-hoc networks using dynamic angle selection. In: IEEE Premier International Conference for Military Communications (MILCOM), New York, N.Y., U.S.A., vol. 1, pp. 501–506, October 2001. doi:10.1109/MILCOM.2002.1180493

13. Huang, C., Chiu, Y., Wen, C.: Using hybrid angle/distance information for distributed topology control in vehicular sensor networks. Sensors **14**(11), 20188–20216 (2014). Basel, Switzerland, doi:10.3390/s141120188

14. NS3. https://www.nsnam.org/. Accessed 28 Jan 2017

15. Moser, S., Behrendt, L., Slomka, F.: MIMO-enabling PHY layer enhancement for vehicular ad-hoc networks. In: IEEE Wireless Communications and Networking Conference Workshops (WCNCW), New York, N.Y., U.S.A., pp. 142–14 (2015). doi:10.1109/WC-NCW.2015.7122544

16. Kristiana, L., Schmitt, C., Stiller, B.: Survey of angle-based forwarding methods in VANET communications. In: IEEE Wireless Days (WD), Toulouse, France, pp. 1–3, March 2016. doi:10.1109/WD.2016.7461505

17. Kristiana, L., Schmitt, C., Stiller, B.: Predictive forwarding scheme in three-dimensional vehicular communication scenarios. In: International Conference on Selected Topics in Mobile and Wireless Networking (MoWNeT), Avignon, France, pp. 1–6, May 2017

18. Kristiana, L., Schmitt, C., Stiller, B.: V2VUNet - a filtering out concept for packet forwarding decision in three-dimensional inter-vehicular communication scenarios. In: IEEE 27th Annual International Symposium on Personal, Indoor, and Mobile Radio Communications (PIMRC), New York, N.Y., U.S.A., pp. 1–6, September 2016. doi:10.1109/PIM-RC.2016.7794600

19. Kolici, V., Oda, T., Spaho, E., Barolli, L., Ikeda, M., Uchida, K.: Performance evaluation of a VANET simulation system using NS-3 and SUMO. In: IEEE 29th International Conference on Advanced Information Networking and Applications Workshops (WAINA), New York, N.Y., U.S.A., pp. 348–353, March 2015. doi:10.1109/WAINA.2015.121

20. Simulation of Urban MObility, SUMO. http://www.dlr.de/ts/en/desktopdefault.aspx/tabid-9883/16931_read-41000/. Accessed 16 Mar 2017

21. Kristiana, L., Schmitt, C., Stiller, B.: Survey of angle-based forwarding methods in VANET communications. In: IEEE Wireless Days, New York, N.Y., U.S.A., pp. 1–3, March 2016. https://doi.org/10.1109/WD.2016.7461505

Towards Internet Scale Quality-of-Experience Measurement with Twitter

Dennis Kergl$^{(\boxtimes)}$, Robert Roedler, and Gabi Dreo Rodosek

Department of Computer Science, Universität der Bundeswehr München,
85577 Neubiberg, Germany
{dennis.kergl,robert.roedler,gabi.dreo}@unibw.de
http://www.unibw.de

Abstract. At present, Quality of Experience (QoE) measurements are accomplished by interrogating users for the perceived quality of a service they just have used. Influenced by many factors and often limited by domain or geographical region, this technique has several drawbacks when a general state of QoE for the internet as a whole is prospected. To achieve such a general metric, we leverage user complaints that we observe in real-time in social media. Such approaches have been successfully applied for the monitoring of specific and single services. We aim to extend existing methods in order to create an overall metric, define an internet wide QoE baseline, monitor changes and hence, provide a context for assessing smaller scale findings against a ground truth. The contribution of this work is to demonstrate the feasibility of using social media analysis for generating a meaningful value for quantifying the actual QoE of the internet.

1 Introduction

Management and operation of communication and networking services rely on holistic knowledge of interrelationships between technical values and perceived service quality. Especially perceived quality of internet services is fundamental for both developing web applications and planning network infrastructure [1]. The shift from technology-oriented to user-centric development, operation and measurement correlates with the trends of network architectures that evolve from host-oriented to information-centric models, and infrastructure networks from static to Software Defined Network (SDN) technologies [22].

On a technical level, there exist plenty of measured parameters that can describe characteristics of network links, protocols, connected systems and applications and form the well-defined Quality of Service (QoS) concept [16]. Although the International Telecommunication Union (ITU) definition of QoS includes the ability to satisfy stated and implied needs of the user of the service, the QoS concept does not provide insights to users' satisfaction on consumed services. To close this gap and to provide specific and measurable objectives to application and infrastructure developers, the concept of QoE was introduced.

D. Tuncer et al. (Eds.): AIMS 2017, LNCS 10356, pp. 108–122, 2017.
DOI: 10.1007/978-3-319-60774-0_8

There are many different application domains of the QoE concept resulting in slightly different understandings. Basically, existing work can be classified in either concentrating on specific network technologies, e.g., mobile networks like 3G [20], 4G [28], 5G [22], on specific media (e.g., video [32], voice [12]), on specific services like Internet Protocol television (IPTV) [31], Mobile Social Networks (MSN) [6] and YouTube [33], or on the type of service deployment like cloud services [2] or peer-to-peer networks [11]. Also combinations of the aforementioned categories are actively researched, e.g., in [5].

QoE can be thought of as QoS plus a human factor. This simple definition might be misleading, as modeling of the human factor is an unresolved issue, that includes different fields of psychology like cognitive psychology, memory psychology, and psychophysics [30]. That is why QoE measurements often include conducting real-world experiments with test persons, asking them in various ways for their opinion on used services. Using this black box test setting, the inscrutability of the human mind is bypassed and the aimed value is achieved. The disadvantage is the requirement of strictly controlled testing procedures, high personnel demand and lack of scalability.

In order to address these shortcomings, this paper is about the question of whether it is possible to turn complaints of globally distributed social media users into valuable signals for inferring perceived levels of web service quality. With a positive outcome, continuous QoE measurement at large scale would become feasible and advanced questions might be identified. With Twitter, people can publish messages (tweets) using various devices and follow other users to subscribe to their tweets. The public Twitter Application Programming Interfaces (APIs) offer programmatic access to public tweets in a well-documented JavaScript Object Notation (JSON) format. Twitter is the most widespread service of its kind and, due to its openness and popularity, current subject of research in several disciplines covering a broad range of examined topics [34]. In this work, we investigate the feasibility of using tweets as an indicator for QoE drops. Twitter users are not a representative share of all internet users. More than that, we expect the population to be biased in various ways. This is a restriction to our approach, which let us detect only complaints about problems without providing an unbiased base line. Nevertheless, we expect the outcome to be actionable in a way that subsequent work can build upon it and support the presented use cases.

The remainder of this paper is organized as follows. Section 2 gives an overview of QoE metrics for web services, how measurements are performed, and which shortcomings exist in current methods. Also, use cases are presented and requirements to the solution are derived. In Sect. 3 we investigate existing approaches on leveraging social media content for detecting disruptions of web services. A description of our experimental setup, message processing and signal extraction methods to receive correlations between web services and user experience are presented in Sect. 4. In Sect. 5, we give insights to the generated data and evaluate our findings with respect to the research question that is raised. The results are concluded in Sect. 6 and future work is outlined.

2   Problem Statement

Assessing accurate QoE metrics is a challenging problem. Schatz et al. give comprehensive insights in [29]. They define two different kinds of testing techniques for QoE: The first kind is made of *subjective* tests, typically conducted in a controlled laboratory setting but also as field tests or using crowdsourcing methods. All of these methods aim to gather answers from humans to predefined questions and include the downside of being costly, time-consuming and require careful planning. The second kind of tests is *objective* measurement that include measuring physiological aspects of test persons or technical parameters of the utilized systems and infrastructure. These assessment methods need to be mapped to a resulting user experience score, requiring a proper model. Whilst also being affected by the drawbacks of the subjective methods, the big advantage of objective methods is the possibility of automation and therefore, some degree of scalability.

2.1   Modeling and Formalization of QoE

QoE is defined as a metric for the relationship of a person that interacts as user with an application [21,25]. While QoS focuses on the relationship between systems, the authors recognize that a change in QoS only affects QoE if a person's expectation is affected. Analogous to this approach, also the concept of Quality of Business (QoBiz) is introduced, the value of which only is affected by changes in QoE if a company's revenue is impaired. The key finding of these publications is that values of different quality aspects can be seen independent, even though they build upon each other, so that only weak coupling between these metrics can be assumed.

2.2   Web QoE Metrics and Assessment

In contrast to QoS that is well defined and standardized [16], and even adapted to specific technologies like mobile networks [17], QoE is much harder to quantify. A common factor of most approaches, is the assignment of an average value for perceived quality on a scale from 1 to 5 (representing *bad*, *poor*, *fair*, *good*, and *excellent*), what is known as the Mean Opinion Score (MOS) [14].

Streijl et al. give a comprehensive summary of methods, applications, limitations and alternatives of the MOS in [30]. They describe the influence of psychological aspects, test design, testing methods and even the choice of scales to the result of MOS measurement. Stating the costly and time-consuming nature and limited scope of subjective quality tests, they also review objective models that exist in various types (e.g., arithmetic models, statistical models, parametric network planning models). While these models can be considered correct, as long as the calculated MOS lies within the confidence interval of the subjective MOS, the authors conclude that slight broadening of distortions results in higher complexity and disagreement between perceived qualities.

2.3   Challenges of Objective Methods for Network Related QoE

The ITU outlines a framework for estimating end-to-end-performance in IP networks in [15] and recommends to focus on technical metrics like bandwidth, delay and packet loss rate in order to gain insights to perceived web quality. While concluding that perceived quality can be derived with a correlation that is high enough for most use cases (>0.9), more detailed methods for addressing factual challenges and considering a higher number of variables have been published during the last years. Most of these approaches incorporate in some way the complexity of human emotion, that are not considered in the framework of the ITU. Some of the human mind's complex relationships have been researched in context of QoE: Egger et al. show in [8] the direct applicability of the Weber-Fechner Law (see [10] for a brief historical outline) to the relationship of waiting time and download experience. They proof this finding empirically for simple waiting tasks and furthermore, they also investigate the applicability of logarithmic relations between bandwidth and mean opinion score for more complex tasks like web browsing. Instead of a logarithmic relationship, rather an exponential relationship was discovered, as has also been shown before by Fiedler et al. in [9]. The explanation for this outcome lies in the complex, non-linear models of network-level page load times, which were investigated in detail by Belshe [4]. Also, a memory effect has to be considered as psychological influence factor as described in [13]. With [7] Egger et al. provide a condensed summary of many of the intertwined aspects. From these insights into technical and psychological background of perceived web quality, we can derive that a purely technical approach to measure web QoE is a hard problem.

2.4   Use Cases

To demonstrate the tangibility of the problem statement, we look at the following exemplary stakeholders that can benefit from internet wide QoE measurements.

Network Providers need to optimize investments on new infrastructure in a way that costs are minimized while turnover is maximized, aiming at ultimately maximizing profit. QoE is a valid metric for customer satisfaction, which in turn we imply is positively correlated with turnover. Due to this correlation, optimizing for QoE is more target-oriented than optimizing for technical QoS parameters. The knowledge of a base level of customer satisfaction and the ability to detect changes is key either to assess the effect of investments already carried out and to identify weak points in network infrastructure that are most in need for further investments.

Service Providers that offer their business to worldwide customers, often rely on both own and third-party infrastructure to deliver contents. Ensuring continuous availability and convenient response times, as two key service level metrics, is business-critical to them. Their challenge in monitoring customer experience is manifold: Services are frequently added and changed so that automatic or synthetic monitoring of technical key performance indicators often lags behind and covers only a small fraction of all service functions. Also a service provider would like to be aware of a shift of customers' experience during the lifetime of a service. Challenging is that the underlying infrastructure is very heterogeneous in most times, not only because of third-party services but also because of implementing novel cloud technologies as demanded by service expansion. In case of a problem, they also want to identify whether the problem affects only their own service or services of other providers as well to communicate accordingly to their customers.

Security Actors may observe disruptions of network segments or services of central importance for the reliability of internet infrastructure as a result of large-scale attacks. In such scenarios, it is crucial to gain as much information as possible as quickly as possible. This is to make up the information advantage of the attackers and become able to successfully deploy counter measures in a timely manner. To know whether, which, where and to what extend web services are affected, can support this process effectively.

2.5   Requirements

To conclude the former stated shortcomings and limitations of current approaches, we derive the following requirements on real-time QoE measurement at internet scale, matching the demands of the presented use cases.

1. Identify an overall baseline for web service QoE.
2. Recognize changes in customer experience with web services, especially drops.
3. Monitor for QoE problems independently of underlying network technology.
4. Monitor new services immediately after deployment and adapt to changes.
5. Provide continuous insights to changes and affected service.
6. Provide measurements near real-time.

3   Related Work

In order to examine to which extend the identified requirements are met by existing approaches and also to eventually identify the open points that have to be considered, we give the necessary overview of the most significant work in the relevant fields.

3.1   Measuring QoE

There are several approaches to derive MOS for specific applications from measurable network parameters and traffic monitoring, most of which include elaborate field trials interviewing test persons. In [5] Casas et al. present YOUQ-MON, an approach to calculate the MOS for YouTube videos in 3G networks by passively monitoring network packets within the network core. To evaluate the model, they conducted a field trial with 16 different videos to compare the calculated MOSs with the ones perceived by test persons.

Mok et al. investigate how network path qualities (i.e., bandwidth, roundtrip time (RTT) and loss rate) affects QoE of Hypertext Transfer Protocol (HTTP) video streaming [23]. They measure the MOS in a sophisticated experimental setup under strictly controlled test conditions. Furthermore, they present first results for a correlation between video category (i.e., sports, news, comedy, music video) and the perceived quality, while keeping technical attributes like stall times and re-buffering frequency fixed. The dependency between MOS and video category is a good example of the human factor in MOS measurement and shows the non-linear connection between technical values and perceived quality. Both publications show the need for access to core network components to automatically measure a QoE score. While fulfilling some of the requirements, these approaches cannot adapt to new services and are strongly dependent on the underlying network topology.

The same authors investigate in a recent work the quality of crowd-sourced approaches to QoE measurement [24]. Though being relatively cost-effective, for long running settings, costs are still a disadvantage. Advantages over one-time experiments are, e.g., the ability of conducting an ongoing assessment of certain services, and due to using humans as sensors, adaptability to changes in the assessed services. A disadvantage is still the management effort for planning, supporting and evaluating the questionnaires. Also the quality can be an issue, as the authors investigate in the paper.

3.2   Using Twitter to Detect Outages

Principally, not only Twitter is suited as a data source for detecting opinions about web services. Other social media platforms offer also a wealth of user generated content. The decisive criterion for choosing Twitter is easy accessibility of data. This is meant in a technical manner, as Twitter offers a well-documented API with free and open access for many use cases. Apart from that, using Twitter is motivated in the text-focused format of the data that can be exploited with well-established techniques.

Motoyama et al. were the first to leverage the unique characteristics of Twitter messages for detecting outages of internet services [26]. They identified terms that qualify tweets to report about service outages by investigating tweets that occurred in temporal correlation with major service outage reports in the media. To further refine their filter, they developed a heuristic that leveraged customs of Twitter users, like using hashtags that include the word *fail*. To clean up the derived signals, they made use of exponential smoothing and gave insights into their chosen parameters to achieve optimal results. Their outcome is to be able to identify outages of online services by observing between 4 and approximately 200 reports about a specific service outage. The suggested solution was later implemented by Augustine and Cushing [3]. They used the approach to monitor outages and network problems of the NETFLIX content delivery network. They were able to evaluate the accuracy of their system because a list of outages of the monitored web service was available to them and showed the practical applicability and value of leveraging tweets for their use case.

Qiu et al. evaluated the relationship between tweets and customer care tickets that both address mobile network experience issues [27]. They found that tweets, relating to the same problem, preceded customer care tickets by approximately 10 min. Furthermore, tweets reported a wider range of problems while also addressing a slightly different set of problems. Qiu et al. mapped the problems reported via Twitter to incidents they knew from the ticket system. In addition to the already known incidents, they were able to identify short-term problems that have not been reported via the ticket system. Summing up their findings, we emphasize that these correspond with our motivation to exploit tweets for measuring QoE in real-time: Timely detection of drops in experience, high sensitivity for a broad range of problems and open availability of continuous monitoring data.

3.3 Open Points

We conclude the review of related work with summarizing how the formulated requirements are met in Table 1. A global baseline for an internet wide QoE score is not provided by any of the mentioned publications. Furthermore, to the best of our knowledge, there is no such approach in existing scientific literature. While the approaches that use network parameter measurements to obtain an MOS are able to map the results to a continuous scale between 1 and 5, the approaches that leverage social media messages to detect outages are only able to make a binary decision between service *available* and *not available*. Also to the best of our knowledge, there is no approach so far that would investigate other service disruptions like increased latency. Network measurement based approaches have an obvious dependency on the underlying technology. In contrast, approaches that use humans as sensor are free of this dependency. Also, human based test methods are able to adapt to new services and service changes. In the case of crowd-sourced test methods, questionnaires and manuals have to be adapted. Provided that services and technology conditions are stable, all methods can be used for continuous monitoring. Though crowd-sourcing methods have limited real-time response times, as the setup and management overhead can be significant.

Table 1. Assessment how the requirements are met by existing work.

Requirement (see Sect. 2.5)	Casas [5]	Mok'11 [23]	Mok'16 [24]	Motoyama [26]	Qiu [27]	Augustine [3]
1: Global baseline	○	○	○	○	○	○
2: Detect score changes	●	●	●	◑	◑	◑
3: Independent of technology	○	○	●	●	●	●
4: Adapt new services	○	○	◑	●	●	●
5: Continuous monitoring	●	●	●	●	●	●
6: Results in real-time	●	●	◑	●	●	●

Requirement ○=not met, ◑=partially met, ●=fully met

4 Internet Scale QoE Measurement

We address the identified open points in the following way. In contrast to existing work, our approach aims to isolate a signal that is suitable for inferring an internet wide QoE score, rather than concentrating on a specific service. Furthermore, we add distinction between a total loss of availability and response time of a service, which can be used to derive a graduated score of disruption, rather than a binary decision. According to existing approaches that use social media content and therefore humans as sensors, we also use tweets to meet the remaining requirements.

4.1 Experimental Setup

In this section, we briefly describe the source of the analyzed data, the ETL process (i.e., extract, transform, load), and used methods of feature isolation, data smoothing and signal extraction. All steps were performed using two mid-class notebooks and one office workstation, equipped with 4–12 CPU cores at 2.7 GHz–3.16 GHZ and 8 GB–32 GB RAM. For loading and analyzing the data, these systems formed a small cluster running Elasticsearch on Apache Lucene as main database supported by a powerful indexing and search environment, and Kibana for gaining insights into the data. Once the data has been loaded, typical requests involving a keyword filter took approximately 60–80 s.

4.2 Data Source

In order to gather a reasonable data set for our analysis, we used Twitter's public API. Combining several API methods, we captured and requested tweets that have been created in the time interval from 13-Feb-2017 12:00:00.000 UTC to 02-Mar-2017 08:59:59.999 UTC. The obtained data set is not complete in the sense that a complete data set would include every single tweet that has been published during the considered period. First reason is, for being able to analyze textual content efficiently, we dropped all tweets with a language attribute that differs from *en* (i.e., English). This restriction is not as strict as it may seem. First, English is the most used language on Twitter, and second, internet related issues are often reported in English, even if it is not the native language of the reporting user. A possible reason might be that error messages are mostly in English and are simply cited by reporting users. We have observed this behavior very often in our data set. In addition, there are several more reasons for the data set not being complete: Besides public tweets there are direct tweets between users. Direct tweets are private and not accessible by anyone else but the sending and the receiving user. Another category of tweets that we missed consists of such tweets that have already been deleted at the time of our request. Ultimately our data set lacks of tweets that we simply did not cover with our query parameters.

Taking into account that a productive implementation of our findings, if appropriate, would most certainly also use the public Twitter API, working on an equivalent data set with common shortfalls appears to be justified. Beyond this, an eventual implementation should be able to work on a much smaller data set than we used to examine the feasibility of the concept.

Figure 1(a) shows a typical Twitter-Day for English content of our data set. We are able to show the amount of total tweets in the firehose (i.e., the stream of all public tweets), taking advantage of the nature of Twitter's sample stream that we described in [19] and also captured for this analysis. Also the proportion of our data set can be derived from the figure.

Furthermore, we have the requirement to our data of being as random as possible. This is due to a limitation in Twitter's Streaming API: If requested with a set of keywords (that seems appropriate for our problem at the first glance), Twitter will deliver all tweets that contain these keywords, applying a logical *OR* between the requested keywords and there is no possibility to use a *NOT* operator for this request. However, according to the documentation of the Streaming API, Twitter caps the delivery rate of this stream to 1% of the current firehose rate. Hence, if the hit rate of our filter exceeds this limit, we would not be able to derive an accurate result value due to capped measurement values. Whether this limitation is a real problem or practical systems could rely on Twitter's Streaming API, can be derived from Fig. 1(b): The histogram shows the distribution of the resulting percentage of the firehose for all 5 min intervals of our data set when we use the keywords that are presented in the next section. According to this analysis, we would hit the limit of one percent in more than a half of the time.

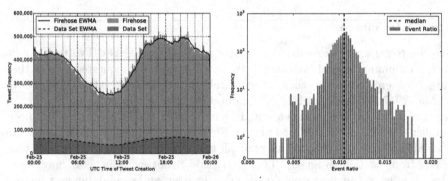

(a) Tweet Frequency for 5-minute-bins for a typical English subset of 24 hours.

(b) Event ratio using *OR*-linked keywords.

Fig. 1. Properties of the derived data set

Data Extraction. The extraction challenge is typically twofold: First, we have to identify relevant terms, that appear in tweets of our interest. Second, tweets containing the identified terms have to be collected from the data set to form generating components for the desired signal.

Inevitably, at first we have to define what characterizes a *tweet of interest*. As Twitter is to be leveraged as a sensor for drops in web QoE, tweets that represent a suitable signal combine the following **Properties**:

1. Related to a specific web service (no need to mention which in particular).
2. Describe present reduction of availability or speed of (parts of) a web service.
3. May be formulated as a question, may use humor, sarcasm, or irony.
4. Do not notify about intentional down time.

Hereinafter the occurrence of a tweet of interest will be referenced as *event*. As a starting point for suitable terms to identify events, we analyzed and used phrases presented in [26]. The first filter approach used the following **Conditions** for tweet content (not case sensitive):

1. Must contain: *website* OR *site* OR *server*
2. Must contain: *down* OR *unreachable* OR *error*

While Condition 1 identifies tweets about web services, Condition 2 restricts the result set to terms that most likely describe the problem component of Property 2. Using only these two conditions, a one-time training set of 400 tweets showed a selectivity of 0.77.

After this manual review we optimized the filter choice for selectivity. As a result, these additional **Conditions** were added to the filter:

3. Must NOT contain: (*going to be* OR *will be* OR *was* OR *is not*) *down*
4. Must NOT contain: (*close** OR *shut** OR *take** OR *took* OR *torn*) *down*
5. Must NOT contain: (*clean* OR *count** OR *dress* OR *low* OR *right* OR *scroll* OR *settle* OR *sit* OR *top* OR *written*) *down*
6. Must not be a retweet of an original tweet.

Condition 3 was added to ensure the temporal relation of Property 2. To address Property 4, Condition 4 was introduced. The conditions were further restricted by introducing Condition 5, covering the most common semantic ambiguities of the term *down*, and by Condition 6 as retweets in the training set in most instances did not fulfill the listed properties. Finally, this set of conditions was evaluated against a test set of 840 tweets that is distinct to the training set. For the refined condition set, a selectivity of 0.88 was identified, yielding 12% false positives. We consider this rate as being sufficient for conducting a proof of concept, considering the simplicity of our approach.

Data Smoothing. The time resolution we applied for this analysis is 5 min. We could have chosen smaller intervals, but then occasional random disconnections of the Twitter stream, network anomalies or other random errors, would have a more significant effect on the results. Hence, we have chosen this general smoothing. Furthermore, we can observe increased activity at every full hour and also at every half hour. The latter does not weight as much as the first. To address the artificially generated bursts in the data set, we applied an exponential weighted moving average (EWMA) with a half-life period of 15 min ($\alpha \approx 0.206$) and used this value for further calculations. The frequency of the analyzed tweets also shows a typical variation during a day.

5   Evaluation

For determining a baseline of reports about service outages or service restrictions like increased response time, we need to apply an appropriate metric. Due to the nature of tweet distribution that is not unique across a day, we cannot simply count the number of event occurrences and use this value as a baseline. Since reports of events underlie the same daily rhythm as the firehose and are correlated with the biological rhythm of the sensors, we have to normalize the event count to the current activity. This is achieved by using the proportion between all events and all non-event tweets as metric. Hence, the ratio of event occurrences in a specific time interval in comparison to the total number of tweets in the same time interval qualifies as the desired metric. The simple formula for the wanted score in time interval n is

$$\text{event-ratio}_n = \frac{|\text{events}|_n}{|\text{EWMA}(\text{tweets})|_n - |\text{events}|_n}. \tag{1}$$

To address temporal spikes in the total tweet number, we applied the smoothing described in the preceding section to the total number of tweets and Fig. 2(a) show the distribution of the event ratio in our data set for the outage event defined above. Figure 2(b) shows the event ratio distribution for *slow* events, for that we changed Condition 2 to the term *slow* only.

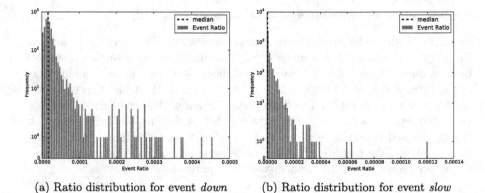

(a) Ratio distribution for event *down*   (b) Ratio distribution for event *slow*

Fig. 2. Event ratios of the analyzed data set. The right most spikes, that constitute a multiple of the average ratio, are related to Amazon's S3 outage during the capture time of the data set.

The mean value for the *down report* ratio can be identified as 2.25×10^{-5}, while the median is 1.66×10^{-5}. Using the median as a baseline seems appropriate, as there have been major outages taken place during the capturing of the data set. The mean value for the *slow report* ratio is 1.58×10^{-6}, while the median is 2.56×10^{-7}. The significant difference between median and mean is a clear indicator for outliers, that can be confirmed by the event ratio histogram that shows occurrences of event ratios that are multiples of the median. Table 2 lists an excerpt from the top 50 event ratios and informs about the causing event, that we identified by textually analyzing the specific period.

Table 2. Excerpt from top 50 highest event ratio intervals. Events manually evaluated.

#	Time	Event ratio	Median multiplier	Causing event
1	28-Feb-17 18:30	0.000456	27.5	Amazon S3 outage
2	28-Feb-17 18:10	0.000424	25.6	Amazon S3 outage
3	28-Feb-17 18:15	0.000374	22.5	Amazon S3 outage
4	28-Feb-17 18:00	0.000371	22.4	Amazon S3 outage
5	28-Feb-17 18:25	0.000352	21.2	Amazon S3 outage
16	27-Feb-17 11:30	0.000275	16.6	Error message on hilton.com
24	02-Mar-17 10:50	0.000246	14.8	Vainglory game server maintenance
37	02-Mar-17 12:25	0.000204	12.3	Booking problem on qatarairways.com
42	27-Feb-17 12:10	0.000188	11.3	Booking problem on klm.com
50	02-Mar-17 12:35	0.000141	8.5	Amazon S3 outage

6   Conclusion and Future Work

We have been able to define a global baseline for *down report* and *slow report* frequencies. Therefore, there are two main contributions of this work to mention: 1. A practical system for monitoring the overall internet web QoE is feasible and can be implemented using Twitter analysis. This fulfills Requirement 1 that most likely has not been addressed by any existing work. 2. Not only outages of web services, but also degradation of web service quality can be detected. This fulfills Requirement 2 that has not been completely covered by existing publications. The remaining requirements have been matched by using humans as sensors.

The presented primary findings about the feasibility of using social media posts for gaining internet wide insights to QoE aspects in real-time denote an important step towards more detailed analysis of affected networks, domains and technologies, constituting a necessary requirement for novel approaches to improve overall network and internet security, e.g., as suggested in [18]. As follow up research questions, we are already investigating whether root causes of drops in QoE can be identified by using additional information contained in tweets, for instance, analyzing geographical origin of the complaints might lead to insights about regional problems and using the contained information about which client software was used to create the tweet might give further hints on whether mobile or fixed networks or both are affected by drops in perceived web service quality. Furthermore, mapping complaints to specific web services in an automated fashion seems to become feasible, while still being a complex problem. This would allow to drill down the QoE measurements to individual domains and accordingly to underlying networks and technologies.

References

1. Ahmad, A., Floris, A., Atzori, L.: QoE-aware service delivery: a joint-venture approach for content and network providers. In: 2016 Eighth International Conference on Quality of Multimedia Experience (QoMEX), pp. 1–6. IEEE (2016)
2. Al-Shammari, S., Al-Yasiri, A.: Defining a metric for measuring QoE of SaaS cloud computing. In: Proceedings of PGNET, pp. 251–256 (2014)
3. Augustine, E., Cushing, C., Dekhtyar, A., McEntee, K., Paterson, K., Tognetti, M.: Outage detection via real-time social stream analysis: leveraging the power of online complaints. In: Proceedings of the 21st International Conference Companion on World Wide Web, pp. 13–22. ACM (2012)
4. Belshe, M.: More Bandwidth Doesn't Matter (much) (2010)
5. Casas, P., Seufert, M., Schatz, R.: YOUQMON: a system for on-line monitoring of YouTube QoE in operational 3G networks. ACM SIGMETRICS Perform. Eval. Rev. **41**(2), 44–46 (2013)
6. Dong, M., Kimata, T., Sugiura, K., Zettsu, K.: Quality-of-Experience (QoE) in emerging mobile social networks. IEICE Trans. Inf. Syst. E **97D**(10), 2606–2612 (2014)
7. Egger, S., Hossfeld, T., Schatz, R., Fiedler, M.: Waiting times in quality of experience for web based services. In: 2012 Fourth International Workshop on Quality of Multimedia Experience, pp. 86–96 (2012)
8. Egger, S., Reichl, P., Hossfeld, T., Schatz, R.: 'Time is bandwidth'? Narrowing the gap between subjective time perception and quality of experience. In: IEEE International Conference on Communications, pp. 1325–1330 (2012)
9. Fiedler, M., Hossfeld, T., Tran-Gia, P.: A generic quantitative relationship between quality of experience and quality of service. IEEE Netw. **24**(2), 36–41 (2010)
10. Hecht, S.: The visual discrimination of intensity and the Weber-Fechner law. J. Gen. Physiol. **7**(2), 235–267 (1924)
11. Hei, X.H.X., Liu, Y.L.Y., Ross, K.: IPTV over P2P streaming networks: the mesh-pull approach. IEEE Commun. Mag. **46**(February), 86–92 (2008)
12. Ho, T., Hock, D., Tran-gia, P., Tutschku, K., Fiedler, M.: Testing the IQX hypothesis for exponential interdependency between QoS and QoE of voice codecs iLBC and G.711. In: Proceedings of the 18th ITC Specialist Seminar on Quality of Experience, pp. 105–114 (2008)
13. Hossfeld, T., Biedermann, S., Schatz, R., Platzer, A., Egger, S., Fiedler, M.: The memory effect and its implications on Web QoE modeling. In: 2011 23rd International Teletraffic Congress (ITC), pp. 103–110 (2011)
14. International Telecommunication Union: P.800: Methods for subjective determination of transmission quality. Technical report, International Telecommunication Union (1996)
15. International Telecommunication Union: G.1030: Estimating end-to-end performance in IP networks for data applications. Technical report, International Telecommunication Union (2005)
16. International Telecommunication Union: E.800: Definitions of terms related to quality of service. Technical report, International Telecommunication Union (2008)
17. International Telecommunication Union: E.804: QoS aspects for popular services in mobile networks. Technical report, International Telecommunication Union (2014)

18. Kergl, D., Roedler, R., Rodosek, G.D.: Detection of zero day exploits using real-time social media streams. In: Pillay, N., Engelbrecht, A.P., Abraham, A., Du Plessis, M.C., Snášel, V., Muda, A.K. (eds.) Advances in Nature and Biologically Inspired Computing. AISC, vol. 419, pp. 405–416. Springer, Cham (2016). doi:10.1007/978-3-319-27400-3_36

19. Kergl, D., Roedler, R., Seeber, S.: On the endogenesis of Twitter's Spritzer and Gardenhose sample streams. In: 2014 IEEE/ACM International Conference on Advances in Social Networks Analysis and Mining (ASONAM 2014), pp. 357–364. IEEE (2014)

20. Ketykó, I., De Moor, K., Joseph, W., Martens, L., De Marez, L.: Performing QoE-measurements in an actual 3G network. In: 2010 IEEE International Symposium on Broadband Multimedia Systems and Broadcasting (BMSB), pp. 1–6. IEEE (2010)

21. Kilkki, K.: Quality of experience in communications ecosystem. J. Univ. Comput. Sci. **14**(5), 615–624 (2008)

22. Liotou, E., Elshaer, H., Schatz, R., Irmer, R., Dohler, M., Passas, N., Merakos, L.: Shaping QoE in the 5G ecosystem. In: 2015 Seventh International Workshop on Quality of Multimedia Experience (QoMEX), pp. 1–6 (2015)

23. Mok, R.K.P., Chan, E.W.W., Chang, R.K.C.: Measuring the quality of experience of HTTP video streaming. In: 2011 IFIP/IEEE International Symposium on Integrated Network Management (IM), pp. 485–492 (2011)

24. Mok, R.K., Chang, R.K., Li, W.: Detecting low-quality workers in QoE crowdtesting: a worker behavior based approach. IEEE Trans. Multimedia **19**(3), 530–543 (2016)

25. Moorsel, A.V.: Metrics for the internet age: quality of experience and quality of business. Quantitative evaluation in the internet age: what is different? Perspective **34**, 26–31 (2001)

26. Motoyama, M., Meeder, B., Levchenko, K., Voelker, G.M., Savage, S.: Measuring online service availability using twitter. In: Proceedings of the 3rd Conference on Online Social Networks (WOSN 2010) (2010)

27. Qiu, T., Feng, J., Ge, Z., Wang, J., Xu, J., Yates, J.: Listen to me if you can: tracking user experience of mobile network on social media. In: Proceedings of the 10th ACM SIGCOMM Conference on Internet Measurement, Melbourne, Australia, pp. 288–293. ACM (2010)

28. Rengaraju, P., Lung, C.H., Yu, F.R., Srinivasan, A.: On QoE monitoring and E2E service assurance in 4G wireless networks. IEEE Wirel. Commun. **19**(4), 89–96 (2012)

29. Schatz, R., Hoßfeld, T., Janowski, L., Egger, S.: From packets to people: quality of experience as a new measurement challenge. In: Biersack, E., Callegari, C., Matijasevic, M. (eds.) Data Traffic Monitoring and Analysis. LNCS, vol. 7754, pp. 219–263. Springer, Heidelberg (2013). doi:10.1007/978-3-642-36784-7_10

30. Streijl, R.C., Winkler, S., Hands, D.S.: Mean opinion score (MOS) revisited: methods and applications, limitations and alternatives. Multimedia Syst. **22**(2), 213–227 (2016)

31. Takahashi, A., Hands, D., Barriac, V.: Standardization activities in the ITU for a QoE assessment of IPTV. IEEE Commun. Mag. **46**(2), 78–84 (2008)

32. Venkataraman, M., Chatterjee, M.: Inferring video QoE in real time. IEEE Netw. **25**(1), 4–13 (2011)

33. Wamser, F., Casas, P., Seufert, M., Moldovan, C., Tran-Gia, P., Hossfeld, T.: Modeling the YouTube stack: from packets to quality of experience. Comput. Netw. **109**, 211–224 (2016)

34. Zimmer, M., Proferes, N.J.: A topology of Twitter research: disciplines, methods, and ethics. Aslib J. Inf. Manag. **66**(3), 250–261 (2014)

Short Papers: Security, Intrusion Detection, and Configuration

Hunting SIP Authentication Attacks Efficiently

Tomáš Jansky[1], Tomáš Čejka[2(✉)], and Václav Bartoš[2]

[1] FIT, CTU in Prague, Thakurova 9, 160 00 Prague 6, Czech Republic
`janskto1@fit.cvut.cz`
[2] CESNET, a.l.e., Zikova 4, 160 00 Prague 6, Czech Republic
{`cejkat,bartos`}`@cesnet.cz`

Abstract. Extended flow records with application layer (L7) information allow for detection of various types of malicious traffic. Voice over IP (VoIP) is an example of technology that works on L7 and many attacks against it cannot be reliably detected using just basic flow information. Session Initiation Protocol (SIP), which is commonly used for VoIP signalling, is a frequent target of many types of attacks. This paper proposes and evaluates a novel algorithm for near real time detection of username scanning and password guessing attacks on SIP servers. The detection is based on analysis of L7 extended flow records.

1 Introduction

Voice over IP (VoIP) is a technology that replaces classic telephone services and is used to transfer multimedial data such as voice or video over common packet switched networks. One of the core protocols used in VoIP services is Session Initiation Protocol (SIP), which is used for signalling between communicating parties.

There are many types of attacks against SIP infrastructure. The most dangerous attacks often compromise Private Branch Exchange (PBX) devices and cause a significant financial loss to the owner of PBX. According to [3], a total worldwide loss due to VoIP hacking and calling to premium rate services goes to billions of dollars per year.

Even though there are standards that describe security considerations and extensions of the SIP protocol, it is still often observed unencrypted in real network traffic. This allows for security analysis of SIP traffic at a network level using a network passive monitoring. The analysis may detect malicious SIP traffic so that a network operator can inform owners of the target device about a potential threat or take appropriate actions to mitigate malicious traffic.

Network traffic monitoring in large networks is usually done using so called flow records, i.e. aggregated information about communicating hosts that is computed from observed packets. A typical flow record consists of information from packet headers up to the transport protocol. This approach is feasible and it allows for detection of various types of malicious traffic. However, as it was presented in [2], many types of attack at application protocol (L7) cannot be reliably detected using just the basic flow records. This paper shows usage of

© The Author(s) 2017
D. Tuncer et al. (Eds.): AIMS 2017, LNCS 10356, pp. 125–130, 2017.
DOI: 10.1007/978-3-319-60774-0_9

application layer flow records [6], in this case flows extended by L7 information about SIP traffic, for detection of brute-force password guessing and scanning for user accounts (called *extensions* in SIP terminology) on PBX. This work is a continuation of [2] and an improvement of detection abilities of the previous detection mechanism.

2   SIP Attacks

This work focuses on two types of network attacks by an unauthenticated external attacker against a SIP server – extension scanning (i.e. finding valid usernames) and password guessing.

Both are based on sending large amount of requests (usually REGISTER) to the server. When a client sends the request requiring authentication, server challenges it with a response code 401 Unauthorized. Normally, the client sends valid credentials and server responds with 200 OK. If the username is not valid, server responds with 404 Not Found or 401 Unauthorized, depending on configuration[1]. In case of correct username but wrong password, 401 Unauthorized is returned.

Therefore, both types of attacks are characterized by a high number of REGISTER requests and 401 Unauthorized (or 404 Not Found) responses, using either different extensions (extension scanning) or a single extension but different passwords (passwod guessing). Combination of both is also possible. More details about these SIP attacks can be found in [4].

3   Detection Algorithm

In line with the L7 flow monitoring approach, our monitoring probes use a plugin which is able to extract necessary SIP information from traffic (*response code*, *To* and *CSeq*). As it is shown in Fig. 1, flow records are sent from probes to a collector in the IPFIX format and afterwards analyzed by the detection algorithm which is implemented as a part of the NEMEA [1] system.

The detection method is designed to work without any prior knowledge of VoIP infrastructure or existing extensions. It is based on an analysis of 401 responses from SIP servers. By aggregating these responses by a PBX IP address, an extension (username) and a client IP address, the detection algorithm can detect non-standard and potentially malicious traffic.

The algorithm shifts between two stages. In the first stage, it receives data and stores it into data structures. For each SIP server (i.e. IP address sending SIP responses), the following data is stored – a list of client IPs, a list of usernames, and a mapping between them that tells which clients tried which usernames and a number of such attempts.

---

[1] The former is considered insecure since it eases the extension scanning as it immediately discloses existence of the extension on the server.

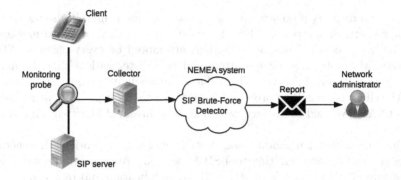

Fig. 1. Monitoring infrastructure.

After a certain time period, the algorithm gets to the second stage where it evaluates the stored data. First a type of (potential) attack is determined. If a single client attempts to register one certain extension, it is classified as a brute-force attack. This attack can be reclassified as a distributed brute-force attack if more clients attempt to register the particular extension on the same server. When a client tries to register more than one extension, the behavior is classified as a scan. When the number of attempts exceeds a threshold, the attack is reported. If 200 OK response code is detected as part of the communication, the attack is considered successful. If no communication between the server and the client is observed for a certain amount of time, the corresponding structures are released from memory.

The algorithm was implemented as a module for open-source NEMEA system and published at GitHub[2].

4   Evaluation

Since the algorithm is threshold based, it was necessary to estimate some key values based on the behavior on a real network. We temporarily captured SIP traffic from CESNET2 network[3].

After the analysis of the captured data, we discovered that more than **99.9 %** of all successful register attempts use **20** messages or less. We therefore set 20 attempts as a threshold for deciding whether the communication is malicious or not.

We also examined the frequency of malicious requests in individual attacks and discovered that only **0.01 %** have more than **30 min** delay between individual requests. Therefore an information about a communication is released from

---

[2] https://github.com/CESNET/Nemea-Detectors/.
[3] CESNET2 network is monitored at all its 7 peering links at the 10 and 100 Gbps wire speeds. Average total amount of traffic: 110,000 flows/s, average SIP traffic: 1,500 flows/s.

the program memory if no new message is observed for 30 min. It also means that an elapsed attack is reported after this delay since the last observed message.

Finally, we counted unique extensions attempted by every client in 30 min windows. Most observed clients attempted to register as less than **10** unique extensions on a certain server. This value is surprisingly high, but it is possible that the client is actually a proxy server or there are multiple SIP clients hidden behind NAT. We used 10 distinct extensions as a threshold for extension scanning detection.

First, the detection module was tested on a real network with generated malicious traffic using auditing tool SIPVicious [5]. All generated attacks were successfully distinguished from other SIP communication and reported.

Then, the module was run for one week to capute real attacks in the CES-NET2 network. Total number of 7,008 events were reported. Table 1 shows some statistics about reported events. One of the most interesting findings is that **46.3 %** of all 200 and 401 SIP responses to REGISTER requests are a malicious traffic and are directly related with one of reported alerts.

Table 1. Statistics after one week of flow detection

Brute-force events	6,488 (92.6 %)
Extension scanning events	520 (7.4 %)
Successful brute-force events	7
Strongest brute-force	6,930,911 attempts
Largest scan	9,360 extensions
SIP flows observed	718,627,758
SIP flows analyzed (401 & 200 responses)	40,909,352 (5.7 %)
Number of malicious flows	18,945,291 (46.3 %)

Detection results were stored to a log file during the week. Thorough examination showed that most attackers perform either brute-force attacks or extension scanning. However, some of the attackers combine these two attacks to one, usually trying a small number of password guesses (between 20 to 100) to a large number of extensions. This behavior indicates that these attackers use some sort of a set of common and frequently used passwords.

To confirm that the detection module is working correctly, we manually analyzed traffic of some of the reported attacks. Most of them are certainly scanning or brute-force attempts. In just a few cases were the traffic did not look like any of the attacks and can be viewed as false positive (we estimate total FP rate to 0.1%), however, it was still an unusual traffic, probably caused by misconfiguration of some devices, which is worth inspecting. To prove practical usefulness of the detection, we chose one of the attacks marked as successful and contacted the administrator of the attacked PBX. He confirmed that, indeed, the account was compromised and informed us that appropriate steps to fortify the PBX will be taken.

5   Conclusion

We designed a method for detection of SIP attacks, namely username scanning and password guessing, based on an analysis of SIP headers in extended flow records. The algorithm works without any prior knowledge of VoIP infrastructure. Its key parameters and thresholds can be adjusted by network administrators in accordance to the characteristics of their network to reach optimal detection results. It is efficient and it is able to process data from an NREN-sized network (several 10 and 100 Gbps links) in real time.

Using the algorithm, we were able to detect thousands of scanning and password guessing against SIP infrastrucutre. The software is also capable of detecting distributed guessing of user's password, however, this type of attack was not observed in our network yet. Some of the attacks, which were identified as successful, were reported to network administrators who subsequently confirmed the attacks. Analysis of detection results showed only a small amount of false positive reports with frequency around 0.1% of all reported events. Most of the false positives are caused by a few clients that communicate in an unusual way and can be easily filtered using a whitelist.

Acknowledgments. This work was supported by *Packet analysis based network diagnostics (DISTANCE)* project No. TH02010186 granted by Technology Agency of the Czech Republic, project Reg. No. CZ.02.1.01/0.0/0.0/16_013/0001797 co-funded by the MEYS of the Czech Republic and ERDF and the CTU grant No. SGS17/212/OHK3/3T/18 funded by the MEYS of the Czech Republic.

References

1. Cejka, T., Bartos, V., Svepes, M., Rosa, Z., Kubatova, H.: NEMEA: a framework for network traffic analysis. In: 12th International Conference on Network and Service Management (CNSM 2016), Montreal, Canada, October 2016
2. Cejka, T., Bartos, V., Truxa, L., Kubatova, H.: Using application-aware flow monitoring for sip fraud detection. In: Latré, S., Charalambides, M., François, J., Schmitt, C., Stiller, B. (eds.) AIMS 2015. LNCS, vol. 9122, pp. 87–99. Springer, Cham (2015). doi:10.1007/978-3-319-20034-7_10
3. Communication Fraud Control Association: Global fraud loss survey (2015). http://www.cfca.org/pdfsurvey/2015_CFCA_Global_Fraud_Loss_Survey_Press_Release.pdf
4. Dwivedi, H.: Hacking VoIP: Protocols, Attacks, and Countermeasures. No Starch Press, San Francisco (2009)
5. Gauci, S.: SIPVicious. Tools for auditing sip based VoIP systems (2012). https://code.google.com/p/sipvicious/
6. Velan, P., Čeleda, P.: Next generation application-aware flow monitoring. In: Sperotto, A., Doyen, G., Latré, S., Charalambides, M., Stiller, B. (eds.) AIMS 2014. LNCS, vol. 8508, pp. 173–178. Springer, Heidelberg (2014). doi:10.1007/978-3-662-43862-6_20

MoDeNA: Enhancing User Security for Devices in Wireless Personal and Local Area Networks

Robert Müller[1(✉)], Marcel Waldvogel[1], and Corinna Schmitt[2]

[1] Distributed Systems Laboratory,
Department of Computer and Information Science, University of Konstanz,
78457 Konstanz, Germany
{robert.mueller,marcel.waldvogel}@uni-konstanz.de
[2] Communication Systems Group CSG, Department of Informatics IfI,
University of Zurich UZH, Binzmühlestrasse 14, 8050 Zurich, Switzerland
schmitt@ifi.uzh.ch

Abstract. Today most used devices are connected with each other building the Internet of Things (IoT). A variety of protocols are used depending on the underlying network infrastructure, application (e.g., Smart City, eHealth), and device capability. The judgment of the security feeling of the data sharing depends on personal settings (e.g., easy to use, encrypted transmission, anonymization support). MoDeNA – a Mobile Device Network Assistant – was developed offering an opportunity for understanding the judgment of security by bringing the user's concerns and their technology understanding of used devices and protocols into relation. MoDeNA provides a transparent overview over the used wireless security of the user's device giving concrete advices for improving the connection security and usability of mobile device security.

1 Motivation

The Internet of Things (IoT) not only includes servers, computers, and routers anymore, but also personal "smart" devices that everyone uses frequently, such as smartphone, sensors, tags, and tablets. All devices collect many data in different application areas and are connected to share the data [1,2]. It is envisioned that the variety of devices will grow in the future as well as the number of participating devices in the IoT [3]. Usually, a user is just a user of the device or the application, trusting in the pre-installed security mechanisms.

In order to allow a judgment of the used security, MoDeNA—our **Mo**bile **De**vice **N**etwork **A**ssistant—was developed addressing the aforementioned views of the users abilities and the deployed network infrastructure in a smart city environment. MoDeNA is an operating system independent application based on a classification algorithm taking into account all available security information from user's device and used infrastructure to make the security setting transparent to the user. Further it recommends the user updates of security settings to improve the mobile device security for the current situation without requiring in-depth know-how. The overall goal of MoDeNA is to raise the user's awareness of security lacks when using WPANs and WLANs to provide countermeasures to avoid data theft.

© The Author(s) 2017
D. Tuncer et al. (Eds.): AIMS 2017, LNCS 10356, pp. 131–136, 2017.
DOI: 10.1007/978-3-319-60774-0_10

2   Related Work

While there are calls for novel security challenges for the services of the IoT like encryption and authentication [4], proposals for securing the IoT with protocols like Lithe [5], TinyDTLS [6,7] are available. Additionally, analyzes exist that investigate the technical challenges and limitations of the IP-based IoT [8,9], though the aspect of involving the user in the security of the connection between IoT devices is not considered. To our knowledge there is no known approach to involve the user in the wireless network security, particularly not for IoT devices.

Work in the field of discovering network topology without network assistance is described in [10]. A user study analyzing security and privacy habits as well as willingness to apply countermeasures is provided by [11]. Another interesting approach is investigated in [12] by moving privacy-sensitive tasks to remote security servers which offer higher protection capabilities than smartphones.

3   MoDeNA's Security Classification Algorithm

Based on the presented challenges in Sect. 2 with existing solutions, the following goals were set for MoDeNA to build a security classification scheme: (1) Central Overview of connected IoT devices, (2) **Automatic Identification** of applied security requirements, (3) **User Interaction** support when no automatic identification happens, and (4) **Control Wireless Radio Connections** to keep track of own IoT devices.

In order to address the first goal the connected IoT devices are classified according to the security standard required by the data transmitted. Reading device specific information, such as shared services for communication, applications used, and identifying device classes can achieve this without user interaction required for an automatic identification. Additional information provided by the user about the pairing process, if available, is used for a more precise identification of security requirements.

The classification itself is a process that needs to be adopted for the various available device types and WPAN/WLAN protocols. Therefore, existing parameters for classification were used building the "static input (e.g., device identifiers, announced services, Universally Unique Identifier UUID) and if necessary "dynamic input" based on the user's manual input. The general security classification algorithm is illustrated in a flow diagram in Fig. 1.

The MoDeNA classification algorithm takes the protocol type, device type and application of the device to be connected with as input values. They are obtained automatically by the WPAN/WLAN network sensors and connection information published in the network (e.g. via network service) by the device. If there is input regarding connection purpose available from the user ("Dynamic Information"), this information is considered for a dynamic risk level calculation. Otherwise a static risk level calculation without additional user input is applied. Afterwards the newly established connection is displayed together with its security classification. If new user input becomes available (i.e. the user confirms a security improvement measure within the application) a new dynamic risk level calculation is executed. Otherwise the algorithm terminates.

Four levels for application security requirements are distinguished: (1) High (green) - key exchange mechanism with no design flaws and transmission encryption, (2) Acceptable (yellow) - key exchange mechanism with design flaws and transmission encryption, (3) Low (red) - insufficient data security, and (4) Undetermined (grey) - by default accepted. This grading can be seen in the **Overview Screen** shown in the shown in the upper part of Fig. 2. It presents the user with an Security classification state per connected smart device. Clicking on a row opens the device's **Detail View Screen** shown in the lower part of Fig. 2. It advises the user with practical security hints and asks for input of environmental parameters to improve classification. The application back-end provides adapter implementations for the supported physical network interfaces and listens asynchronously for connected devices available. First, it identifies whether a device was previously connected. For new detected devices, the MoDeNA application collects the protocol - and device specific information and creates a new entry in the devices database. Previously known devices can be recognized and the security classification is based on the available device history. For each device the database stores a dataset consisting of: device name, type, address, last security classification, performed security improvements by the user and used application. Based on this information, the MoDeNA algorithm is applied to determine the security requirements and obtain the security classification. This is then used to provide the user with recommendations for each specific combination of device type and security requirement (e.g., Smart watch + WiFi and/or Bluetooth indi-

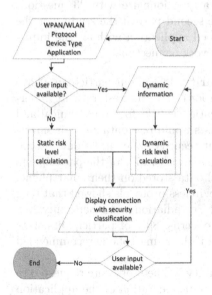

Fig. 1. Classification algorithm

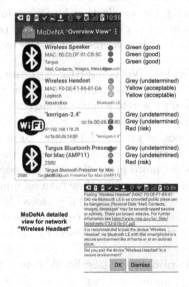

Fig. 2. MoDeNA views (Color figure online)

cating High security, wireless mouse + WiFi or Bluetooth indicating Acceptable security, hearing aid + Bluetooth indicating Low security).

An example for improving the security of a connection is shown for the WLAN "kerrigan-2.4". The WLAN is automatically detected by the smartphone with activated Wi-Fi service as someones private network, which does not require authentication and the smartphone connects to it automatically. When a user of MoDeNA application detects it in the Overview Screen, it is listed as a network interfaced with. Since there is no authentication provided, it is rated not secure by the MoDeNA application. The three bullets indicator is used to show the maximum possible grading available. If the user now clicks on the list entry, he/she is brought to the detail view, which shows the reason for this security classification (red indicator) and what measures can be applied to improve connection security with "kerrigan-2.4" by adopting them. Settings and measurements made for known networks can be saved automatically by MoDeNA. Further information about the security risk of using specific wireless technologies is provided with links to useful web pages that provide background information and educate the user.

4 User Study

A prototype of the application MoDeNA is realized on the Android OS platform, since it is the most widely used operating system to date for smartphones.

We conducted a two-part user study to analyze usage of IoT devices connected to smartphones via WPAN/WLAN and to rate the use of our application. The participants were asked to fill in a questionnaire with 23 questions while using the application MoDeNA for the second part of the study. For the evaluation, we used a mock-up of our proposed application without the implementation of the classification of the real network connections.

(1) **Wireless Network Smartphone Security.** 48% of our participants have a technical background (work or education). The interest rate in understanding wireless smartphone communication is 91% for non-technical and 67% for technical users. 87% of participants would rate data on their smartphones as private data. 70% know about security concerns of data stored on smartphones but they accept the possible risks. 87% of the participants ask for more protection of their personal data stored on their smartphone. Asking the users if they turn off unused wireless protocols showed that 65% do turn off radio, but for reasons like battery, radiation and others, only 22% of them do it also because of security concerns. 83% of participants state that they would apply security measures, if their smartphone recommended them to do so.

(2) **"Application Specific Wireless Security".** The users were requested to play around and evaluate our prototype implementation of the application MoDeNA. Thus, this received feedback was user-specific and highly influenced by individual knowhow. 74% of participants state that they gained

insight in the security of wireless smartphone communication. The same percentage of participants also claimed, that they think the application MoDeNA would improve the security when used. 87% expect MoDeNA would improve the WPAN/WLAN security of their smartphones.

5 Conclusions and Future Work

We present MoDeNA, a framework for detection and classification of WPAN/WLAN connection security and a prototype smartphone application for Android OS to (semi-)automatically rate the security of connected WPAN/WLAN devices and provide advices to the user. In our user study with 23 participants we observed that 70% of participants are generally aware of security risks when transmitting data wirelessly from a smartphone to any other device but nevertheless use the functionality. 78% of our participants have heard or know about security risks for WPAN/WLAN protocols. MoDeNA is rated by 90% of our user study participants to be helpful to feel more secure with smart devices in WPAN/WLAN.

References

1. Greengard, S.: The Internet of Things (MIT Press Essential Knowledge). The MIT Press, Cambridge (2015)
2. International Telecommunication Union: The internet of things. ITU Internet Reports (2005)
3. Vesola, A., Schulte, W., Lheureux, B.: Hype cycle for the internet of things, 2016. Technical report, Gartner Inc., July 2016
4. Roman, R., Najera, P., Lopez, J.: Securing the internet of things. IEEE Comput. J. **44**(9), 51–58 (2011)
5. Raza, S., Shafagh, H., Hewage, K., Hummen, R., Voigt, T.: Lithe: lightweight secure CoAP for the internet of things. IEEE Sens. J. **13**(10), 3711–3720 (2013)
6. Schmitt, C., Kothmayr, T., Hu, W.: Two-way authentication for the internet-of-things. In: Acharjya, D., Kalaiselvi Geetha, M. (eds.) Internet of Things: Novel Advances and Envisioned Applications, pp. 27–56. Springer, Heidelberg (2017)
7. Kothmayr, T., Schmitt, W., Hu, C., Bruenig, M., Carle, G.: DTLS based security and two-way authentication for the internet of things. ELSEVIER Ad Hoc Netw. **11**(8), 2710–2723 (2013)
8. Heer, T., Garcia-Morchon, O., Hummen, R., Keoh, S.L., Kumar, S.S., Wehrle, K.: Security challenges in the IP-based internet of things. Wirel. Pers. Commun. **61**(3), 527–542 (2011). http://dx.doi.org/10.1007/s11277-011-0385-5
9. Hummen, R., Shafagh, H., Raza, S., Voigt, T., Wehrle, K.: Delegation-based authentication and authorization of the IP-based internet of things. In: 11th Annual IEEE International Conference on Sensing, Communication, and Networking, SECON, pp. 1–9, June/July 2014
10. Black, R., Donnelly, A., Fournet, C.: Ethernet topology discovery without network assistance. In: 12th IEEE International Conference on Network Protocols, ICNP, pp. 328–339, October 2004

11. Chin, E., Felt, A.P., Sekar, V., Wagner, D.: Measuring user confidence in smartphone security and privacy. In: 8th Symposium on Usable Privacy and Security, SOUPS, pp. 1–16. ACM, July 2012
12. Portokalidis, G., Homburg, P., Anagnostakis, K., Bos, H.: Paranoid android: versatile protection for smartphones. In: 26th Annual Computer Security Applications Conference, ACSAC, pp. 347–356. ACM, December 2010

Flow-Based Detection of IPv6-specific Network Layer Attacks

Luuk Hendriks[1]([✉]), Petr Velan[2], Ricardo de O. Schmidt[1],
Pieter-Tjerk de Boer[1], and Aiko Pras[1]

[1] Faculty of Electrical Engineering, Mathematics and Computer Science,
University of Twente, Enschede, The Netherlands
{luuk.hendriks,r.schmidt,p.t.deboer,a.pras}@utwente.nl
[2] CESNET, a.l.e, Zikova 4, 160 00 Prague 6, Czech Republic
petr.velan@cesnet.cz

Abstract. With a vastly different header format, IPv6 introduces new
vulnerabilities not possible in IPv4, potentially requiring new detection
algorithms. While many attacks specific to IPv6 have proven to be possible and are described in the literature, no detection solutions for these
attacks have been proposed. In this study we identify and characterise
IPv6-specific attacks that can be detected using flow monitoring. By constructing flow-based signatures, detection can be performed using available technologies such as NetFlow and IPFIX. To validate our approach,
we implemented these signatures in a prototype, monitoring two production networks and injecting attacks into the production traffic.

1 Introduction

Monitoring network traffic is an essential aspect in today's Internet. With the
ever-growing collection of possible network-based threats, security officers need
to stay up to date and be aware of what is possibly coming towards their networks and services. Intrusion Detection Systems (IDSs) play a critical role in this
scenario, offering the first insight into malicious traffic, *e.g.* brute-force attacks
on SSH daemons [2], or large numbers of DNS responses caused by a Distributed Denial of Service (DDoS) attack. Currently, the adoption and deployment
of IPv6 in the Internet is increasing: 16.4% of users of Google's services have
IPv6 connectivity. North-America and Germany feature an adoption of around
30%, and Belgium is almost at 50%. With the increasing amount of IPv6 traffic
in mind, we want to know whether the flow-based detection approaches from
IPv4 are applicable, and moreover, fully covering the spectrum of IPv6 attacks.

In this paper, we ask ourselves 1. which new threats are introduced by these
changes in the network layer; 2. how fundamental these threats are; and 3. how
flow-based monitoring solutions should be adapted in order to enable detection
of these new attacks.

© The Author(s) 2017
D. Tuncer et al. (Eds.): AIMS 2017, LNCS 10356, pp. 137–142, 2017.
DOI: 10.1007/978-3-319-60774-0_11

2   Methodology

We focus on a subset of threats: we inquire the literature, and select (Sect. 2.1) the vulnerabilities that are expected to be a long-term threat not easily mitigated. With the selection of threats at hand, we analyze (Sect. 2.2) their packet-based forms, to construct flow-based signatures. The signatures are implemented and tested on flows collected on two production networks: (1) the National Research and Educational Network (NREN) CESNET, with 8 vantage points, totalling 2.5G of flows (87G packets, 81.2Ti bytes); and (2) the campus network UTNET, with a single vantage point, with 2.2G of flows (158.6G packets, 140.7Ti bytes).

2.1   Threat Selection Process

The comprehensive overview in [3] functions as a starting point in our selection process. In that paper, Tables II and III list Security Vulnerabilities and Privacy Vulnerabilities, respectively, indicating the origin of each threat. **Step 1:** We only consider threats originating from the *design* of IPv6, and not any threats based on *implementation* or *configuration* mistakes. We continue by looking at Table V of that same paper, which is a matrix linking threats to *detective*, *preventative* and/or *reactive* countermeasures. **Step 2:** We only consider threats that have either no forms of countermeasure, or only a *reactive* countermeasure, as our goal is detection of attacks. Lastly, we rule out threats that are not actually in IPv6 itself, but merely in other (supporting) protocols. **Step 3:** Dismiss threats based on DNS and ICMP6.

2.2   Threat Analysis Process

For each threat, the following steps are carried out:

1. At the packet-level, pinpoint the protocol fields and their respective values that make up the essence of the vulnerability.
2. Determine if the essential features found in the previous step are still available in the aggregated form (flow level). **N.B.:** availability of these features depends on which Information Elements are exported by the flow exporter. Furthermore, the flow cache should in some cases use these fields in its cache key, in order to distinguish and export separate flow records. More details on this follow in Sect. 3.
3. If an attack is not distinguishable based on information of a single flow, determine the relationship between malicious flows, as well as the relationship between the malicious and benign flows.
4. Formalize a signature based on the previous two steps, resulting in a per-attack detection approach.

3   Attack Signatures

Our selection process described in Sect. 2.1 yields six attacks (Table 2), categorized as *covert channels* (exfiltration of information), *DoS* attacks (aiming to overload and impair functioning of systems) and *middlebox evasion* (getting around *e.g.* firewalls). The constructed signatures, along with their formal explanation, are listed in Table 1. Note that we describe signatures **from the perspective of the collector**, not aggregation by the flow cache on the exporter.

The Denial of Service (DoS) signatures have two variants: the *multi-flow* kind describes an attack where a large number of destination addresses is generated randomly, as opposed to the kind where a single destination address is used. Naturally, different destination addresses lead to different flow records, and therefore different signatures.

Table 1. Signatures and notation explanation

f_i	Field in packet, *e.g.* Source Address	$5t$	Shorthand for the 5-tuple flow-key
$\{f_1, \dots f_n\}$	Flow-key based on fields $f_1 \dots f_n$	FL	Flow Label (IPv6 header field)
$\#$	Number of flows for flow-key or set	TC	Traffic Class (IPv6 header field)
ppf	Packets per flow	pr_n	Protocol Number n
$pps(S)$	Packets per second in flow set S	τ	Threshold, relative to context

$(FK|F+)$	Set of flows aggregated on FK filtered on one or more filters F
F	Selection filter, *e.g.* $ppf = 1$ for flows with a single packet, or pr_0 for Protocol 0

Flow Label Covert Channel	$\#(\{FL, 5t\}|FL > 0, ppf = 1) - \#\{5t\} > \tau_{flow\_diff}$
Traffic Class Covert Channel	$\#(\{TC, 5t\}|TC > 0, ppf = 1) - \#\{5t\} > \tau_{flow\_diff}$
Multi-flow Flow Label DoS	$S = (\{src\_ip\}|FL > 0, ppf = 1)\,,\ pps(S) > \tau_{pps}$
Multi-flow Fragmentation ID DoS	$S = (\{src\_ip\}|pr_{44}, ppf = 1)\,,\ pps(S) > \tau_{pps}$
Multi-flow Hop-by-Hop DoS	$S = (\{src\_ip\}|pr_0, ppf = 1)\,,\ pps(S) > \tau_{pps}$
Flow Label DoS	$\#\{FL, 5t\} - \#\{5t\} > \tau_{flow\_diff}$
Fragmentation ID DoS	$S = (\{5t\}|pr_{44}, ppf > \tau_{ppf})\,,\ pps(S) > \tau_{pps}$
Hop-by-Hop DoS	$S = (\{5t\}|pr_0, ppf > \tau_{ppf})\,,\ pps(S) > \tau_{pps}$
Fragmentation Overlap	$\{5t|0 < \text{fragMinOffset} \le 20\}$

An overview of requirements for flow exporters is presented in Table 2. These requirements include certain fields to be incorporated in the flow cache key (distinguishing flows on those fields), and a new IPFIX Information Element to be implemented. Note that not all IANA assigned fields are exported per se.

Table 2. Flow record requirements for implementation of signatures

Threat	Flow key	IANA	New IE
Flow Label CC	$\{\mathbf{FL}, 5t\}$	id31	
Traffic Class CC	$\{\mathbf{TC}, 5t\}$	id5	
Flow Label DoS	$\{\mathbf{FL}, 5t\}$	id31	
Fragmentation ID DoS	$\{5t\}$	id4, id54	
Hop-by-Hop Option DoS	$\{5t\}$	id4	
Fragmentation Overlap	$\{5t\}$	id4	**minFragOffset**

4   Evaluation of the Signatures

The proposed signatures are evaluated on real production traffic, in which we inject generated attacks. As the DoS attacks could harm the routers, a safe number of packets is used, likely lower than a real attack but still allowing verification of our signatures. We describe the generated attacks, and discuss the performance of the signatures with respect to both these attacks and the production traffic, below.

Generated Attacks:

Flow Label and Traffic Class Covert Channels: Sending 100, 500, 1000 packets, within a 5 min time-frame, towards a single host.

Flow Label, Fragmentation ID, Hop-by-Hop Option DoS: Sending 500 packets at line rate, towards a single host; Sending 500 packets at line rate, towards randomly generated hosts in a /64 network.

Fragmentation Overlap: Sending flows of 2, 10, 20 packets, with second packet offsets of 1, 4, 10, 20 towards a single host.

Performance:

Flow Label Covert Channel: The flow records related to the covert channel are successfully distinguished, using a threshold of $\tau_{pkt} = 50$. No other positives were found in the dataset, meaning the signature has a low false positive rate but possibly a non-zero false negative rate.

Traffic Class Covert Channel: The Traffic Class can hold different values within a single flow, and we do observe this in production traffic. Most commonly, these are a zero and a non-zero value: including the TC-field in the aggregation thus results in two flows. Using $\tau_{fl} = 10$, *i.e.* marking flows with 10 or more different Traffic Class values as attacks, the signature distinguishes all the injected attacks from the production traffic. Similar to the Flow label Covert channel, no other positives where marked, pointing out a low false positive rate but a possible non-zero false negative rate.

Flow Label Flood: Detection of a Flow Label flood to a single destination address is similar to detecting a Flow Label covert channel, thus results are equivalent. Distinguishing the covert channel from the DoS attack is challenging. Multi-flow signature has a false positive rate, albeit because it marks other threats and not benign traffic. For example, a SYN scan has, on the flow level, vast similarities when compared to the flow label flood attack: a large number of end hosts is being connected to from a single source address, with every initiated connection having a new (thus different) Flow Label.

Hop-by-Hop Flood: As the Hop-by-Hop Options are not widely used (most of it is link local traffic, with only one or two packets per flow), simplistic thresholds for detection work: $\tau_{ppf} = 10$ suffices. This means scalable detection without the need for extra Information Elements or extra processing at the exporter is trivial. A possible form of false positives exists however, as we observed two times on the

NREN: ping sweeps with Hop-by-Hop Options match this signature. Marking the spread version of the attack is successful, without any other positives.

Fragmentation Flood: Detection of flooding based on the Fragmentation ID has several caveats. By definition, a flow with fragmented packets consists of more than one packet, but an exception of this characteristic are the atomic fragments. Signatures based on fragmented but single packet flows therefore yield false positives. As the sending rate and number of sent packets are crucial in the success of a flooding attack, we can choose thresholds that eliminate these false positives: $\tau_{pps} = 5000/s$, $\tau_{ppf} = 200$. Our attacks are identified without any other flows being marked, again pointing out a low false positive rate but a possible false negative rate. The case where destination addresses were generated and the flooding attack was hidden in a large number of different 5-tuple flows, is successfully detected.

Fragmentation Overlap: The approach based on *fragMinOffset* marks all our injected attacks. The lowest value observed in the production traffic was 64, so no positives other than our injected attacks were marked.

5   Conclusions

IPv6 comes with a plethora of threats specific to this new version of the IP protocol. By systematically characterising threats described in literature, we found six of these threats to be fundamental, *i.e.* based on the protocol specification and without detection approaches for attacks as of yet. In this study, we proposed flow-based signatures to perform such detection. By implementing a prototype, we proved the validity and limitations of these signatures, and defined the requirements for flow measurement equipment to allow for applying detection of attacks based on these signatures. These requirements show adaptations to flow equipment are necessary to enable for detection of these new attacks.

By deploying our prototype on two production networks and injecting attacks into the production traffic, we showed our signatures are able to successfully distinguish the attacks from benign traffic without any false negatives. We provide both the detection prototype as well as the code used for generation of attacks as free and open source software [1].

Acknowledgments. This work has been supported by the project Reg. No. CZ.02.1.01/0.0/0.0/16_013/0001797 co-funded by the Ministry of Education, Youth and Sports of the Czech Republic and European Regional Development Fund, and the Ministry of the Interior of the Czech Republic under project no. VI20162019029.

References

1. IPv6 L3 Threat Detection. https://github.com/ut-dacs/IPv6-L3-threat-detection/
2. Hofstede, R., Hendriks, L., Sperotto, A., Pras, A.: SSH compromise detection using NetFlow/IPFIX. ACM SIGCOMM CCR **44**(5), 20–26 (2014)
3. Ullrich, J., Krombholz, K., Hobel, H., Dabrowski, A., Weippl, E.R.: IPv6 security: attacks and countermeasures in a nutshell. In: USENIX WOOT (2014)

Towards a Hybrid Cloud Platform
Using Apache Mesos

Noha Xue, Hårek Haugerud[(✉)], and Anis Yazidi

Department of Computer Science,
Oslo and Akershus University College of Applied Sciences, Oslo, Norway
harek.haugerud@hioa.no

Abstract. Hybrid cloud technology is becoming increasingly popular as it merges private and public clouds to bring the best of two worlds together. However, due to the heterogeneous cloud installation, facilitating a hybrid cloud setup is not simple. Despite the availability of some commercial solutions to build a hybrid cloud, an open source implementation is still unavailable. In this paper, we try to bridge the gap by providing an open source implementation by leveraging the power of Apache Mesos. We build a hybrid cloud on the top of multiple cloud platforms, private and public.

Keywords: Opensource hybrid cloud · Apache Mesos · Data segmentation · Fault tolerance

1   Introduction

The use of cloud computing is becoming more common, bringing along the advantages of flexibility and abundance of available resources, but also a higher degree of complexity along with privacy and security concerns. The concepts of *multicloud* and *hybrid cloud* are not new and several companies explore and capitalize these concepts. Most of the available solutions are commercial. Different vendors including Dell, IBM and HP provide hybrids cloud solutions [1,2]. The *MODA-Clouds* project [3] utilizes several tools to provide an environment for utilizing multiple cloud providers. Several large companies are offering hybrid cloud solutions, often in conjunction with their existing product portfolio. VMWare is offering a hybrid cloud solution called *vRealize suite* which provides one interface to manage the entire hybrid cloud platform [4,5]. Other companies like *Cisco* [6], *IBM* [7] and *RackSpace* [8] are also offering hybrid cloud solutions. Another attempt addresses the challenges of managing heterogeneous virtual environments to create a hybrid cloud platform [9]. *PaaSage* is an interesting initiative for building a hybrid cloud solution using a defined deployment model, *Cloud Application Modeling and Execution Language* (CAMEL) [10]. However, there has been no practical demonstration of using open-source and freely available clustering technology to attempt to address the multitude of challenges

© The Author(s) 2017
D. Tuncer et al. (Eds.): AIMS 2017, LNCS 10356, pp. 143–148, 2017.
DOI: 10.1007/978-3-319-60774-0_12

when creating a hybrid cloud platform that is available and supports data segmentation. This paper outlines an attempt to prototype such a solution in addition to facilitate cloud bursting using spot price instances. Borja et al. introduced OpenNebula in [11], which is one of the most popular open source Virtual Infrastructure Manager (VIM). OpenNebula permits to abstract resources of an existing local Grid and a cloud infrastructure. At the heart of OpenNebula we find Haizea [12] which is a VM-based Lease Manager that enhances the resource scheduling manager with advanced reservation of resources and queueing of best effort requests. Nevertheless, OpenNebula suffers from the single point failure problem [13]. In this paper, we present a lightweight solution, that is tolerant to different failure scenarios. Similarly, it is also possible to create a Hybrid Cloud With AWS and Eucalyptus.

This paper will explore and document the attempts at designing and prototyping a possible opensource solution for constructing a computer cluster built on top of private servers and external cloud providers.

2   Design and Implementation

An Apache Mesos cluster including both master nodes and slaves nodes were successfully installed and configured in Altocloud, with slave nodes correctly registering themselves to the cluster through the leading master node. However, when attempting to register a slave node running at Amazon Web Services EC2 peculiar activity was observed. The traffic from the slave node located at EC2 managed to successfully send a registration request to the leading master node, passing through multiple layers of network abstraction including two layers of NAT. Although the master node receives the registration requests, no registration acknowledge is ever sent back. Eventually, the cause was discovered to be a combination of the use of NAT and the way Mesos nodes communicates between each other. When a slave node sends a registration request, it includes information about the resources available and an IP-address. The IP-address sent along is the one that is defined on the network interface bound by the Apache Mesos process. Furthermore, in a cloud environment like Altocloud and Amazon Web Services EC2, the public IP-addresses are loosely coupled with the virtual machine and functions similarly as NAT does. Consequently, the Mesos master attempts to send the acknowledgement and other internal traffic meant for that slave node to the non-routable private IP-address. The communication flow is illustrated in Fig. 1.

By using VPN tunneling, the need for allocating public IP-addresses for each node disappears for the purpose of maintaining the cluster, as the private IP-addresses becomes routable within the hybrid cloud platform. With the exception of the extra infrastructure to maintain a VPN, the prototype is identical to the proposed proposed design. Figure 2 illustrates the final implementation of the prototype, showing how the Mesos master nodes are distributed between the different availability regions.

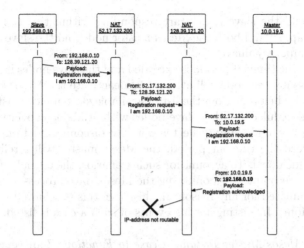

Fig. 1. Communication flow between an Apache Mesos slave node and master node with the registration attempt failing due to how public IP-addresses are handled in cloud platforms.

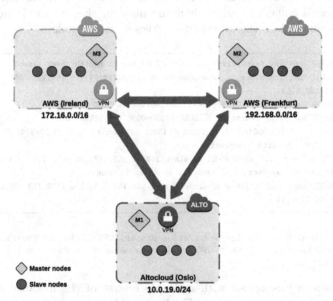

Fig. 2. Prototype 1: Maximizing availability. Distributing the master nodes and thereby the risks.

Test Scenarios

A Mesos Slave Process Becomes Unavailable. In the event of a Mesos slave node becoming unavailable for some reason, the Mesos master node allows a default timeout period of 75 s to pass before procedures for deactivating the slave node is begun. Should the slave node start responding within this timeout period, nothing will happen and both the Mesos master node and the slave node simply ignores the temporary unavailability.

However, if the timeout period is exceeded and the slave nodes is still unavailable, the Mesos master node will attempt to deactivate the Mesos slave process on the slave node before it from the list of available slave nodes. Tasks that were lost will be rescheduled to other slave nodes with available capacity.

Should a slave node simply be temporarily disconnected from the master node, but exceed the timeout period, the Mesos master will forcibly shut the Mesos slave node down. To account for such scenarios, the official Apache Mesos documentation recommends monitoring the Mesos slave process and restart if it should be terminated for any reason. In this case, this is achieved with a simple check using Monit. In Listing 1.1 log events of such a case is listed.

The Working Mesos Master Instance Cease to Function. ZooKeeper maintains an active connection to the participants of the quorum and will after a very short timeout lasting a few seconds, will initiate a new leader electing for choosing a new leading Mesos master node. As long as the number of functional Mesos master nodes is equal or higher than the quorum size, a new leader will be elected and will replace the unresponsive Mesos master node.

```
1 17:34:23.298998 Shutting down slave ...5050-5669-S3 due to health check timeout
2 17:34:23.300134 Removing slave ...5050-5669-S3 at slave(1)@192.168.187.205:5051
  ↪ (192.168.187.205)
3 17:34:23.301009 Removed slave 20150501-230056-2407081856-5050-5669-S3
4 17:34:23.536837 Notifying framework ...5050-27030-0006 (marathon) at
  ↪ ...473b-b57a-83121a00a01c@128.39.121.140:43217 of lost slave ...5050-5669-S3
  ↪ (192.168.187.205) after recovering
5 17:34:29.017205 Slave ...5050-5669-S3 at slave(1)@192.168.187.205:5051 (192.168.187.205)
  ↪ attempted to re-register after removal; shutting it down
6 17:34:57.329751 Registering slave at slave(1)@192.168.187.205:5051 (192.168.187 .205) with
  ↪ id ...5050-5669-S4
```

Listing 1.1: Excerpt from /var/log/mesos/mesos-master.INFO showing the forced shut down of the Mesos slave process at 192.168.187.205 and the registration as new slave at end. Truncated for increased readability.

This scenario was tested with a simple reboot of the instance where the leading Mesos master was running. The backup Mesos masters quickly discovers the loss of connection to the leading Mesos master and promptly, with the use of ZooKeeper elects a new leading Mesos master node. The rebooted Mesos master node later joins the cluster as a backup node after coming back online.

The setup proposed in this prototype has three Mesos master nodes, with the quorum size set to two. This means that among the Mesos master nodes, one can fail without crippling the cluster, as the quorum size dictates the number of election participants that has to be able to communicate to be able to elect a new leader.

An Entire Region within the Hybrid Cloud Becomes Unavailable. If an entire region becomes unavailable, the Mesos nodes located within those regions will by extension also become unavailable. In this particular case, the loss of one single site equals the loss of one Mesos master node and four slave nodes. Each node, depending on the type, is handled as specified in the test scenarios mentioned above.

This was tested by taking down the VPN tunnels at the VPN gateway of the concerned region. This cuts all communication between the affected region and the other ones. As expected the Mesos master nodes continued without any issues, as the current leader was not the affected one. As for the affected Mesos slave nodes, after the timeout of 75 s, the leading Mesos master node determined that the slave nodes were unresponsive deactivated them.

The Hybrid Cloud Splits and Semi-isolates Part of the Platform. In the event of split in the hybrid cloud, resulting in a partly isolated availability region, the quorum mechanics will prevent inconsistencies of the cluster and avoid issues like the split-brain problem.

To test this scenario, two simple `iptables` DROP rules was added on the Mesos master node located in Frankfurt with the IP address `192.168.0.5`.

```
iptables -A INPUT -s 10.0.19.5 -j DROP
iptables -A OUTPUT -d 10.0.19.5 -j DROP
```

The leading Mesos master node at the current time was `10.0.19.5`, with nothing occurring immediately as a result of the `iptables` DROP rules. The leading master continued with no issues and other two standby Mesos masters correctly redirected to the leading master node. However, after rebooting the ZooKeeper process and Mesos master process on the master nodes, the cluster is unable to elect a new leader. Immediately after the `iptables` DROP rules were removed, a new leading Mesos master was elected and operations continued as normal.

3   Conclusion

This paper presents a prototype of a hybrid cloud platform using Apache Mesos to weave together heterogeneous clouds and geographical locations into a unified platform. The prototype proposed focuses on a specific perspective, namely, maximizing availability.

References

1. Connor, T.R., Southgate, J.: Automated cloud brokerage based upon continuous real-time benchmarking. In: 2015 IEEE/ACM 8th International Conference on Utility and Cloud Computing (UCC), pp. 372–375. IEEE (2015)

2. Breiter, G., Naik, V.K.: A framework for controlling and managing hybrid cloud service integration. In: 2013 IEEE International Conference on Cloud Engineering (IC2E), pp. 217–224. IEEE (2013)
3. MODAClouds. Modaclouds. http://www.modaclouds.eu
4. VMWare, Inc. vrealize suite. http://www.vmware.com/products/vrealize-suite/features.html
5. VMWare, Inc., Cloud Computing. http://www.vmware.com/cloud-computing/hybrid-cloud.html
6. Butler, B.: Re-examining ciscos intercloud strategy, January 2015. http://www.networkworld.com/article/2864857/cloud-computing/re-examining-cisco-s-intercloud-strategy.html
7. IBM. Private and hybrid cloud. http://www.ibm.com/cloud-computing/uk/en/private-cloud.html
8. Rackspace, Inc., Hybrid cloud computing, hybrid hosting by rackspace. http://www.rackspace.com/cloud/hybrid
9. Breiter, G., Naik, V.: A framework for controlling and managing hybrid cloud service integration. In: 2013 IEEE International Conference on Cloud Engineering (IC2E), pp. 217–224, March 2013
10. PaaSage. Paasage: Model-based cloud platform upperware. http://www.paasage.eu
11. Borja, S., Ruben, M., Ignacio, M., Ian, F.: An open source solution for virtual infrastructure management in private and hybrid clouds. IEEE Internet Comput. 1, 14–22 (2009)
12. Kovács, Á., Lencse, G.: Modelling of virtualized servers. In: 2015 38th International Conference on Telecommunications and Signal Processing (TSP), pp. 241–245. IEEE (2015)
13. Feller, E., Rilling, L., Morin, C.: Snooze: a scalable and autonomic virtual machine management framework for private clouds. In: 2012 12th IEEE/ACM International Symposium on Cluster, Cloud and Grid Computing (CCGRID 2012), pp. 482–489, May 2012

Visual Analytics for Network Security and Critical Infrastructures

Karolína Burská[✉] and Radek Ošlejšek

Faculty of Informatics, Masaryk University, Brno, Czech Republic
burska@mail.muni.cz, oslejsek@fi.muni.cz

Abstract. A comprehensive analysis of cyber attacks is important for better understanding of their nature and their origin. Providing a sufficient insight into such a vast amount of diverse (and sometimes seemingly unrelated) data is a task that is suitable neither for humans nor for fully automated algorithms alone. Not only a combination of the two approaches but also a continuous reasoning process that is capable of generating a sufficient knowledge base is indispensable for a better understanding of the events. Our research is focused on designing new exploratory methods and interactive visualizations in the context of network security. The knowledge generation loop is important for its ability to help analysts to refine the nature of the processes that continuously occur and to offer them a better insight into the network security related events. In this paper, we formulate the research questions that relate to the proposed solution.

Keywords: Visual analytics · Network security · Knowledge generation

1 Introduction

Although network security is strongly connected with technology (e.g., network infrastructure, cloud computing), the context is usually much broader and must be mediated by human interaction. While some of the known attack methods may be detectable rather easily, many attacks can be identified only with the participation of a human, by analysis. The analysts' goals are to identify, track, and understand these attacks. One of the viable approaches is to combine the human flexibility, creativity, and background knowledge with the enormous storage and processing capacities of today's computers to gain insight into complex problems and to understand causality. Especially, when involving large and complex data sets that require a high degree of interaction, the support of knowledge generation techniques is likely to prove as very beneficial.

In what follows, we formulate research questions that are related to the loop of exploratory visual analysis in the context of cyber security. Each question aims to describe a broader motivation and current state and then formulates approaches enabling us to tackle the goals in proposed PhD thesis.

D. Tuncer et al. (Eds.): AIMS 2017, LNCS 10356, pp. 149–152, 2017.
DOI: 10.1007/978-3-319-60774-0_13

2   Research Questions and Proposed Approaches

How to Model Cyber-Security Data and Its Semantics? Cyber security data has a strong heterogeneous nature. Data sets can be temporal, geospatial, multivariable, or graph-based, for instance. And also, mixed together. Although there exist some formalizations that describe how various data types can be mapped to visual properties [8] in general, a clear taxonomy of data types used in cyber security domain is missing. However, a formal classification scheme is necessary if we want to build an adaptive data gathering and construct a knowledge base – two mandatory parts of any visual analysis loop.

In our research, we initially focus on the design of taxonomies for cyber security data and corresponding analytical processes. We plan to utilize formal OWL ontologies to provide semantically correct vocabulary enabling as to (semi)automatically construct adaptable data sets and derived knowledge models. Using existing taxonomies and approaches, e.g. those described in [1,6,13], we aim to unite the different perspectives and apply them in the visual analysis loop in the cyber security domain.

How to Provide Insight into Cyber Security Processes via Exploratory Visualizations? Many works confirm that the involvement of the human factor in the process of data analysis may contribute to revealing new information in a significant way [5,12]. One of the basic principles used in this field is the *visual analytics process* by Keim et al. [7], which is described as an approach that combines data analysis, visualization, and human factor, as well as the areas of cognition and perception. This approach follows the Shneiderman's visual information-seeking mantra: "Overview first, zoom and filter, then details-on-demand" [11]. By applying this mantra in the visual analysis domain, Sacha et al. [10] proposed an approach enabling the visual analytic theories to go beyond the inclusion of the human factor in the process, to the theory where human is a part of the loop [3].

Our approach to the cyber security knowledge management and its visual analysis would combine the Keim's and Sacha's approaches. Their models have to be significantly adapted since the cyber security domain requires a wide range of network-related manipulation techniques. Our model would consist of two parts. The first part would deal with the automated processes connected to data monitoring and knowledge management, while the second part would involve human interactions by means of exploratory visualizations. Unfortunately, there is no clear separation between the two parts since the whole model for exploratory visual analysis attempts to connect the benefits of both – humans are creative and able to find subtle connections between two seemingly unrelated events, but they miss the ability to deal with large data sets. On the contrary, computers offer large storage spaces and fast data processing, but they lack the human reasoning and the background knowledge of the problem domain. Therefore, finding a balanced solution based on the feasible technical background makes this goal challenging.

How to Utilize Exploratory Visualizations for Efficient Protection of Critical Information Infrastructures? Protection of critical information infrastructures is ensured by security experts. Their skills and the ability to react to incidents quickly and correctly are affected by two factors: a training and an online situation awareness. In general, decision making is viewed as consisting of an analyst's state of knowledge in a dynamically changing environment [4].

To facilitate a cyber protection training and to evaluate benefits of visualization techniques for situation awareness, we attempt to use KYPO Cyber Range [9], where various attacks and threats can be easily simulated. KYPO enables us to focus on linking the knowledge base with suitable visualizations and to evaluate their benefits. New approaches can be tested and evaluated by means of cyber defense exercises focused on improving skills of participants [2].

Acknowledgements. This research was supported by the Security Research Programme of the Czech Republic 2015–2020 (BV III/1 VS) granted by the Ministry of the Interior of the Czech Republic under No. VI20162019014 Simulation, detection, and mitigation of cyber threats endangering critical infrastructure.

References

1. Chi, E.H.: A taxonomy of visualization techniques using the data state reference model. In: IEEE Symposium on Information Visualization 2000 (2000)
2. Čeleda, P., Čegan, J., Vykopal, J., Tovarňák, D.: KYPO - a platform for cyber defence exercises. In: M&S Support to Operational Tasks Including War Gaming, Logistics, Cyber Defence. NATO Science and Technology Organization (2015)
3. Endert, A., et al.: The human is the loop: new directions for visual analytics. J. Intell. Inf. Syst. **43**(3), 411–435 (2014)
4. Endsley, M.R.: Toward a theory of situation awareness in dynamic systems. Hum. Factors: J. Hum. Factors Ergon. Soc. **37**(1), 32–64 (1995)
5. Fischer, F.: Visual analytics for situational awareness in cyber security (2016)
6. Gao, J., et al.: Ontology-based model of network and computer attacks for security assessment. J. Shanghai Jiaotong Univ. (Sci.) **18**(5), 554–562 (2013)
7. Keim, D.A., Mansmann, F., Stoffel, A., Ziegler, H.: Visual Analytics. Springer, Heidelberg (2009)
8. Kott, A., Wang, C., Erbacher, R.F.: Cyber Defense and Situational Awareness. Springer, New York (2014)
9. Kouřil, D., et al.: Cloud-based testbed for simulation of cyber attacks. In: IEEE Network Operations and Management Symposium (NOMS), pp. 1–6, May 2014
10. Sacha, D., et al.: Knowledge generation model for visual analytics. IEEE Trans. Vis. Comput. Graph. (Proc. Vis. Anal. Sci. Technol.) **20**(12), 1604–1613 (2014)
11. Shneiderman, B.: The eyes have it: a task by data type taxonomy for information visualizations. In: Proceedings 1996 IEEE Symposium on Visual Languages (1996)
12. Sun, G., Wu, Y., et al.: A survey of visual analytics techniques and applications: state-of-the-art research and future challenges. J. Comput. Sci. Tech. **28**(5), 852–867 (2013)
13. Zareen, S., et al.: UCO: a unified cybersecurity ontology. In: Proceedings of the AAAI Workshop on Artificial Intelligence for Cyber Security (2016)

Preserving Relations in Parallel Flow Data Processing

Tomáš Čejka[1]([⊠]) and Martin Žádník[2]

[1] FIT, CTU in Prague, Prague, Czech Republic
cejkato2@fit.cvut.cz
[2] CESNET, a.l.e., Prague, Czech Republic
zadnik@cesnet.cz

Abstract. Network monitoring produces high volume of data that must be analyzed ideally in near real-time to support network security operations. It is possible to process the data using Big Data frameworks, however, such approach requires adaptation or complete redesign of processing tools to get the same results. This paper elaborates on a parallel processing based on splitting a stream of flow records. The goal is to create subsets of traffic that contain enough information for parallel anomaly detection. The paper describes a methodology based on so called witnesses that helps to scale up without any need to modify existing algorithms.

1 Introduction

Common architecture of monitoring large networks contains multiple observation points measured by monitoring probes and a central collector with captured data. This approach creates a global view of the network traffic. In addition, it allows for analysis and detection of global events that are less visible from a local view.

This approach works well on small networks, however, since the network traffic grows, processing all data on one place reaches limits of resources such as memory capacity. In addition, various network events produce data that reach maximal performance of a single machine. Altogether, network monitoring becomes a Big Data processing and some scalable approach must be considered.

As it is described later in Sect. 2, Big Data principles are being studied for last years. However, a general methodology of splitting network data into subsets is missing. The aim of this work is to describe a principle how to split data with respect to internal relations and used processing algorithms in order to analyze balanced data subsets while the needed information still remains together.

The goal is to allow processing huge amounts of flow data using analysis tools that are not designed for a distributed environment. A correct selection of data subsets can improve current mechanisms of data distribution or sampling without loosing information needed by detection algorithms.

© The Author(s) 2017
D. Tuncer et al. (Eds.): AIMS 2017, LNCS 10356, pp. 153–156, 2017.
DOI: 10.1007/978-3-319-60774-0_14

2   Related Work

MapReduce was used for network data processing e.g. in [6,7], however, the authors used a distributed database or a distributed filesystem to store data files. Paper [4] analyzes IP, TCP and HTTP traffic stored in offline files using Hadoop and MapReduce. Paper [1] analyzes campus network using several types of MapReduce jobs (e.g. measuring volume of traffic per subnet).

Authors of [5] try to use Apache Spark framework with Netmap to extract traffic features for a packet-based detection of different types of DDoS attacks in real-time. The detection uses machine learning methods. The authors rely on a distributed storage and an abstraction of objects called Resilient Distributed Dataset, however, no efficient data splitting is discussed. The paper notes that usage of sampled data produces many false-positives.

Semantic relations in data and possible negative effects of splitting data were mentioned in [3]. The authors present experiments with Hashdoop, an improved Hadoop, that splits data using CRC hashes of src and dst IPs. The authors chose a simple packet counting and ASTUTE algorithm for parallel processing. The splitting based just on IP addresses is a single case in our methodology.

3   Proposed Approach

The main requirement is to identify which parts of data must stay together to preserve data relations and which parts can be split into subsets.

A **detection algorithm** can be described as a function with data about network traffic as its input and alerts (detected events) as its output. Generally, the input data is a mixture of benign and malicious traffic. The goal of a detection algorithm is to identify the malicious traffic and to generate an alert that describes the detected event. The algorithm is successful if it observes at least a **minimal subset** of malicious traffic which triggers the alert. Lets call the instance of a minimal subset a **witness**. If a witness gets divided, the malicious traffic is not detectable with the same detection algorithm anymore because there is not enough information for decision. As a result, data can be divided for parallel processing in any way that does not break witnesses.

In practice, there are many different detection algorithms processing the same data to detect various types of malicious traffic. As a result, multiple different witnesses must be preserved at the same time which complicates data splitting.

Data can contain many witnesses that identify the same malicious traffic, while any of them is sufficient for a successful detection. In order to design a data splitter a particular type of witness should be characterized. This kind of characterization describes what data an algorithm analyzes, how the malicious traffic looks like and what is the configuration of an algorithm.

4   Evaluation

To evaluate the witness-based splitting, we analyze data distribution among computation nodes and overall detection results. We need to compare results of a single instance and results of a distributed environment. As the distributed processing generates some alerts multiple times a deduplication based on timestamps, type of events and other information contained in the alerts is necessary.

For the evaluation, we use a NEMEA framework [2] which can be easily run in a single instance as well as in a distributed configuration. There are several detection modules in NEMEA and some of them were presented in our previous work. However, the presented principle can be used with any system that allows to modify an algorithm of data splitting.

The first experiments with splitting flow data with respect to potential witness showed that it is possible to distribute flow data almost uniformly and there is no significant difference between detection results of a single instance and the distributed environment. The measured difference was about 1% which is caused by inaccurate timing of stream-wise real-time analysis during our experiments.

5   Conclusion

This paper addressed a network traffic analysis in a distributed environment. There are many papers focusing on existing Big Data frameworks but, to our best knowledge, a general methodology of splitting a stream of flow data is missing. This research aims to describe data relations that must be preserved for the parallel analysis. The data relations, types of malicious traffic and used detection algorithms with their parameters define so called witnesses. Since this research is rather a work-in-progress, we have some preliminary results. However, the experiments with real data show that respecting witnesses allow for distributed processing without significant impact on detection results.

As a future work, we are going to explore the principle of witnesses in more detail. Moreover, based on witnesses, an algorithm of real-time reconfiguration of the splitter to scale up the distributed system would be useful.

Acknowledgments. This work was supported by the Technology Agency of the Czech Republic under No. TA04010062 *Technology for processing and analysis of network data in big data concept* and grant No. SGS17/212/OHK3/3T/18 funded by Ministry of Education, Youth and Sports of the Czech Republic.

References

1. Bumgardner, V.K., el al.: Scalable hybrid stream and Hadoop network analysis system. In: Proceedings of the 5th ACM/SPEC ICPE (2014). doi:10.1145/2568088. 2568103
2. Cejka, T., et al.: NEMEA: a framework for network traffic analysis. In: Proceedings of CNSM (2016). doi:10.1109/CNSM.2016.7818417
3. Fontugne, R., et al.: Hashdoop: A MapReduce framework for network anomaly detection. In: Proceedings of INFOCOM (2014). doi:10.1109/INFCOMW.2014. 6849281

4. Ibrahim, L.T., et al.: A study on improvement of internet traffic measurement and analysis using Hadoop system. In: Proceedings of ICEEI (2015). doi:10.1109/ICEEI. 2015.7352545
5. Karimi, A.M., et al.: Distributed network traffic feature extraction for a real-time IDS. In: Proceedings of EIT (2016). doi:10.1109/EIT.2016.7535295
6. Lee, Y., et al.: Toward scalable internet traffic measurement and analysis with Hadoop. ACM SIGCOMM Comput. Commun. Rev. **43**(1), 5–13 (2013). doi:10. 1145/2427036.2427038
7. Zhang, J., Zhang, Y., Liu, P., He, J.: A spark-based DDoS attack detection model in cloud services. In: Bao, F., Chen, L., Deng, R.H., Wang, G. (eds.) ISPEC 2016. LNCS, vol. 10060, pp. 48–64. Springer, Cham (2016). doi:10.1007/ 978-3-319-49151-6_4

Ph.D. Track: Autonomic
and Self-Management Solutions

SmartDEMAP: A Smart Contract Deployment and Management Platform

Markus Knecht[(✉)] and Burkhard Stiller

Communication Systems Group CSG, Department of Informatics IfI,
University of Zürich, Binzmühlestrasse 14, 8050 Zürich, Switzerland
markus.knecht2@uzh.ch

Abstract. Smart contracts on a blockchain behave exactly as specified by their code. To be sure that a smart contract behaves as expected, the end-user has to either analyze its code or trust a potentially anonymous developer or auditor to do so. This approach proposes a smart contract deployment and management platform that can execute development tools and code quality tools in a trusted way and uses this to reduce the trust required into the smart contract developer or auditor. Additionally, such a platform can provide new capabilities for developers aiding them in the creation of smart contracts.

1 Introduction

Smart contracts are programs which run in a trusted execution environment provided by a blockchain [2]. The code of smart contracts can dictate how valuable assets, associated with a smart contract, are handled. A flaw in the code can lead to the loss or theft of the handled assets [10]. Developing bug-free software is challenging even for skilled professionals [7]. Programming languages and tools like formal verification or automated tests can support that process. Before a smart contract is trusted with assets, such as cryptocurrency coins or a owner-ship certificate, it must be ensured that the code implements the expected and specified behavior. A end-user can ensure this by analyzing the code, by trusting the developer to have implemented the specified behavior, or by trusting an auditor to verify that the code implements the specified behavior. Analyzing the code is not an option for most end-users, because of the complexity of the task as well as the required time.

This paper proposes *SmartDEMAP* a smart contract deployment and management platform which reduces the trust required into smart contract developers and auditors by imposing restrictions on the smart contracts that can be deployed on it. The restrictions are enforced by executing formal verifiers [1,4], compilers, automated bug-finders [8], or other development and code quality tools on smart contracts. Such restrictions could consist of a formal proof of some specified properties, enforcing a programming language, or requiring a negative result from an automatic bug finder. *SmartDEMAP* can reduce the trust needed into third parties, without requiring expertise in software auditing.

© The Author(s) 2017
D. Tuncer et al. (Eds.): AIMS 2017, LNCS 10356, pp. 159–164, 2017.
DOI: 10.1007/978-3-319-60774-0_15

SmartDEMAP allows to run development and code quality tools in a trusted way to do deploy-time and run-time checks to increase smart contract quality and robustness. To accelerate the integration into the development process, we propose to develop a custom smart contract programming language that is aware of the existence of *SmartDEMAP*. Such a language can generate code that facilitates the provided functionality and gives a developer easy access to it. Existing languages can integrate *SmartDEMAP* by providing libraries to interact with it.

2   Hypotheses

An investigation into the current state of smart contract development has shown that there currently is a high risk for end-users when interacting with smart contracts, as shown by the "The DAO" incident [10], where an attacker exploited a bug to steel 3.6 million in ether. The following hypotheses are premises for developing and analysing *SmartDEMAP*. In the project it should be researched how well these premises can mitigate the respective risks.

Hypothesis 1: A platform on the blockchain, which provides access to trusted execution of development and code quality tools, enables the development of smart contracts which can manage, verify, and analyze the code of other smart contracts in order to increase their robustness as well as reducing the trust required in developers and auditors.

Sub-hypothesis 1.1: The ability to associate attributes with a smart contract based on a trusted analysis of its code, where the results can be queried and analyzed by other smart contract or external sources, enables the detection of misbehaving smart contracts.

Sub-hypothesis 1.2: A smart contract that controls the compilation and deployment of other smart contracts by using development and code quality tools, allows a developer to add new features or bug fixes to a smart contract after it has been deployed, without the need for end-users to trust the developer.

Sub-hypothesis 1.3: A custom smart contract programming language with the ability of accessing code analysis at run-time can prevent certain exploits.

3   Related Work

There are two categories of work related to *SmartDEMAP*. On one hand there are smart contract specific development and code quality tools including programming languages. On the other hand there is research on how resource intensive computations can be executed in a trusted way despite the resource limitations of smart contract enabled blockchains [2,11].

For the tools it is important that they work in a reliable way and can not be fooled by a fine tuned input. If a compiler guarantees a certain semantic which do not hold in the generated byte code, then a trusted execution of the compiler will not help either. An earlier Solidity version had such a problem [9]. Formal verification [1,4] and automatic bug-finding [8] are other relevant research topics for *SmartDEMAP*. Research into these topics is relatively new and the developed tools are not in wide use and geared more towards trained professionals. *SmartDEMAP* could change that by allowing users not trained in these tools to still benefit from their results.

Theoretical results already exist concerning the execution of complex computations in a way, such that the results can be trusted [3,5]. Their currently is a project developing a concrete implementation [6] based on the theoretical foundations from [3,5], and will allow smart contracts to trigger a trusted computation and access the result.

One part of the current research promises new tools that can be used to improve the development process and reduce the exploitability of smart contracts. Another part promises ways to run complex computations in a trusted way, which can be utilized during the execution of smart contracts. There is no research investigating if and how these two approaches could be combined. *SmartDEMAP* will close that research gap.

4   Smart Contract Exploits

In recent years, different exploits have been found which are usable against some of the existing smart contracts [8]. The most prominent example is the "The DAO" theft [10]. Contrary to centralized software development, smart contracts operate in an open environment where arbitrary adversaries can exist [8] and thus attacks can originate from inside the same virtual machine. Additionally, it is substantially harder to correct a bug because smart contract code is unchangeable after it is deployed on a blockchain [2,11]. Most problems occur when unknown code is executed, because it may have been deployed by an adversary. Such vulnerabilities can lead to loss or theft of valuable assets and are often hard or even impossible to fix. Most users of such smart contracts do not have the expertise and time to ensure that it is safe to trust the smart contract with their assets.

5   Platform-Based Smart Contract Management

The auditors and developers of smart contracts are often anonymous and their trustworthiness is unknown. Some smart contracts include code which allows a privileged entity to exchange parts of the code. This is done to make it possible to replace code containing a flaw with a fixed version. On the other hand this could be used to inject code that violates a specified behavior.

SmartDEMAP determines a new mechanism, which allows only code to be deployed that does not violate an associated behavior specification. The behavior can be specified as a formal specification and on deployment needs a proof that it conforms to the specification. Other approaches like defining a test suite and only allow code to be deployed that passes the test suite will be investigated in addition to the formal verification approach. This has only a benefit if the formal verification tool or test suite can be run in a trusted way. This reduces the trust required in developers and auditors and replaces it with trust into the tools and their input (formal specification or test suite).

To achieve this, the approach to be designed will follow a blockchain-based path, with a platform for management, analysis, and deployment of smart contracts (*SmartDEMAP*). The platform will manage a set of tools and use them to enforce that smart contracts deployed on it fulfill as set of specifiable criteria. Such a tool set contains formal verifiers, compilers, automatic test suites, and automatic bug-finders. These tools are often complex and *SmartDEMAP* will provide a way to ensure that these tools fulfill their purpose. This indicates that each *SmartDEMAP* instance needs a entity fulfilling this role. This may be another instance or a known third party (e.g. Microsoft, Amazon, Google) as well as a consortium of people founded exclusively for that purpose. This system reduces the trust needed in the code quality tools and replaces it with trust in the tool verification entity.

6   Improved Smart Contract Programming Language

SmartDEMAP benefits from a custom programming language, which is aware of it and uses its features during compilation or at run-time. Such a custom programming language can incorporate *SmartDEMAP* to give additional guarantees by generating the respective run-time checks based on the platforms capabilities. Further it provides a simple way for developers to access the platforms services. A new programming language provides the opportunity to analyze existing languages as well as common exploits of smart contracts programmed in these languages. A smart contract programming language covering this aspect could prevent some exploits and common pitfalls by design.

One currently preferred approach is a language based on a process calculi as suggested in [4]. This does prevent by design some of the common exploits, such as the reentrancy exploit that brought "The DAO" to its knees [10]. This exploit is prevented because no state is shared between different processes and unlike a function a process cannot be called again if it is still running, and thus, no unexpected state change can occur. This work evaluates if such a language efficiently can be compiled to existing smart contract virtual machines and which exploits could be prevented on the language level.

7   Methodology

This project is of high importance if smart contract should become safe to use by non-experts. On one hand *SmartDEMAP* can give them a higher degree of certainty, that it is safe to interact with a smart contract without the risk of unexpected behavior. On the other hand *SmartDEMAP* and the custom programming language help the developer to deliver smart contracts that are harder to exploit.

The project is approached by developing a model of *SmartDEMAP* and the custom programming language that describes their respective capabilities and guarantees. Beside the model the platform as well as a compiler for the language are implemented as a proof of the practical feasibility.

The biggest risk involved in the project is that the currently developed tools like formal verifiers as well as the trusted execution infrastructure will not be available in time or do not satisfy the needs of *SmartDEMAP*. The developed models are used to prove that certain exploits can be prevented fully or at least to which degree if the described platform and the custom programming language is used. The expected proofs are:

1. A proof that it is possible to decide if a unknown smart contract can be called without the risk of becoming vulnerable to certain exploits.
2. A proof that a developer can only deploy code that result in a behavior that conforms to a formal specification.
3. A proof that smart contracts programmed in the custom language are not vulnerable against certain exploits.

The evaluation of which exploits are preventable this way is another expected result from this project. Beside the theoretical results an implementation of *SmartDEMAP* on the EVM [11] is expected.

References

1. Bhargavan, K., Delignat-Lavaud, A., Fournet, C., Gollamudi, A., Gonthier, G., Kobeissi, N., Kulatova, N., Rastogi, A., Sibut-Pinote, T., Swamy, N., Zanella-Béguelin, S.: Formal verification of smart contracts: short paper. In: 2016 ACM Workshop on Programming Languages and Analysis for Security, PLAS 2016, Vienna, Austria, pp. 91–96 (2016)
2. Buterin, V.: A next-generation smart contract and decentralized application platform. Technical report (2014). Accessed 15 Nov 2016
3. Canetti, R., Riva, B., Rothblum, G.N.: Practical delegation of computation using multiple servers. In: 18th ACM Conference on Computer and Communications Security, CCS 2011, Chicago, Illinois, USA, pp. 445–454 (2011)
4. Edstroem, R., Pettersson, J.: Safer smart contracts through type-driven development. Master's thesis, Chalmers University of Technology and University of Gothenburg (2016)
5. Jain, S., Saxena, P., Stephan, F., Teutsch, J.: How to verify computation with a rational network, June 2016
6. Teutsch, J., Reitwiessner, C.: A scalable verification solution for blockchains (2017). http://people.cs.uchicago.edu/%7Eteutsch/papers/truebit.pdf
7. Anand, K., Rai, K., Madan, L.: Software crisis. Int. J. Innov. Res. Technol. 1 (2014)
8. Luu, L., Chu, D.-H., Olickel, H., Saxena, P., Hobor, A.: Making Smart Contracts Smarter. Cryptology ePrint Archive, Report 2016/633 (2016)

9. Reitwiessner, C.: Security alert solidity variables can be overwritten in storage (2016). https://blog.ethereum.org/2016/11/09/analysis-storage-corruption-bug. Accessed 03 Dec 2016
10. Vessenes, P.: Deconstructing the DAO Attack: A Brief Code Tour (2016). http://vessenes.com/deconstructing-thedao-attack-a-brief-code-tour. Accessed 03 Dec 2016
11. Wood, G.: Ethereum: A Secure Decentralised Generalised Transaction Ledger (2015). http://gavwood.com/paper.pdf. Accessed 03 Dec 2016

Optimizing the Integration of Agent-Based Cloud Orchestrators and Higher-Level Workloads

Merlijn Sebrechts[(✉)], Gregory Van Seghbroeck, and Filip De Turck

IDLab, Department of Information Technology, Ghent University - imec,
Technologiepark-Zwijnaarde 15, 9052 Ghent, Belgium
merlijn.sebrechts@ugent.be

Abstract. The flexibility of cloud computing has put significant strain on operations teams. Manually installing and configuring applications in the cloud simply isn't an option anymore. Configuration management automation solves the issue of getting a single application into a certain state automatically and reliably. However, the issue of automatic dependency management between multiple applications is still an "open, hard problem" according to researchers at Google. Agent-based modeling and orchestration tools like Juju solve the issue of getting from zero to a working set of correctly clustered and connected frameworks. The shortcomings of these state-of-the-art tools are that they don't provide efficient ways to model and orchestrate workloads running on top of these frameworks. This paper presents a number of ways to deploy and orchestrate workloads with Juju, compares their performance and overhead, and suggests how this overhead can be minimized.

Keywords: Cloud modeling languages · Service orchestration · Juju

1 Introduction

There is a big need to make IT operations easier. Take the field of data science for example. There is an ever-growing set of tools and platforms that support data scientists. The prevalence of open-source software in that field has shifted the barrier of entry from licensing costs to operations costs. The tools are available and free to use, but actually running them in production requires a team of system administrators that have expert knowledge on both the tools themselves and IT operations in general. Even industry-standard companies such as Google state that the issue of automatic dependency management between multiple services is still an "open, hard problem" [1].

The devops world has spawned a number of useful tools that help operations teams. Configuration management systems help automate the task of installing, configuring and managing applications. Automating these tasks reduces errors and saves a lot of time when scaling an application. This process, called

© The Author(s) 2017
D. Tuncer et al. (Eds.): AIMS 2017, LNCS 10356, pp. 165–170, 2017.
DOI: 10.1007/978-3-319-60774-0_16

infrastructure as code, allows businesses to quickly react to changes in usage of their application. These languages are less suited to lower the time to market because each new application requires new management code. Moreover, these tools don't really abstract away the complexity of operations. This means that operators using these tools now have to be experts in three fields: Configuration management, IT operations and the applications they're maintaining.

Cloud modeling languages aim to reduce complexity and time to market by providing an abstraction layer on top of IT operations. Instead of changing the applications themselves, the operator changes a model that represents the application. The orchestrator then translates actions on the model into actions on the application. This is a great step forward to manage the complexity of IT operations. The current generation of cloud modeling languages such as OASIS TOSCA [2] also improve flexibility and re-usability of operations code by dividing the operations code of an entire cloud application into a number of reusable isolated pieces connected to each other using dependencies.

Monolithic cloud orchestrators have a tendency to become very complex [3]. This results hard-to-maintain and hard-to-scale bottlenecks. Agent-based orchestrators such as Juju [6] are the solution to this problem. All the dependency resolution and operations logic is put into a series of agents that communicate with each other over predefined interfaces. The only responsibility of the orchestrator is to install the agents and set up communication channels between them [5]. The actual dependency resolution happens in the agents. This has the added benefit that the implementation of the agent is hidden. This makes it possible for two agents that manage services using two different configuration management tools to communicate with each other, exchange information, and feed that information into the config management tools.

The combination of agent-based cloud orchestrators and cloud modeling languages makes IT operations a lot easier but there is still a lot of work to be done. All the aforementioned tools have a strong focus on the operations of an application as a combination of services. What is left out are the actual workloads running on top of these services. It's great that orchestrators allow an operator to setup a MySQL database, but what about the tables in the database? It's easy to model and orchestrate an Apache Hadoop cluster, but what about the jobs running on top of that Hadoop cluster? This isn't only about creating the table and submitting the job. The MySQL table will be used by some software or algorithm and the Hadoop job will get data from somewhere and put the extracted information somewhere else. Configuring all these workloads by hand isn't a viable option due to the same reason that running the operations of an entire application isn't a viable option: it's error-prone, it slows innovation down to a crawl, and requires a very competent team with highly specialized skills.

Since agent-based cloud orchestrators solve these challenges for the operation of services and applications, they form a great start to explore solutions for the operation of high-level workloads.

2   Modeling High-Level Workloads in Juju

The authors' previous work proposed the workflow component as a way to model and manage high-level workloads with Cloud Modeling Languages [4]. Each workflow component is a Charm that contains both the workload itself and a workflow agent that manages the workload. This approach provides a lot of flexibility without adding any additional logic to the Juju orchestrator itself. The tricky part of this approach is that each workload requires at least one agent, and this agent needs to run somewhere. Juju provides two ways to run additional agents: co-locate the workflow agent and the framework agent without any isolation and isolate the workflow agent from the framework agent by running it inside an LXD container.

Both methods aren't ideal. It clearly shows that Juju is not built with such use in mind. The issue with co-location is that Juju doesn't allow two co-located agents to run in parallel. This is to avoid conflicts when two agents try to manage the same machine at the same time. This significantly slows down the agents because each agents needs to wait for the other agents to finish executing. Isolating the agents using LXD containers solves this issue but introduces a new one: the overhead of the LXD container. In many cases the overhead of the LXD container is larger than the resources used by the actual workload.

3   LimeDS Big Data Model

This paper evaluates both methods for running additional agents in order to get a better grasp on what the actual overhead is and how it compares to the resources used by the workload. The evaluation is done using the LimeDS Big Data model[1]. This model and its components is further explained in this section.

LimeDS is a modular platform to create and run data-driven services[2]. The LimeDS Big Data model is perfect for validating the flexibility of modeling workloads for a number of reasons. First of all, **LimeDS is both a workload and a platform**. The LimeDS Docker container is a workload running on top of the Docker host, but it is also a host to services and modules running on top of LimeDS. It is important to support such flexibility. Having LimeDS and the Docker runtime be two different Charms also has the advantage that you can swap out the single Docker host and plug in for example a Kubernetes cluster. Secondly, **workloads running on LimeDS need to connect to other services,** for example external datastores or load balancers. These connections require a workload agent communicating with other services to exchange the correct information and to resolve possible dependencies such as the workload having to wait for MongoDB to start. Lastly, **LimeDS needs to run in a scaled-out setup** to handle Big Data workloads. The agents make this incredibly easy. An operator specifies how many instances of LimeDS are needed. The Orchestrator installs an agent for each LimeDS instance, and the agents communicate

---

[1] https://jujucharms.com/u/tengu-team/limeds-bigdata/.
[2] http://limeds.be/.

with the Docker host agent to deploy LimeDS correctly. Since each LimeDS agent implements the http interface, the agents don't need any additional clustering logic. Each agent connects to the agent managing the HAProxy load balancer, and that agent configures the proxy correctly to loadbalance requests over the LimeDS cluster.

4   Evaluation

The **deploy-time overhead** is measured as the time it takes from the model to scale. The tests start with a running LimeDS Big Data cluster with two units. This cluster is then scaled to n units, and the time until the scaling action is complete is measured and compared.

The results in Fig. 1 show that the deploy-time overhead is initially greater for the isolated setup than for the co-located setup. This is due to the overhead of spinning up an LXD container for the new agent. However, when more units are requested, the isolated setup scales faster than the co-located setup due to the sequential nature the co-located setup. Only one co-located agent is allowed to execute actions at any given moment.

For the **runtime overhead** of the agents, the memory and disk usage of the agent are recorded as shown in Fig. 2. Here the disadvantage of the isolated setup is clearly visible, it has a much bigger runtime overhead. The +200 MB of RAM usage per agent is especially worrisome since the LimeDS container itself uses about 300 MB of RAM.

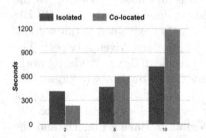
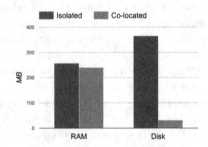

Fig. 1. The deploy-time overhead of the agents; LXD vs co-located.

Fig. 2. The runtime overhead of the agents; LXD vs co-located.

5   Conclusion and the Road Forward

Neither of the solutions has satisfactory performance. The co-located setup compromises heavily on deploy-time overhead and both setups compromise on runtime overhead. There are a few advantages to these solutions. Having the ability to write arbitrary logic in the agent enables complex dependency resolution without adding complexity to the orchestrator itself. Containers successfully stop the workload agents from accessing or changing the machine where the framework is running. This forces agents to communicate using the relationships. This enables other frameworks to implement the same relationship, making the solution pluggable. The ability to model higher-level workloads as a combination of components related to each other gives operators a clear view of what is actually running, and allows the workloads themselves to be pluggable. The challenge will be to find a solution that addresses the performance issues described here without compromising on the stated advantages. Future research will explore the road forward in a few directions.

Agentless Agents: The advantage of the agents is that they allow running arbitrary dependency handling code, thus keeping the orchestrator simple. A possible solution might be to have a way for giving snippets of dependency handling code to other agents instead of spinning up new agents.

Slim Agents: Instead of reducing the amount of agents, another path forward is to investigate if the overhead of the agent itself can be reduced. This approach requires thorough investigation into where the overhead comes from. There is also potential to use more lightweight process containers such as Docker instead of the full-blown operating system containers that LXD provides.

Parallel co-located Agents: Enabling co-located containers to run in parallel is a possible solution to the deploy-time overhead of co-located agents. This would need each agent to specify what kind of operations the agent will execute. The orchestrator can then use that information to determine whether or not two agents are allowed to run at the same time.

Acknowledgment. Part of this work has been funded by the iFest project, cofunded by imec and VLAIO.

References

1. Burns, B., Grant, B., Oppenheimer, D., Brewer, E., Wilkes, J.: Borg, Omega, and Kubernetes. Queue **14**(1), 70–93. http://dl.acm.org/citation.cfm?doid=2898442.2898444
2. OASIS: TOSCA Simple Profile in YAML Version 1.0, August 2016. https://docs.oasis-open.org/tosca/TOSCA-Simple-Profile-YAML/v1.0/TOSCA-Simple-Profile-YAML-v1.0.html
3. Schwarzkopf, M., Konwinski, A., Abd-El-Malek, M., Wilkes, J.: Omega: flexible, scalable schedulers for large compute clusters. In: Proceedings of the 8th ACM European Conference on Computer Systems, EuroSys 2013, NY, USA, pp. 351–364 (2013). http://doi.acm.org/10.1145/2465351.2465386
4. Sebrechts, M., Borny, S., Vanhove, T., Seghbroeck, G.V., Wauters, T., Volckaert, B., Turck, F.D.: Model-driven deployment and management of workflows on analytics frameworks. In: 2016 IEEE International Conference on Big Data (Big Data), pp. 2819–2826, December 2016

5. Sebrechts, M., Vanhove, T., Van Seghbroeck, G., Wauters, T., Volckaert, B., De Turck, F.: Distributed service orchestration: eventually consistent cloud operation and integration. In: Proceedings of the 2016 IEEE International Conference on Mobile Services (MS 2016). IEEE (2016)
6. Tsakalozos, K., Johns, C., Monroe, K., VanderGiessen, P., Mcleod, A., Rosales, A.: Open big data infrastructures to everyone. In: 2016 IEEE International Conference on Big Data (Big Data), pp. 2127–2129, December 2016

Ph.D. Track: Methods for the Protection of Infrastructure and Services

Situational Awareness: Detecting Critical Dependencies and Devices in a Network

Martin Laštovička$^{(\boxtimes)}$ and Pavel Čeleda

Institute of Computer Science and Faculty of Informatics,
Masaryk University, Brno, Czech Republic
lastovicka@ics.muni.cz, celeda@ics.muni.cz

Abstract. Large-scale networks consisting of thousands of connected devices are like a living organism, constantly changing and evolving. It is very difficult for a human administrator to orient in such environment and to react to emerging security threats. With such motivation, this PhD proposal aims to find new methods for automatic identification of devices, the services they provide, their dependencies and importance. The main focus of the proposal is to find novel approaches to building cyber situational awareness in an unknown network for the purpose of computer security incident response. Our research is at the initial phase and will contribute to a PhD thesis in four years.

Keywords: Situational awareness · Cybersecurity · Device importance evaluation · Threat impact estimation · Graph theory · Network monitoring

1 Introduction

The impacts of cyber threats became more serious with organisations increasing dependency on computer infrastructure. To defend against such threats, system administrators must build situational awareness which allows them to understand and orient in the complex networks [6]. The aim of this PhD thesis is to find new ways to automatically build situational awareness to help administrators understand possible impacts of a cyber threat.

Situational awareness means the knowledge and understanding of the current situation. It is possible for a system administrator to know what is going on in a small network, but with the growing number of connected devices, this becomes more and more difficult. A basic solution is to manually create a list of all devices in the network. But it is impossible to maintain such list throughout time and keep it updated with the dynamic changes of the network. Moreover, the trend of nowadays networks, containing mobile devices or IoT (Internet of Things), and cloud environments goes directly against the idea of device list and makes it useless in practice An automated approach is needed to deal with the constantly changing environment [6].

© The Author(s) 2017
D. Tuncer et al. (Eds.): AIMS 2017, LNCS 10356, pp. 173–178, 2017.
DOI: 10.1007/978-3-319-60774-0_17

The current approach for device and service identification focus on very specific networks, e.g., industrial control systems, or selected subset of services [1,2] which reduces their value in modern networks described above. Manual evaluation by security expert is still prevalent in the field of dependency detection and importance estimation. These risk assessment methods are not automated [5] or need active cooperation of the devices [8].

In our work, we intend to find new methods of building situational awareness based on data from network monitoring that will not depend on a specific type of network. We will define a computer network model containing information about devices and services, their dependencies and importance for the organisation. The importance of a device can then be expressed as how the device outage or compromise would impact other devices and goals of the host organisation. The nature of continuous information gathering from the network also overcomes the ever-changing nature of large networks and allows us to evaluate the data throughout time.

2   Research Questions

This research aims to discover new ways of threat impact estimation with respect to current situation, devices and services. To achieve this goal we attempt to answer following research questions:

1. **How can device and its services be identified in a complex network using passive network monitoring?**
   Many devices are not willing (end-user devices) or not able to (IoT) provide information about themselves in large networks. But every device communication over network could be analysed [3] and used to identify the type of the device, its operating system and provided services. However, current trends in modern networks, e.g., encrypted communication, port obfuscation, high transfer rate, make such identification hard. We plan to investigate those issues and propose methods to handle them.
2. **How can device dependencies be detected in a network?**
   To understand the situation in a network, it is not enough to know only what a device is and what services it provides. It is important to know which devices it depends on and how many devices depend on it. To answer this research question, we will study relationships between devices in internal network and propose new methods for their detection from network monitoring data.
3. **How can device importance be estimated from the perspective of reaction to cyber threats?**
   The importance of a particular device for organisation mission differs according to the provided services and the number of clients depending on the device. We plan to take these factors into account to build a model for importance estimation and we will find new ways of automatic importance evaluation based on traffic monitoring.

3   Proposed Approach

Our first step towards the building of situational awareness will be the definition of a network model. The natural representation of a computer network is a graph, where each node stands for a device in the network. Edges between nodes represent device communication, while another type of edge can represent dependencies or the presence of a cyber threat. This model allows us to separate the mostly static nature of what device is from its dynamic behaviour on the network.

3.1   Identification of Devices and Services

The knowledge of what a device is and what services it provides is a fundamental part of understanding the network. The goal of this part is to research methods of processing network traffic data to identify the type of the device (server, workstation, mobile, IoT), its operating system (Windows, Linux) and its services (web, mail, database).

Easiest way to determine a device type and services is to simply ask it. To do it in an organised way, many Service Discovery Protocols have been implemented [7] and deployed. They build a directory of all devices and their services, as an example, we can name well-known protocols such as BitTorrent or UPnP. However, this approach require active cooperation of the devices and hence we will not focus on them. Another way is to use active scanning. Our plan is to focus on passive methods only, yet we can use outputs of network scanning projects, e.g., Shodan, Censys, as a verification or an enhancement of our methods.

To achieve passive classification described above a sophisticated method must be used. Simple methods using protocol and port numbers currently falls short in classifying services with a dynamic port assignment or port obfuscation, e.g., hiding behind TCP port 80 [10]. To overcome these issues, more characteristics need to be taken into consideration.

The current trend of traffic encryption makes the analysis of its content hard, but on the other hand, it opens new ways of host identification. A client needs to send a lot of data to establish encrypted communication. For example, supported ciphersuites can be used to identify communicating clients during TLS (Transport Layer Security) handshake [4]. Similarly, we plan to investigate other properties of encrypted communication to identify the client device.

The most promising service identification method nowadays is the use of machine learning algorithms to classify the network traffic. Current methods perform well in a controlled environment where every application is known in advance, but cannot efficiently handle unknown traffic. Zhang et al. [11] presented an iterative method to improve identification accuracy, yet this field is still not fully explored. The two challenges we plan to address are the accuracy of identification in real network and performance of such algorithms when processing large amounts of data continuously coming from the monitored network.

3.2 Dependency Detection and Importance Estimation of a Device

The problem of asset criticality evaluation is known as vital for proper decision making during cyber-attacks but is difficult to achieve [5]. Research in this area is mainly focused on finding ways how a group of security experts can determine criticality by following prepared guidelines just like in risk assessment. But this approach is very time-consuming and cannot be repeated very often which leads to the data being outdated.

On the contrary, automatic evaluation is able to run continuously and can provide results when needed. We are aware that some important services or dependencies can be discovered only during exceptional operations or back-up servers become active only after failure of the main one. Automatic detections can still provide good staring point for risk assessment and save resources. Moreover, automatic system can identify operations that the administrators do not know about as presented in [9]. We propose three components to combine in order to estimate the device importance:

1. **Traffic Statistics** – Analysis of ongoing traffic in the network can point out the most used services in the terms of connected clients and data transfer volume. We will link these volumetric statistics to identified services to give them the dynamic context for importance evaluation, e.g., heavily loaded web server will be set as more important than another one scarcely visited. Our research will focus on real-time statistics computations so that it will be possible to dynamically adjust the evaluation as the network usage changes in time.
2. **Dependency detection** – Based on the identification of device type and traffic statistics, the basic dependency between client and server will be modelled. Using graph centrality algorithms we can then estimate the servers importance and the impact of its outage as the number of affected clients weighted by their own criticality. More complex dependencies can be discovered by clique detection. Dependencies forming a clique between servers can indicate strong relationship and exploitation of one will affect the whole group. The first steps towards automatic dependency detection using graph algorithms were made in [9], but they rely on active probing (i.e., Nagios system) to discover effects of service failure and backup detections, whereas we plan to achieve the same with passive network monitoring.
3. **Attacks Statistics** – Network attack is a manifestation of a cyber threat. The understanding of attack targets and discovery of most attacked devices should lead to raising the protection level of those devices. Our assumption is that parts of critical infrastructure will be targeted by attackers more often than user stations. Moreover, the type of the attack should differ and these differences could help to identify the most important devices. However, such assumption needs to be carefully verified before using in the criticality calculations. For example, attackers could target the most vulnerable device instead of critical infrastructure. In that case, such observation should be used as an advisory for the administrator rather than for criticality estimation.

4   Conclusion

In this research, we focus on building situational awareness from passive network observation without the necessity of active device probing. From those data, we intend to determine what a device is, what services it provides, what are its dependencies and how important it is for the network. Our methods will evaluate the situation continuously in order to follow changes in network and will be designed to be autonomic to minimise the need for human administrator assistance. Achieving our goals will help system administrators to better understand the situation in their network and to perceive the possible impacts of cyber threats.

Acknowledgement. This research was supported by the Security Research Programme of the Czech Republic 2015–2020 (BV III/1 VS) granted by the Ministry of the Interior of the Czech Republic under No. VI20172020070 Research of Tools for Cyber Situation Awareness and Decision Support of CSIRT Teams in the Protection of Critical Infrastructure.

Martin Laštovička is Brno Ph.D. Talent Scholarship Holder – Funded by the Brno City Municipality.

References

1. Callado, A., Kamienski, C., Szabó, G., Gero, B.P., Kelner, J., Fernandes, S., Sadok, D.: A survey on internet traffic identification. IEEE Commun. Surv. Tutorials **11**(3), 37–52 (2009)
2. Franke, U., Brynielsson, J.: Cyber situational awareness - a systematic review of the literature. Comput. Secur. **46**, 18–31 (2014)
3. Hofstede, R., Čeleda, P., Trammell, B., Drago, I., Sadre, R., Sperotto, A., Pras, A.: Flow monitoring explained: from packet capture to data analysis with NetFlow and IPFIX. IEEE Commun. Surv. Tutorials **16**(4), 2037–2064 (2014, Fourthquarter)
4. Husák, M., Čermák, M., Jirsík, T., Čeleda, P.: HTTPS traffic analysis and client identification using passive SSL/TLS fingerprinting. EURASIP J. Inf. Secur. **2016**(6), 1–14 (2016)
5. Kim, A., Kang, M.H.: Determining asset criticality for cyber defense. Technical report, Naval Research Lab, Washington DC (2011)
6. Kott, A., Wang, C., Erbacher, R.F.: Cyber Defense and Situational Awareness. Springer, Heidelberg (2014). ISBN: 978-3-319-11390-6
7. Meshkova, E., Riihijärvi, J., Petrova, M., Mähönen, P.: A survey on resource discovery mechanisms, peer-to-peer and service discovery frameworks. Comput. Netw. **52**(11), 2097–2128 (2008)
8. Weintraub, E., Cohen, Y.: Continuous monitoring system based on systems's environment. In: Proceedings of the Conference on Digital Forensics, Security and Law, p. 151. Association of Digital Forensics, Security and Law (2015)
9. Zand, A., Houmansadr, A., Vigna, G., Kemmerer, R., Kruegel, C.: Know your achilles' heel: automatic detection of network critical services. In: Proceedings of the 31st Annual Computer Security Applications Conference, pp. 41–50. ACM (2015)

10. Zander, S., Nguyen, T., Armitage, G.: Automated traffic classification and application identification using machine learning. In: The IEEE Conference on Local Computer Networks 30th Anniversary (LCN 2005), pp. 250–257. IEEE (2005)
11. Zhang, J., Chen, C., Xiang, Y., Zhou, W.: Robust network traffic identification with unknown applications. In: Proceedings of the 8th ACM SIGSAC Symposium on Information, Computer and Communications Security, pp. 405–414. ACM (2013)

A Framework for SFC Integrity in NFV Environments

Lucas Bondan[1,2(✉)], Tim Wauters[2], Bruno Volckaert[2], Filip De Turck[2], and Lisandro Zambenedetti Granville[1]

[1] Institute of Informatics (INF), Federal University of Rio Grando do Sul, Porto Alegre, Brazil
{lbondan,granville}@inf.ufrgs.br
[2] Department of Information Technology (INTEC), Ghent University, Ghent, Belgium
{tim.wauters,bruno.volckaert,filip.deturck}@intec.ugent.be

Abstract. Industry and academia have increased the deployment of Network Functions Virtualization (NFV) on their environments, either for reducing expenditures or taking advantage of NFV flexibility for service provisioning. In NFV, Service Function Chainings (SFC) composed of Virtualized Network Functions (VNF) are defined to deliver services to different customers. Despite the advancements in SFC composition for service provisioning, there is still a lack of proposals for ensuring the integrity of NFV service delivery, *i.e.*, detecting anomalies in SFC operation. Such anomalies could indicate a series of different threats, such as DDoS attacks, information leakage, and unauthorized access. In this PhD, we propose a framework composed of an SFC Integrity Module (SIM) for the standard NFV architecture, providing the integration of anomaly detection mechanisms to NFV orchestrators. We present recent results of this PhD regarding the implementation of an entropy-based anomaly detection mechanism using the SIM framework. The results presented in this paper are based on the execution of the proposed mechanism using a realistic SFC data set.

Keywords: Service function chaining · Network functions virtualization · Anomaly detection

1 Introduction

Network Functions Virtualization (NFV) was proposed to deal with the virtualization of network functions usually performed by dedicated hardware devices (*e.g.*, firewalls, session border controllers, load balancers) [1]. In NFV, Virtual Network Functions (VNF) are connected to each other, composing Service Function Chainings (SFC) for service delivery. Any anomaly in SFC operation, such as missing elements, misconfiguration, and redirection, could lead to the interruption of the service delivery and, in some cases, could indicate attacks to the

D. Tuncer et al. (Eds.): AIMS 2017, LNCS 10356, pp. 179–184, 2017.
DOI: 10.1007/978-3-319-60774-0_18

network. For this reason, in this PhD, we propose an additional SFC Integrity Module (SIM) to the NFV architecture [2]. SIM is a framework that allows the implementation of different anomaly detection mechanisms and the integration of such mechanisms into any NFV network under the control of NFV Orchestrators (NFVO). In this PhD, our focus resides in: (*i*) the applicability of existent and new anomaly detection mechanisms for SFC integrity in NFV environments, (*ii*) how to integrate such mechanisms to the NFV Management and Orchestration (MANO) architecture [3], and (*iii*) the evaluation of anomaly detection solutions in realistic NFV scenarios using the proposed SIM framework.

1.1 Motivation

In virtualized environments, vulnerabilities and exploits can lead to different SFC threats, since virtualization elements of NFV environments are susceptible to exploits. Examples of exploitable elements are container engines [4], hypervisors [5], and virtual machines [6]. Therefore, solutions have been proposed to detect anomalies in different NFV elements, such as VNFs [7], NFV services [8], and SLA violations [9]. However, there is still a lack of proposals dealing with security and integrity issues in the context of SFC [10]. In this PhD, we consider both the lack of solutions for SFC integrity and the potential vulnerabilities of NFV environments as research opportunities to be properly explored. To do so, we first investigated and proposed a framework that allows the implementation of anomaly detection techniques based on the NFV MANO information model.

2 SFC Integrity Framework

The NFV MANO architecture does not consider security-related tasks to protect functions and services. In this PhD research, we seek to guarantee the integrity of SFC operation for service delivery. Our proposal is designed to operate in NFV networks ruled by NFVOs according to the standard NFV MANO architecture.

2.1 Proposed Approach

The NFVO sends cataloged and monitored information to an Orchestrator Abstraction Driver (OAD), depicted in Fig. 1 along with all SIM internal components. The information is then processed and analyzed according to the anomaly detection mechanisms implemented in the Detector component. If no anomalies are detected, the results are stored in the Library for further access. Otherwise, the results are filtered using the Filter module to specify the sources of such anomalies. Once identified, SIM stores it in the Library and forwards a report message to NFVO with the filtered results and suggestions from the Advisor module for overcoming such anomalies, *e.g.,* turn off unregistered VNFs.

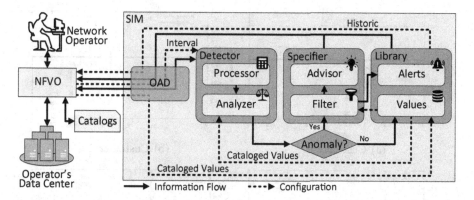

Fig. 1. Detailed SIM architecture [2] – The SIM communicates directly with NFVOs, using standard northbound APIs for requesting information regarding NFV elements operation and also to forward the results of the anomaly detection analysis.

2.2   Methodology

SIM was designed with specific elements for processing, analyzing, and filtering, enabling the design and implementation of different anomaly detection mechanisms. In this paper, we advance our first investigation using entropy-based anomaly detection [2] in two ways: (i) evaluating our solution using realistic NFV data sets [11] and (ii) improving the entropy-based anomaly detection mechanism to work with the current data set. These improvements enabled us to analyze each customer individually, increasing the accuracy of the anomaly detection mechanism. The data set was generated based on realistic information regarding the number of network functions composing SFCs on lager scale enterprise networks (with around 100 VNFs) [11]: 2 to 7 VNFs per SFC, mostly 2 to 5 [12]. So the number of VNFs for a given customer follows a truncated power-low distribution with exponent 2, minimum 2 and maximum 7. Following enterprise reports, anomalies were injected in the data set with a likelihood of 60% [13]. We considered three anomaly types: (i) unregistered SFCs, (ii) missing SFCs, and (iii) unauthorized changes in the SFC, such as additional or missing VNFs.

2.3   Results Obtained

Figure 2 shows the entropy results of the anomaly detection mechanism considering 4 customers with different sets of SFCs. The detector creates a merged list with cataloged and monitored information. As the number of elements with low probability increases in the list, *i.e.*, highly uncertain elements, the merged entropy changes, indicating a disorder in the monitored elements. The merged entropy varies according to the number and type of anomalies detected (represented by markers). In our experiments, anomalies of type (i) and (ii) decreased the entropy value, since they involve adding or subtracting information, while anomalies of type (iii) (changes in existing values) increased the entropy value. It may lead to situations where anomalies of type (i) and (ii) cancel the entropy

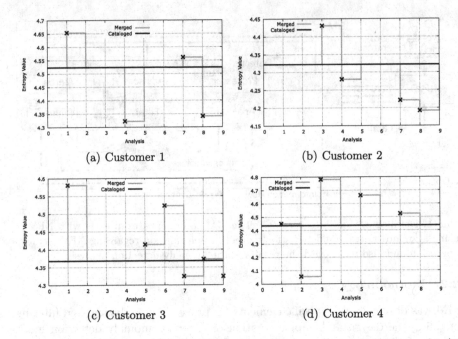

Fig. 2. Entropy results per customer. When anomalies occur (represented by markers), the entropy values varies, according to the amount of anomalies and their type.

variations caused by anomalies of type (*iii*) and vice-versa. Despite rare to occur, this problem should be properly addressed to avoid false negatives. With the two-level approach of SIM (detection and filtering) it is possible to avoid false negatives with fine-grained filters comparing monitored and cataloged information. After each analysis the entropy values go back to normal (cataloged).

3   Conclusions and Future Work

This PhD aims to propose efficient solutions for maintaining the integrity of service delivery in NFV environments. As first step, we proposed a SIM framework that allows the implementation of different anomaly detection mechanisms to analyze the network operation. The SIM modular architecture has the ability to operate with different NFVOs, requiring only to adapt one specific block. For future research, we foresee the following topics as good directions to follow.

Detection on Different Information Levels. SIM was designed to operate at different levels of information. In this way, we foresee the possibility to analyze information regarding real-time resource consumption by virtual machines (*e.g.*, CPU, RAM, disk) and network information (*e.g.*, SFC traffic flows, bandwidth).

Evaluation of Different Detection Mechanisms and Network Scenarios. Different anomaly detection mechanisms could be more suitable for a given network scenario, according to its characteristics. Analyzing the operation of different mechanisms in different environments will lead to important insights.

Deployment on Production Networks. Our results are based on realistic data sets generated according to real-world observations. However, production networks may present unpredicted behaviors, such as communication problems between NVFOs and other network elements. In this way, analyzing SIM operation in production networks is another important step of this PhD.

Acknowledgements. This research was performed partially within the FWO project "Service-oriented management of a virtualised future internet".

References

1. Chiosi, M., et al.: Network Functions Virtualisation (NFV). White Paper 1, ETSI NFV ISG (2012). https://portal.etsi.org/NFV/NFV_White_Paper.pdf
2. Bondan, L., Wauters, T., Volckaert, B., Turck, F.D., Granville, L.Z.: Anomaly detection framework for SFC integrity in NFV environments. In: IEEE Conference on Network Softwarization (NetSoft), (July 2017, to appear)
3. Quittek, J., et al.: Network Functions Virtualisation (NFV) - Management and Orchestration. White paper, ETSI NFV ISG (2014)
4. Combe, T., Martin, A., Pietro, R.D.: To docker or not to docker: a security perspective. IEEE Cloud Comput. **3**(5), 54–62 (2016)
5. Thongthua, A., Ngamsuriyaroj, S.: Assessment of hypervisor vulnerabilities. In: International Conference on Cloud Computing Research and Innovations (ICC-CRI), pp. 71–77, May 2016
6. Wang, Z., Yang, R., Fu, X., Du, X., Luo, B.: A shared memory based cross-VM side channel attacks in IaaS cloud. In: IEEE Conference on Computer Communications Workshops (INFOCOM WKSHPS), pp. 181–186, April 2016
7. Giotis, K., Androulidakis, G., Maglaris, B.S.: A scalable anomaly detection and mitigation architecture for legacy networks via an openflow middlebox. Secur. Commun. Netw. **9**, 1958–1970 (2015)
8. Xilouris, G.K., Kourtis, M.A., Gardikis, G., Koutras, I.: Statistical-based anomaly detection for NFV services. In: IEEE Conference on Network Function Virtualization and Software Defined Networks (NFV-SDN) (2016, to appear)
9. Sauvanaud, C., Lazri, K., Kaâniche, M., Kanoun, K.: Anomaly detection and root cause localization in virtual network functions. In: IEEE International Symposium on Software Reliability Engineering (ISSRE), pp. 196–206, October 2016
10. Briscoe, B., et al.: Network Functions Virtualisation (NFV) - NFV Security: Problem Statement. White paper, ETSI NFV ISG (2014)
11. Rankothge, W., Le, F., Russo, A., Lobo, J.: Data modelling for the evaluation of virtualized network functions resource allocation algorithms. Computing Research Repository (CoRR) abs/1702.00369 (2017). http://arxiv.org/abs/1702.00369
12. Sherry, J., Hasan, S., Scott, C., Krishnamurthy, A., Ratnasamy, S., Sekar, V.: Making middleboxes someone else's problem: network processing as a cloud service. In: ACM SIGCOMM Conference on Applications, Technologies, Architectures, and Protocols for Computer Communication, pp. 13–24 (2012)
13. Anstee, D., Bowen, P., Chui, C., Sockrider, G.: Worldwide infrastructure security report. Technical report, Arbor Networks (2017). https://www.arbornetworks.com/insight-into-the-global-threat-landscape

Multi-domain DDoS Mitigation
Based on Blockchains

Bruno Rodrigues[(✉)], Thomas Bocek, and Burkhard Stiller

Communication Systems Group (CSG), Department of Informatics (IfI),
University of Zürich (UZH), Zürich, Switzerland
{rodrigues,bocek,stiller}@ifi.uzh.ch

Abstract. The exponential increase of the traffic volume makes Distributed Denial-of-Service (DDoS) attacks a top security threat to service providers. Existing DDoS defense mechanisms lack resources and flexibility to cope with attacks by themselves, and by utilizing other's companies resources, the burden of the mitigation can be shared. Technologies as blockchain and smart contracts allow distributing attack information across multiple domains, while SDN (Software-Defined Networking) and NFV (Network Function Virtualization) enables to scale defense capabilities on demand for a single network domain. This proposal presents the design of a novel architecture combining these elements and introducing novel opportunities for flexible and efficient DDoS mitigation solutions across multiple domains.

Keywords: Distributed Denial-of-Service (DDoS) · Security · Blockchain · Software-defined Networks (SDN) · Network management

1 Introduction and Motivation

A Distributed Denial-of-Service (DDoS) attack is a large-scale, coordinated attempt to make a target system's resources unavailable. Although being a known category of attack, it remains as one of the major causes of concern for service providers. The increasing number of unsecured connected devices (stationary and portable) and their growing processing capacity, allow attackers to take control of a vast amount of unsecured devices that ranges from connected cameras to smart fridges to generate malicious attacks.

Major causes of concern for service providers is that not only the volume of traffic of DDoS attacks is growing, but also their complexity. Botnets taking advantage of unsecured IoT (Internet of Things) devices are the primary cause of these large-scale attacks. The Mirai botnet [4], for example, exploits default and weak security credentials to spread itself for other devices.

In an attack launched on Krebs Security [1] website in September 2016, Mirai peaked 623 Gbps in volume of traffic. Akamai, the service hosting the website, had to shut down the site because defending it during three days became too costly. It was reported that so many devices were used that the attacker did not have to use any sophisticated strategy.

© The Author(s) 2017
D. Tuncer et al. (Eds.): AIMS 2017, LNCS 10356, pp. 185–190, 2017.
DOI: 10.1007/978-3-319-60774-0_19

2   Problem Description

As DDoS attacks become progressively sophisticated and coordinated, the defense from such attacks likewise needs distribution and coordination. To prevent or reduce damages caused by these DDoS attacks, different detection and mitigation methods are available.

Typical implementation is based on dedicated ASIC-based appliances to analyze flow records exported from edge routers, and further filtering or load balancing traffic. Cloud-based solutions such as Cloudfare [3] and Akamai [1] can take away the burden of detection and mitigation, serving as a proxy able to load balance, reroute, or drop the traffic in case of DDoS attacks.

Many centralized defense systems lack of hardware resources or software capabilities to detect and mitigate attacks themselves. Traditional or cloud-based defenses can become a communication bottleneck due to the need to download and process all the traffic measurements at a single location. Thus, if an attack is highly sophisticated and there is no countermeasure available, legitimate users may be impaired until the attack stops.

An alternative is sharing hardware and defense capabilities with other systems, an approach called cooperative DDoS mitigation. However, existing cooperative approaches involve the proposal of a particular distributed architecture and protocols that usually require the modification of existing hardware and software in its support.

3   State-of-the-Art

Although there are several related works, concepts and technologies guiding the development of the proposal, for brevity in this section we highlight only three main related works. Internet Engineering Task Force (IETF) is proposing a protocol [5] named DOTS (DDoS Open Threat Signaling) covering both intra-organization and inter organization communications. DOTS requires servers and clients organized in both centralized and distributed architectures to advertise black or whitelisted addresses. However, DOTS presents a complex architectural design, which hinders your deployment without the complete standardization of the DOTS protocol. A different approach is [7], proposing a collaborative framework that allows the customers to request DDoS mitigation from ASes. However, the solution requires an SDN controller at customer side interfaced with the service provider, which can change the label of the anomalous traffic and redirect them to security middle-boxes. A similar approach is seen in [6]. The authors propose a cooperation between domains that implements VNFs to alleviate DDoS attacks by redirecting and reshaping excessive traffic to other collaborating domains for filtering. However, the proposal still requires the support of a gossip-based protocol by the network infrastructure to exchange information about attacks.

4   Research Questions

Many research challenges are found in the current scenario to improve current DDoS defense mechanisms not only in a single domain, but in a cross-domain perspective. Expected contributions of this work are categorized herein into three major stages of the DDoS protection: (1) analysis and detection, (2) collaboration across multiple domains, and (3) scalability of the proposed solution. Therefore, contributions of this work are expected to answer the following research questions:

RQ1: How to efficiently identify traffic types avoiding that, in presence of attacks, legitimate users may be hampered by the traffic of attackers? This proposal involves the identification of techniques based on machine learning to promote the signaling of attacks.

RQ2: How to simplify existing cooperative DDoS architectures and protocols so minimal hardware and software modifications are necessary to advertise DDoS information across multiple domains? In addition, it is necessary to investigate an incentive scheme to balance the relationship between cooperative entities, preventing a domain from abusing the cooperative scheme.

RQ3: How does the solution scale to report a number of addresses given the scale of devices involved in large-scale attacks?

5   Approach and Next Steps

A novel approach is presented herein to mitigate DDoS attacks across multiple domains. Recent advances on networking technology, such as Software-defined Networking (SDN) and Network Function Virtualization (NFV) are gaining attention towards the establishment of software-defined infrastructures. Blockchain and Smart Contracts may be used to advertise information across multiple domains, reducing the complexity of distributed protocols and architectures for gossiping DDoS attacks information. Figure 1 illustrates the proposed architecture of the system.

- **Software-Defined Networks (SDN):** enable the development of customizable security policies and services managed in a dynamic, software-based fashion. Among the available SDN controllers, Ryu is an open-source controller providing an well defined API for interacting and managing applications.
- **Network Function Virtualization (NFV):** enforce the security policies of the centralized control through virtualized functions provisioned in generic hardware. The VNF-BC is the virtual appliance deployed both on the network domain and customers, that may interface with network management systems, and optionally import flow-records of widely used network monitoring tools, as sFlow or NetFlow.
- **Blockchain:** Ethereum-based blockchain, which is public, decentralized and provide a trusted consensus in which data of DDoS attacks can be advertised and accessed between the cooperative domains. In an Ethereum blockchain,

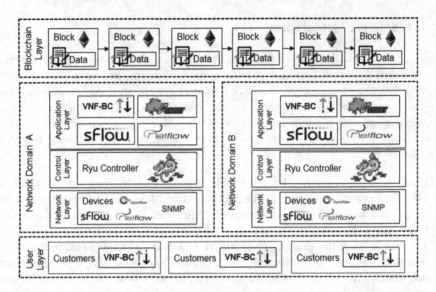

Fig. 1. Proposed architecture

VNF-BC appliances listening to the blockchain may see new addresses reported within a new 14 s, which is the time a block is mined.

- **Smart Contracts:** a Solidity-based contract implementing the logic of the collaborative approach, advertising of white or blacklisted IP addresses of certified customers, as well as information on the reporting entity and attack characteristics.

SDNs optimize the management of flows in response to attacks by enabling the deployment of sophisticated traffic analysis based on global network awareness given by a centralized controller. Aligned, SDN and NFV offer flexible and programmable network infrastructures toward generic network hardware deployed on open software, in which functions of the centralized control can be performed through virtualized network functions (VNF) and capabilities from NFV.

Security policies and thresholds may be defined based on historical records directly obtained from southbound protocols such as OpenFlow or SNMP, or exported from monitoring tools as sFlow or NetFlow. In response to attacks, the SDN controller may dynamically provision virtual functions for firewalling, packet inspection (e.g., Snort), or black-holing malicious traffic.

Blockchain and Smart Contracts can be used to advertise DDoS attacks information across multiple domains [2]. This simplifies existing cooperative DDoS mechanisms by using an existing distributed infrastructure to broadcast black or whitelisted addresses without the need to build specialized registries or other distribution mechanisms/protocols. The Ethereum blockchain supports a Turing-complete contract language [2], such as Solidity. Therefore, a node participating in the Ethereum blockchain runs a Solidity smart contract by executing a script, which is used to store references to the advertised addresses. The contracts is further processed checking if the entity reporting addresses is certified and its result is stored in a block.

However, entities issuing addresses need to have its identity certified. Similar to IETF-DOTS, certificates can be used to ensure authenticity of entities. Therefore, a network domain may issue to its customers a an authentication service to its customers through a registered VNF appliance able to report black or whitelisted addresses to the blockchain. For example, an LDevID certificates signed by the device owner may encode an owner assigned unique identifier and a PKI matching a private key held within the VNF appliance. Inter-domain trust can be established through any of the multi-PKI trust models in use today [8]. Then, information on the registered appliances will be hashed and referenced in the smart contract.

6 Summary

An architecture for multi-domain DDoS Mitigation based on Blockchains, SDN and VNFs was presented. Although designed based on SDN, a VNF appliance to read/write in the blockchain could be integrated with different networking-systems that exports flow records with sFlow or NetFlow. Expected contributions are not limited to the collaborative perspective of the DDoS defense, but also on the detection and mitigation of these attacks in a single domain based on key technologies such as SDN and NFV.

References

1. Akamai: How to Protect Against DDoS Attacks - Stop Denial of Service (2016). https://goo.gl/pfcWph. Accessed 10 Jan 2017
2. Bocek, T., Stiller, B.: Smart Contracts - Blockchains in the Wings, pp. 1–16. Springer, Heidelberg (2017). Tiergartenstr. 17, 69121
3. CloudFare: Cloudflare advanced DDoS protection (2016). Accessed 10 Jan 2017
4. Gamblin: Source code of the mirai botnet available on github, January 2016. https://goo.gl/CB5vx4. Accessed 14 Mar 2017
5. Nishizuka, K., Xia, L., Xia, J., Zhang, D., Fang, L., Gray, C.: Inter-organization cooperative DDoS protection mechanism. Draft, December 2016. https://goo.gl/szsalO
6. Rashidi, B., Fung, C.: Cofence: a collaborative DDoS defence using network function virtualization. In: 12th International Conference on Network and Service Management (CNSM 2016), October 2016
7. Sahay, R., Blanc, G., Zhang, Z., Debar, H.: Towards autonomic DDoS mitigation using software defined networking. In: SENT 2015: NDSS Workshop on Security of Emerging Networking Technologies. Internet Society (2015)
8. Shimaoka, M., Hastings, N., Nielsen, R.: Memorandum for multi-domain public key infrastructure interoperability (2008)

Author Index

Badonnel, Rémi   47
Barcellos, Marinho P.   62
Barshan, Maryam   79
Bartoš, Václav   125
Bocek, Thomas   16, 185
Bondan, Lucas   179
Botero, Juan F.   62
Burská, Karolína   149

Carle, Georg   30
Čejka, Tomáš   3, 125, 153
Čeleda, Pavel   173
Compastié, Maxime   47

de Boer, Pieter-Tjerk   137
de O. Schmidt, Ricardo   137
De Turck, Filip   79, 165, 179
Dorfhuber, Marko   30

Festor, Olivier   47

Gaspary, Luciano P.   62
Gil-Herrera, Juliver   62
Granville, Lisandro Zambenedetti   179

Haugerud, Hårek   143
Hausheer, David   16
He, Ruan   47
Hendriks, Luuk   137
Herold, Nadine   30

Isolani, Pedro H.   62

Jansky, Tomáš   125

Kassi-Lahlou, Mohamed   47
Kergl, Dennis   108
Knecht, Markus   159
Kristiana, Lisa   94

Lareida, Andri   16
Laštovička, Martin   173
Latré, Steven   62
Liebald, Stefan   30

Moens, Hendrik   79
Müller, Robert   131

Neves, Miguel C.   62

Ocampo, Andrés F.   62
Ošlejšek, Radek   149

Pras, Aiko   137

Rafati, Sina   16
Rodosek, Gabi Dreo   108
Rodrigues, Bruno   16, 185
Roedler, Robert   108
Rudolf, Christoph   30

Schmitt, Corinna   94, 131
Sebrechts, Merlijn   165
Stiller, Burkhard   16, 94, 159, 185
Švepeš, Marek   3

Van Seghbroeck, Gregory   165
Velan, Petr   137
Volckaert, Bruno   79, 179

Wachs, Matthias   30
Waldvogel, Marcel   131
Wauters, Tim   179

Xue, Noha   143

Yazidi, Anis   143

Žádník, Martin   153
Zambenedetti, Lisandro   62

Printed in the United States
By Bookmasters